Total Quality Management:
Implications for Higher Education

Edited by
Allan M. Hoffman
and
Daniel J. Julius

Prescott Publishing Company
Maryville, Missouri
1995

Total Quality Management:
Implications for Higher Education
Edited by Allan M. Hoffman and Daniel J. Julius

Copyright © 1995 by Prescott Publishing Company
106 South Main Street, Maryville, Missouri 64468
1/800-528-5197

Printed in the United States of America
First Printing: 1995
10 9 8 7 6 5 4 3 2 1

Publisher's Cataloging in Publication
(Prepared by Quality Books Inc.)

Total quality management: implications for higher education / edited by Allan M. Hoffman, Daniel J. Julius.
   p. cm.
   Includes bioliographical references.
   ISBN 1-886626-00-6

   1. School management and organization. 2. Total quality management. I. Hoffman, Allan M. II. Julius, Daniel J.

LB2805.T68 1995   371.2
                          QBI94-21202
CIP 94-073970

ISBN 1-886626-00-6: $29.95 Hardcover

�֎ �֎ ✖

*This book is dedicated to the men and
women in higher education management
who have a vision for a better world,
who encourage change,
and who establish new traditions
in which teaching and learning can thrive.*

✖ ✖ ✖

Contents

FOREWORD

Is it true, what they've been saying in the nineties about higher education? Are we entering into a period that will demand total restructuring, a virtual (there's that word again) reinventing of the university? Are the experiences of American industry to be relived on our college campuses? I don't know, but I think probably so.

Are we ready to face these challenges, if they are thrust upon us? This I do know; we are not ready.

The reasonable voices of conservatism in higher education should not be ignored. They argue that the enduring strength of the world's great universities is the product of unchanging or very slowly changing policies rooted in grand traditions, and they see danger in radical changes. America's system of higher education, and especially our graduate education, is the best in the world and the best in all of human history. "If it ain't broke, don't fix it!"

When I heard this admonition in a faculty meeting in 1993, I told the story of the pilgrim who was traveling to a monastery high in the Italian Alps. The pilgrim discovered to his dismay that the final step on his journey required that he enter a wicker basket suspended over a deep chasm by a frayed rope on a pulley. Eyeing the ragged rope nervously, he asked the monk in charge how often he changed the rope. "Whenever it breaks," came the reply. "If it ain't broke, why fix it?"

With all respect to the traditionalists, we must begin to fix our colleges and universities, even before we are driven to action by catastrophe. We must recognize that our campus cultures change very slowly for many good reasons, including the diffusion of authority and our historical isolation from the pressures of the marketplace. Unless we work very hard right now to get ready for an uncertain future, we will not be prepared to ride the waves of change when the storms of the global economy finally reach our shores.

Of course it may turn out that tomorrow will be more like yesterday than the alarmists imagine. We must be prepared for any eventuality, including this one. The one thing that is certain about the future is its uncertainty.

So how do we prepare for uncertainty? How can we prepare ourselves to succeed in an environment of continuous, rapid, and unanticipated change? Will this book help?

The first step in such preparation is taking time to think about the fundamental forces at work in modern society and the possible future scenarios for higher education. (Try to concentrate on the learning activity, and not on the teaching institutions.) The overview that begins this book will help to define the context, and subsequent chapters on such fields as learning theory should help you to think creatively about the future.

The next step is to find out how other people have learned through experience, either in educational institutions or in other kinds of organizations. The Total Quality Management (TQM) concept as practiced at Westinghouse has implications for higher education, as described in the chapter by Aris Melissaratos. Ed Coate and Marna Whittington made these concepts work at two quite different universities (Oregon State and Pennsylvania State), and both have moved on to new challenges; their chapters are written by people who have broken new ground in university administration.

Likins

TQM has also been implemented at Fox Valley College in Wisconsin and Rio Salado Community College in Arizona; there are, in this book, new lessons to be learned from their experiences as well.

From the public schools of Virginia to the teaching hospitals of New York City, the basic principles of continuous quality improvement are being applied, as described in chapters that follow.

The lessons of industry are most readily applied to academic administration. But the commitment to quality certainly includes the faculty, most of whom have been conditioned to think of themselves as its final arbiter. In chapters to follow, we'll see how faculty are getting involved in a new vision of quality at UC Berkeley, and examine the implementation of TQM in the classroom at Cal-State Dominguez Hills.

The reader's purpose in reading this book should be exploratory. The search for the final answers will surely not end here. But benchmarking the experiences of others is an important part of the continuous improvement process, and these chapters should facilitate that task.

Finally, the application of the principles of the quality movement is a unique challenge in every individual environment; there is no formula for success. Moreover, it would be a mistake to rush down this path with no clear purpose; these ideas work only if you have clearly established your reasons for going forward. If you understand the first stage of this process well, and fully comprehend the forces for change at work in our society, then you'll have no problem getting motivated. Even if you are doing very well right now, you'll understand the need to get better in a hurry. (We call our continuous improvement initiative at Lehigh University "Getting Even Better.")

Once you find yourself on the path that was pioneered in industry as total quality management, you'll find that it leads to an endless succession of new ideas. In the final chapter we go "Beyond TQM" to see what it takes to thrive in an atmosphere of unremitting and unpredictable change. The quality we need is called "agility," and we must prepare for a future when the notion of an "agile university" doesn't sound like an oxymoron.

PETER LIKINS

President, Lehigh University
Bethlehem, Pennsylvania

Likins

PREFACE

SURMOUNTING THE BARRIERS TO TOTAL QUALTIY MANAGEMENT

Daniel J. Julius

TQM's two biggest lies are that it is a modern concept and a straightforward matter to implement. Readers of this volume might reflect upon early Judaic commentaries on the old testament (set forth in a series of books called the Talmud). These rabbinical treatises adopt the position that the creation was not final. The early prophets argued the essence of man and woman's existence was to improve the world (and to improve themselves) according to standards defined by God. Indeed, there is a philosophical discussion in the Talmud which asks why God created humanity and what the proper role of people and communities should be. It is here, with respect to Judeo-Christian thought, that the concept of continuous improvement finds its Genesis (Chapter 2, verse 3).

Christians, Confucians, Protestants, Taoists, Buddhists, Hindus, and representatives of other world religions have also sought continuous improvement in themselves and their communities through prayer, good deeds, devotion, sacrifice, meditation or a variety of other activities. While not the subject of this book, we find examples of the concept of "quality" and "continuous improvement" in the writings of Aristotle, Socrates and, of course, Plato, who bequeathed the philosophical notion of the "ideal" form. The principle of an "ideal," the belief that actions and objects could be evaluated against the standard of perfection, has had a significant impact on western thought in science, art, literature and mathematics.

From yet another perspective, consider the following excerpt on continuous improvement from the perspective of a Zen Master written approximately eight hundred and fifty years ago:

> Who has no faults? To err and yet be able to correct it is best of all. Since time immemorial, all have lauded the ability to correct faults as being wise, rather than considering having no faults to be beautiful. Thus human actions have many faults and errors—this is something that neither the wise nor the foolish can avoid—yet it is only the wise who can correct their faults and change to good, whereas the foolish mostly conceal their faults and cover up their wrongs. When one changes to what is good, virtue is new every day. This is characteristic of what is called the ideal person. When one covers up one's faults, the evil is more and more manifest. This is characteristic of what is called the lesser person. (Cleary 1989)

World history is replete with examples of individuals who have struggled to improve themselves, their communal organizations, methods of agriculture, mercantile endeavors, warfare, and other activities of human life. Viewed from this vantage point, the continuous quality movement becomes even more meaningful and, certainly, a concept that reflects the thoughts of civilization's most intelligent monarchs, politicians, philosophers, poets, clerics, artists, social scientists, and military strategists.

Of course, the major dilemma associated with quality and continuous improvement was never its efficacy as a worthy goal. The core problem has always involved implementation: how to measure and achieve the desired ends (assuming people agree on the desired ends), how to interpret or reconcile perplexing disparities between what actually occurs in organizations, communities and ourselves, and what we would prefer to occur.

During the earliest years of the twentieth century, management theorists and supervisors embraced principles associated with scientific management (the modern precursor to the total quality movement). They very soon discovered the difficulty of simply making a better product, influencing people to act in more efficient ways, or identifying a core client. Recall that Frederick Taylor, patron saint of scientific management, argued that managers and workers must put aside all that conflicted with efficient production. ("All" in this context was interpreted to mean informal group networks, unions, et al.) With the risk of delving too deeply into the history of managerial behavior and the evolution of the corporate work environment in America, it was not long before Taylor was embroiled in political controversy, replete with congressional hearings, on the fundamental nature of scientific management and its practical manifestations. Later, in what is perhaps one of his most poignant observations, Taylor lamented that his ideas and theories were misused by those who would subvert them for different ends (Wren 1987). Writing in the 1950s, Reinhardt Bendix, a brilliant interpreter of social change and the nature of work, wrote that scientific management demanded no less than a mental revolution with regard to how work was managed (Bendix). Bendix identified barriers to the successful implementation of continuous improvement. He suggested that any quality movement risks falling prey to those who have a vested interest in maintaining the status quo or those who seek to change the status quo to accommodate a specific agenda.

In higher education, TQM will require an "organizational" revolution. After all, as Clark Kerr once observed, the university has become so fragmented it now resembles disparate groups of scholars, housed in separate buildings, connected only by a common grievance over parking privileges (Kerr 1963). Hazard Adams wrote eloquently in *The Academic Tribes,* that behavior in academic organizations could be viewed in an analogous way to tribal societies, complete with symbols, rituals, punishments, and sacrifices, resulting in a culture which promotes exclusive, not inclusive, behavior (Adams 1976). Nor are the private liberal arts colleges or religiously affiliated institutions immune. Deciding on the essence of quality or continuous improvement demands that individuals prioritize values. At its inner core, the quality movement is one which asks that educators adhere to (and implement) a set of ideals; not an easy task!

All of which leads me to state the obvious; anyone who claims it is relatively simple to implement TQM in academe is either a liar, a fool, or both. For example, scholars and administrators have yet to agree on the mission of the university, let alone standards for teaching or scholarship. Nor is there unanimity on the question of who the "client" really is. Medical scientists, philosophers and psychologists do not yet agree how people learn, not to mention what should be learned. The debate on national standards in the secondary school history curriculum or the efficacy of the Goals 2000 legislation, should at least sober those ardent enthusiasts of continuous quality improvement (Katz).

The notion of TQM also challenges us to recognize the constancy of change. Consider a brief passage written by Maureen Clark, an organizational consultant in Silicon Valley, in the forefront of developing solutions to questions concerning the design of work, strategic planning, and employee commitment:

> The world is changing at breakneck speed, propelled by leapfrogging technological advances that leave most people struggling to catch their breath. Just as technology makes the world seem smaller and nations/markets/industries more interdependent, traditional big business structures are shown to be clumsy and not up to the challenge. Organizations are charging in simultaneous (and seemingly opposite) directions, toward such contextual "remedies" as self-managed work teams and the individual telecommuting. Today, a person with a few tools (e.g., computer, modem, fax) can be a complete business of one, an individual contributor/specialist in an organization, an electronic team member, or some combination of all three.

> Technological, organizational and work changes are creating incredible pressures for individuals at all levels in business. Executives, faced with global competition and intense price pressures, are constantly scanning an ever-widening horizon to identify both creative ideas and threats to long-term growth. The constituents they must satisfy are likely to be very diverse, possibly global. They must walk a fine line

between short-term profitability and creating organizations that are both flexible and enduring. While it is obvious that the implicit covenants that have governed employer-employee relationships no longer hold, new covenants are still only tentative and emerging.

(Clark 1994)

Now ask yourself when was the last administrative or faculty meeting you attended (pick a discipline) that included representatives from other divisions or departments and focused on clients, changes in the environment, or the need to redirect the curriculum and institutional policies to accommodate such trends. If you answered affirmatively, you are in the minority.

TQM demands answers to the questions "who is the client?" and "how can the organization and its employees better accomplish work the client desires?" In academic enterprises, a host of subsequent issues must be addressed if TQM is to be effective:

- How can we create the right conditions and rewards in order to enable faculty and administrators to evaluate their own behaviors?
- How do we evaluate work in a manner which fully accepts the "client's" point of view or opinion?
- How can we nurture and utilize teams of employees which may cross disciplinary, teacher-student, or faculty-administrative boundaries?
- Can we agree upon concepts of flexibility, or what it means to create a learning organization?
- How can we motivate employees who are practically guaranteed a salary and job security?
- Can we agree on how to measure what academic organizations do?

- How can concepts of change or accountability be introduced without causing defensive reactions on the part of individuals who may view such concepts as an intrusion into their intellectual freedom?
- How should quality or continuous improvement concepts be approached with those who are genuinely anti-intellectual or members of a state legislature committed to reducing institutional resources?
- How can continuous improvement policies be implemented in organizations where authority and responsibility are highly diffused?
- Can we agree on what it means to make an institution accountable?
- Can we convert our research on learning into solid assessment measures?
- How should we approach the debate on "national standards" for higher education?
- Are concepts associated with TQM compatible with collective bargaining? (Unions now represent at least half of all employees working in American colleges and universities.) (Julius 1993)
- How do we convince institutional leaders that change may be necessary when such individuals view their role (and organizational mission) as an intellectual, religious, or cultural bulwark against societal forces?
- How should faculty be approached who believe their department must "weed out" (flunk) students who do not meet "traditional" entrance criteria?

Solutions to the above questions are difficult. Indeed, extraordinary skill is needed to introduce such matters for debate!

Finding the right answers to the challenges posed by TQM and implementing strategic actions which accommodate organizational and cultural characteristics of colleges and universities are not impossible, but difficult.

TQM has been applied successfully to certain programs and school processes—in particular, those with agreed upon outcomes and a highly committed staff. Sub-units of organizations with relatively uniform (and identifiable) products and clients are also successful candidates. In his new book, Jeffrey Pfeffer, professor at the Stanford Business School demonstrates how efficiency concepts can be applied in corporate environments and argues persuasively that continuous improvement processes refocus the energy of employees and engender efficient work paradigms as well (Pfeffer 1994). Similarly, in *Transforming Post Secondary Education,* Ellen E. Chaffee and Lawrence A. Sherr provide a context for implementing TQM in colleges and universities, with examples of successful programs (Chaffee 1993).

Demanding "quality" can be risky if such ideas are considered controversial. This can lead to social and intellectual isolation for those who bring these concepts forward. While the current climate of "political correctness" has made it easy to attack some time-worn traditions and shibboleths (some of which should be attacked), it has also made it difficult to criticize some of the newer and more perverse manifestations brought about by desires to make the academy more "politically correct."

TQM, in my opinion, forces administrators, scholars, teachers, staff, and presidents to look within, confront, examine, ponder, and—we hope—to act upon the most important reasons our institutions exist. Implementing quality concepts is not something which would be nice to do, but necessary for integrity and organizational survival. It is to these kinds of questions and issues that this book is directed.

Julius

References

Adams, H. 1976. *The Academic Tribes*. Urbana, IL: University of
Illinois Press.

Bendix, R. *Work and Authority in Industry*. Holt, Reinhard & Winston.

Chaffee, E. E. and L. A. Sherr. 1993. *Transforming Post-Secondary
Education*. Association for the Study of Higher Education, ERIC
Clearinghouse on Higher Education, Washington, D.C. (For another
worthwhile volume, see Deborah J. Teeter and G. Gregory Lozier,
*Pursuit of Quality in Higher Education: Case Studies in Total
Quality Management*. San Francisco, CA: Jossey-Bass, Inc., 1993.)

Clark, M. 1994. Proposal for "Society for Work and Change." University of San Francisco (October).

Cleary, T., trans. 1989. Yuanwu letter to Wen Wangbu. In *Zen Lessons:
The Art of Leadership*. Boston, MA: Shambhala Publications, Inc.

Julius, D. J. 1993. "Unions of Academe: 1930s to the 1990s." In
*Managing the Industrial Labor Relations Process in Higher
Education*, edited by D. Julius. Washington D.C.: College and
University Personnel Association.

Katz, S. N. 1994. "Defining Education Quality and Accountability."
The Chronicle of Higher Education (16 November).

Kerr, C. 1963. *The Uses of the University*. New York: Harper & Row.

Pfeffer, J. 1994. *Competitive Advantage Through People*. Boston, MA:
Harvard Business School Press.

Wren, D. A. 1987. *The Evolution of Management Thought*. New York:
John Wiley & Sons, Inc.

Preface   xxi

DANIEL J. JULIUS

Daniel J. Julius is associate vice president for academic affairs and director of the National Center for Employment Studies at the University of San Francisco. Julius received a bachelor's degree from Ohio State University, studied at the New York State School of Industrial Labor Relations at Cornell University, and earned his master of arts and doctorate in education from Teachers College, Columbia University.

Active as a labor arbitrator and management consultant, Julius teaches for the American Arbitration Association and is widely published in the areas of labor-management relations and higher education administration. He is a past-president of the Academy of Academic Personnel Administrators, president of the College and University Personnel Association, and a program chair of the San Francisco Industrial Relations Research Association.

He has also been a visiting scholar at the Graduate School of Business at Stanford University, and a visiting professor at the universities of Hawaii, New Hampshire, and Shanghai.

ACKNOWLEDGMENTS

This book represents the culmination of a long and detailed process of exploring Total Quality Management in many sectors of America and the implications and impact it has on managing higher educational institutions. As I attempted to put together the best research and practice relating to TQM, I had an opportunity to meet and talk with many people involved in Total Quality Management efforts and activities. As such, I would like to personally express a debt of gratitude to several people who provided invaluable guidance, direction, and in some cases, heated, lively discussion:

Yvonne Thayer, Assistant Superintendent, Gloucester County Schools (Virginia), deserves thanks for reminding me to explore K-12 models of TQM and the relevance such models have for all sectors of educational endeavors.

Galen Godbey, Executive Director, Lehigh Valley Association of Independent Colleges, provided insightful thoughts that led to exploring TQM in higher education as a futuristic modality relating to how such organizations could be, albeit should be, managed.

Randal Summers of Eastman Office Depot Inc., Signal Hill, California, deserves a special note of thanks for his feedback regarding TQM from the perspective of business and industry.

Amer El-Ahraf, Executive Vice President, California State University–Dominguez Hills, provided an opportunity to observe and evaluate models of TQM, as it was in the process of being implemented at that institution.

Sam Wiley, Vice President for Academic Affairs at California State University–Dominguez Hills, is to be thanked for his encouragement regarding the completion of this project.

Much appreciation goes to all the chapter authors, who shared the vision and were willing to contribute to this book.

A special acknowledgment goes to Dan Julius, volume co-editor who also provided key concepts relating to the format of this book.

I would especially like to thank Melody Lowe and her staff at Prescott Publishing who clearly should be given a very special "thank you" for their exemplary efforts, their attention to detail, follow-up, and their ultimate production of the product you are holding in your hands. Without Melody's efforts, this book clearly would not have come into existence.

Finally, my family has provided a tranquil environment in which I could work the long hours it took to complete this effort. They have been both an inspiration and the guiding light.

A. M. H.

CHAPTER ONE:

TQM: IMPLICATIONS FOR HIGHER EDUCATION—A LOOK BACK TO THE FUTURE

Allan M. Hoffman and Randal Summers

American higher education, like many institutions and agencies in our culture and society, is being criticized for being inefficient, ineffective, and out of touch with the complex needs of our modern day technical society. The work force that staffs our institutions is changing, becoming more diverse, better educated, more demanding, and less accepting than their predecessors. Academicians, or so the belief is proposed, frequently provide expert guidance to organizations and agencies and laude the benefits of implementing Total Quality Management (TQM), but cannot seem to get it to work within the hallowed walls of the academic enterprise.

Although programs to implement TQM, organizational reengineering, employee empowerment, etc. have been difficult, sometimes highly frustrating, many examples do exist and programs have been implemented. The notion that higher education cannot or will not keep up with the quality standards being implemented in many sectors of our society is erroneous. Perhaps because the quality movement was given birth outside of the higher education cohort, many academicians and managers within higher education have been skeptical regarding its value for the academy. This chapter is designed to briefly examine aspects of the quality movement and provide a backdrop for succeeding sections of this volume. "Whenever a business keeps going downhill despite massive spending and heroic effort . . . the most likely cause is . . . obsolescence of its business theory." This statement was made by Peter Drucker (1993), and considering the rapid and perhaps unprecedented pace of the changing environment in which educational institutions and agencies function, perhaps a radical reform in the way business is conducted is necessary. This change may be an essential ingredient leading to institutional survival and stability. Perhaps human resource work force issues will diminish and people will recognize the need for the shared vision of quality.

A United States Commerce Department's report on competitiveness (1993) indicates, "Except for software and medical equipment, the United States has been losing market share in all products since 1984." Industries that were once dominated by the United States are now largely dominated by Europe and Japan. The cause was alluded to by Tom Peters, author of *In Search of Excellence* and *Thriving on Chaos* (1987). He made the passionate statement, "People like things that work. But the sad fact of the matter is that our cars and semi-conductors and everything else in between, don't work very well" (Peters).

The following three examples from industry support his comment and may have relevance to our discussion concerning education: Motorola lost its global markets to Japan in the areas of semi-conductors, color televisions, and radios; Xerox's share of the low-end market in the copier business fell from 80 percent in 1975 to 8.6 percent in 1984; Canon, Minolta, and Ricoh, all Japanese companies, were building copiers at half the production cost with 10 to 30 times higher quality. In 1980 Milliken, a textile manufacturer, despite its advanced manufacturing technology, found that its foreign competitors had higher quality and greater productivity. Therefore, throughout the 80s the manufacturing sector became preoccupied with the challenge of competing in the global marketplace. They adopted a quality improvement strategy with the ultimate goal of capturing market share by satisfying the customer.

As Tom Peters put it, "To turn around America's position in world trade, American products must earn a reputation as quality products. They don't have that reputation today" (Deming 1992). The strategy involved not only increasing productivity and innovation, but also reducing the costs associated with poor quality and inefficient work processes. In 1987 Motorola instituted their "Sigma Six" program, reducing defects to 3.4 parts per million. Xerox started the "Leadership Through Quality" program in 1984, and Milliken began their "Pursuit of Excellence" customer satisfaction program in 1981. All three of these companies eventually won the Malcolm Baldrige Award from the United States Department of Commerce for excellence in quality.

Where Did It All Begin?

The quality principles in and of themselves are not new. According to Louis Schultz in *Japan Before Deming* (1993), quality began with Homer Sarasohn, not Deming or Juran, and goes back to the post-war years when the American forces, under the direction of General Douglas MacArthur, occupied Japan. Kenichi Koyanagi was the leader of a group of Japanese scientists. This was one of many groups that were set up by the military to support the war effort in Japan. After the war, Koyanagi's group was kept intact. It was dedicated to the rebuilding of Japan and became known as the Union of Japanese Science and Engineering (JUSE).

In 1948, engineers from the Bell Laboratories working on General MacArthur's staff supplied these engineers and scientists with literature on quality control. They explained that statistical methods had improved the accuracy of American weapons. Their literature included Walter Shewhart's book, *Economic Control of Quality of Manufactured Product* (1931), describing the Shewhart Cycle "Plan-Do-Check-Act," which Deming later made popular. Thus, the Japanese acquired an appreciation for quality and productivity. (Shewhart's statistical methods were being taught in America in 1942, but the effort eventually faded out.)

General MacArthur was concerned about the Japanese fear of not being treated well by the conquering Americans. Therefore, it was decided that the Civil Communication Section, (CCS) would be established to inform the populace that the Americans would not terrorize the Japanese. MacArthur asked Homer Sarasohn to head up the industry section of the CCS and communicate the message to the Japanese by radio. There were no radios, and the factories were just piles of rubble. Since the industrial capability of Japan had been leveled with the bombing, the first challenge involved creating new plants at a time when resources were scarce. These new factories were small clay-floor shacks in which radios of low reliability and poor quality were produced.

Sarasohn and his colleagues designated a manager in each company and charged them with setting and achieving production and quality goals. Measurement and standards were applied to production line quality needs and quality inspections were instituted.

Sarasohn and Charles Protzman, an industrial engineer from Western Electric, felt it was necessary to educate Japanese managers if quality and productivity were to be sustained in the fledgling communications industry in Japan so they developed an eight-week curriculum that included Shewhart's Statistical Quality Control (SQC) concepts. The Union of Japanese Science and Engineering (JUSE) was very supportive since they believed SQC was responsible for the Americans winning the war. The first course was offered in 1949.

Later Sarasohn, having promised to bring in SQC experts, invited Walter Shewhart himself. However, since he was not well, an invitation was extended to W. Edwards Deming. Deming was a professor at Columbia University who was familiar with the application of Shewhart's methods. He was also working on consulting projects with the Japanese related to agriculture and demographics. He arrived in Japan in the summer of 1950. As MacArthur became more concerned with Korea, Sarasohn passed the quality torch to Deming and left in the fall of that same year.

Meanwhile, the Japanese managers who attended the Civil Communication Section seminars were becoming the new industrial leaders. Juran came later and made his contribution, but the pioneering post-war radio quality work gave rise to the high-tech communications industry with companies such as Sony, Toshiba, Matsushita, Sharp, and Fujitsu.

With JUSE support, Deming conducted eight-day courses with over 400 engineers on his visits in 1951. The teaching of consumer research (statistical sampling) began that year. Door-to-door surveys were done on the need for bicycles, pharmaceuticals, and sewing machines.

A Look Back to the Future   5

In 1954, JUSE invited Joseph Juran whose teaching emphasized that improving quality was management's responsibility. According to Deming, between 1950 and 1970, over 14,000 engineers and thousands of foremen were taught statistical methods and consumer research. In 1960 Dr. Ishikawa introduced "Quality Circles" which were small groups used to eliminate quality flaws and improve design and systems. Within five years the Japanese were involved in world markets and eventually dominated many of them. Their standard of living rose to that of the most prosperous in the world. In North America the loss of market share to the Japanese forced manufacturers to focus on quality. This triggered a renewed interest in the work of Deming and Juran, and later, Philip Crosby. World Class Manufacturing and the ISO 9000 standards became the "quality" targets and processes for United States manufacturers.

The principles and approaches of the quality proponents and authorities such as Deming, Juran, and Crosby became the tools for fashioning the great quality Renaissance.

W. Edwards Deming

Deming worked on quality at Western Electric in the 1930s. He helped the Japanese in 1950 but apparently had no audience in America until 1980 when he appeared on an NBC television documentary entitled "If Japan Can, Why Can't We?"

Deming was noted for his statistical approach to analyzing and improving the way a company does business through its operational systems or processes. His approach revolved around statistical process control and his 14 point quality philosophy. In *Out of the Crisis* (1992), Deming outlines his 14 points:

Deming's 14 Points for Management

1) Constancy of purpose creates constancy of purpose toward improvement of product and service, with the aim to become competitive, to stay in business, and to provide jobs.
2) Adopt a new philosophy. We are in a new economic age. Western management must awaken to the challenge, must learn their responsibilities, and take on leadership for change.
3) Cease dependence on inspection to achieve quality. Eliminate the need for inspection on a mass basis by building quality into the product in the first place.
4) End the practice of awarding business on the basis of price tag. Instead, minimize total cost. Move toward a single supplier for any one item, on a long-term relationship of loyalty and trust.
5) Improve constantly and forever the system of production and service, to improve quality and productivity, and thus constantly decrease costs.
6) Institute training on the job.
7) Institute leadership. The aim of supervision should be to help people and machines and gadgets do a better job. Supervision of management is in need of overhaul as well as supervision of production workers.
8) Drive out fear so that everyone may work effectively for the company.
9) Break down barriers between departments. People in research, design, sales, and production must work as a team to foresee problems of production that may be encountered with the product or service.
10) Eliminate slogans, exhortations, and targets for the work force asking for zero defects and new levels of productivity. Such exhortations only create adversarial

A Look Back to the Future   7

relationships, as the bulk of the causes of low quality and low productivity belong to the system and thus lie beyond the power of the work force.

11) Eliminate work standards (quotas) on the factory floor. Substitute leadership. Eliminate management by objectives. Eliminate management by numbers, numerical goals. Substitute leadership.

12) Remove barriers that rob the hourly worker of his right to pride of workmanship. The responsibility of supervisors must be changed from sheer numbers to quality.

13) Institute a vigorous program of education and self-improvement.

14) Put everybody in the company to work to accomplish the transformation. The transformation is everybody's job. (Deming 1992)

Joseph Juran

Joseph Juran was another quality pioneer who assisted the Japanese in their dramatic post-war recovery. In his book, *Juran on Leadership for Quality* (1989), he pointed out that managing for quality in the way we do business encompasses three essential processes:

1) Quality Planning—focusing product development and service on meeting customer needs.

2) Quality Control—by comparing performance to quality goals and not by the quality control department inspections.

3) Quality Improvement—raising quality of performance to new "breakthrough" levels.

Juran (1989) defined quality as "fitness for use," and believed quality improvement is a project-by-project endeavor. His approach to each project followed a particular sequence:

Hoffman and Summers

1) Form a Quality Council comprised of upper managers.
2) Solicit project nominations throughout the company.
3) Have the Quality Council screen nominations for a project that relates to a chronic problem and that can be completed in a few months with results that are measurable in money and technological terms.
4) Develop a mission statement that has a measurable goal for each project. Compile a list of projects and include in next year's business plan (Strategic Quality Management).
5) Select a team of six to eight people for each project. The team has no boss, only a chairperson appointed by the Quality Council.
6) Define team responsibilities and a mission statement that includes these steps:
   • analyze the symptoms
   • brainstorm to generate ideas about the causes
   • test these ideas/theories with data analysis
   • establish causes
   • assign the appropriate function to develop a solution
   • test the solution under operating conditions
   • establish controls to maintain the improvement
   • apply solutions to other problems if appropriate
7) Provide recognition/rewards to the project teams
8) Evaluate progress on all projects

Quality in Juran's approach meant freedom from problems that create customer dissatisfaction. These problems are costly because they require the redoing of work and responding to customer complaints. Juran felt that a third of the work done in the United States is work that is being done again because of its deficiencies or the lack of quality. He asserts that this situation will not change unless there is a mandate from the top and a special organizational structure to ensure that quality becomes a high priority.

A Look Back to the Future 9

Philip Crosby

Philip Crosby entered the quality movement in 1979 with the publication of *Quality is Free*. He was the director of quality with International Telephone and Telegraph before he became a quality consultant. He introduced the concept of "zero defects" and popularized the phrase, "Do it right the first time."

He describes his model of quality in "Four Absolutes"

1) The definition of quality is conformance to requirements. Products must be designed to meet customers' needs.
2) The system of quality is prevention. The causes of errors must be determined and then remedied
3) The performance standard is zero defects. Low quality work is not acceptable
4) The measurement of quality is the price of nonconformance. You can measure the costs of bad quality and track the savings from improved quality (Katz 1993).

Crosby (1979) used a 14 point program in approaching quality improvement:

1) Management commitment—be convinced of the need for improving quality.
2) Quality Improvement Team to oversee quality improvement.
3) Quality measurement.
4) Cost of Quality Evaluation—identifying profitable quality improvement opportunities.
5) Quality Awareness—training and education for employees on quality and cost of quality.
6) Corrective Action—employees generate ideas for areas for correction.
7) Zero Defects Planning—committee develops a plan.
8) Supervisor Training—so management can fulfill their role in quality improvement.

9) Zero Defects Day—provides a signal to employees that the organization has a new standard.

10) Goal Setting—goals are posted and meetings held to discuss progress.

11) Error Case Removal—employees report anything that prevents them from doing error-free work.

12) Recognition—public, non-financial rewards for achievement of goals.

13) Quality Councils—employee teams meet to share ideas.

14) Do It All Over Again—emphasis on quality as an on-going process. (Katz 1993)

Each of these quality pioneers, Deming, Juran, and Crosby, felt that quality improvement requires measurement, education, determining and eliminating causes of problems, and a total commitment from management.

Quality in the Public and Service Sectors

The quality revolution became widespread. A recent Gallup Poll done for the American Society for Quality Control suggests that quality is becoming firmly rooted as a way of life in corporate America. The poll found 80 percent of respondents saying some form of team activity occurs in their workplace. Forty percent of established teams indicated their goal is to improve quality.

Because quality improvement was seen as the most advanced approach to customer satisfaction, cost control, and improving work processes, it was quickly embraced by the public in government and service sectors. For example, a survey done in 1993 by the Government Accounting Office indicated that 68 percent of 2,300 federal installations use TQM. On a state level, as a result of the Florida Quality Initiative, 16 of 28 state agencies implement TQM. In the health care sector, hospitals seeking accreditation are now required to have some form of ongoing, continuous quality initiative in place. Many hospitals are reaping substantial bottom line results with their quality projects. For example, Good Samaritan Hospital in Dayton, Ohio, reduced the length of a hospital stay by patients from 12.2 to 7.2 days. We are also seeing the successful implementation of quality programs in our education system, the focus of this book.

An example of a highly successful quality project occurred at Northwest Missouri State University. The quest for quality began in 1984 and continues to this day. Through effective teamwork, the University developed a "Culture of Quality" plan for the improvement of its undergraduate program. Since its inception in 1986-87, the "Culture of Quality" plan incorporates approximately 42 goals and 40 action steps. The University has fully integrated its quality efforts in all aspects of its operations, including formulating a mission statement. Because of the implementation of quality activities, budget for instruction, according to college officials, have increased from 48 percent of the national average for comprehensive universities to over 51.5 percent. Faculty salaries increased from $3,000 below the national norm to the national norm for similar institutions. Other improvements reported the elimination of a backlog of maintenance requests of approximately eighteen months with a cost reduction of $1,700,000 annually. Other quality innovations include, among others:
- the first comprehensive "Electronic Campus" in the nation installed
- writing assignments increased 72 percent
- over 50 campus events that integrate extracurricular life with learning activities
- faculty committees developed a uniform course outline/syllabus

- new faculty evaluation system developed (Hubbard 1993)

Another example, Babson College in Wellesley, Massachusetts, obtained some very impressive results with their quality approach to managing their college. The students, who pay $100,000 to attend this business school, were now viewed as the "customer." Thirty quality teams were formed to improve services to these "customers." They reduced the cost of mailings to accepted students, saving 275 work hours. They reduced the delays in paying financial aid checks from approximately 80 delay-associated incidents to just three in one year. The process for making schedule changes, such as adding or dropping courses, which required students to stand in line for hours was streamlined and the long lines eliminated. The teams were also looking at alternate ways of evaluating faculty and orienting new faculty. These improvements are expected to benefit the college in the future by creating a more generous alumni and getting more student referrals to apply and enter the college. Other examples of quality efforts are detailed in this book.

The Pillars of Quality

Whether the quality improvement endeavor was implemented in the private or public sector, certain elements or "pillars of quality" are usually present. They include a customer focus, continuous improvement philosophy, employee/team participation, supplier partnerships, and management systems.

The 1980s were the hallmark of the industrial renaissance in the United States. At the beginning of the 90s the drum beat spread to the service industries and public sector institutions and agencies. It is at this point that we begin the TQM journey. Succeeding chapters will describe efforts of quality activities.

References

Charters, D. 1993. "U.S. Postal Service Delivers Total Quality." *Quality Digest* (June).

Crosby, P. B. 1979. *Quality is Free.* New York: McGraw-Hill.

Deming, E. W. 1992. *Out of the Crisis.* Cambridge, Mass.: Massachusetts Institute of Technology.

Drucker, P. 1993. *Wall Street Journal* 2 January.

Dusharme, D. 1993. "News You Can Use." *Quality Digest* (April).

Government Accounting Office Survey. 1993. In *Industry Week* 18 January.

Hogan, G. 1993. "Total Quality Management." *Facility Manager* (June).

Hubbard, D. L. 1993. Is Quality a Manageable Commodity in Higher Education? In *Continuous Quality Improvement*, edited by D. L. Hubbard. Maryville, MO: Prescott Publishing Co.

Juran, J. M. 1989. *Juran On Leadership for Quality: An Executive.* New York: The Free Press.

Juran, J. and F. Gryne. 1980. *Quality Planning and Analysis.* New York: McGraw-Hill.

Katz, R. 1993. "The Quality Conflict: Crosby vs. Deming." *Quality Digest* (November).

Peters, T. *A Passion for Excellence.* Nathan/Tyler Productions. Videocassette.

—. 1987. *Thriving on Chaos.* California: Excel.

Schultz, L. E. 1993. "Japan Before Deming." *Quality Perspective* (September).

Shewhart, W. A. 1931. *Economic Control of Quality of Manufactured Product.* New York: Van Nostrand.

ALLAN M. HOFFMAN

Allan M. Hoffman is dean of the School of Health at California State University–Dominguez Hills and is an experienced administrator in higher education and healthcare. He has a doctorate degree from Teachers College, Columbia University, where he was named a Kellogg Fellow and held an appointment in the Institute for the Study of Higher Education. His baccalaureate was earned magna cum laude from the University of Hartford in Connecticut. He holds national board certification as a Health Education Specialist (CHES) by the National Commission on Health Education Credentialing. He is also an active member of the American College of Healthcare Executives, the American Association of Higher Education, the Association for the Advancement of Health Education, and the American Educational Research Association.

Hoffman held academic appointments at the State University of New York at Buffalo and was associate dean for academic affairs at Compton College. Hoffman also held an executive level leadership position with the University of Southern California School of Medicine where he currently holds the rank of clinical professor of family medicine.

RANDAL SUMMERS

Randal Summers is an adjunct senior professor in the School of Business and Health Care Administration at the University of La Verne, California. He is also the Manager of Professional Training and Development for Eastman Inc., an Office Depot Company. Summers has a doctorate in educational psychology from the University of Alberta in Canada and a master of science degree in psychology and counseling from North Dakota State University.

Summers is a member of the American Society for Training and Development in Orange County, California, and a licensed psychologist in Alberta, Canada.

CHAPTER TWO:

TQM:
THE WESTINGHOUSE EXPERIENCE

Aris Melissaratos and Carl Arendt

For the past decade, American business firms have been rethinking their operation and management approaches. Our motives are straightforward—we must find ways to compete with aggressive foreign companies in the global marketplace.

Approaches to this new competitive challenge have coalesced around a group of methods which are collectively called "Total Quality Management" or TQM. Companies who follow this new model of management are demonstrably more successful than those who tread the traditional paths. TQM companies exhibit greater profitability, increased customer satisfaction, lower costs, higher productivity, and superior products and services.

Today, many colleges and universities have begun exploring the ideas of TQM. Their motives are similar to those of industry: they must compete with other institutions to capture a share of the dwindling supply of potential students; costs are escalating wildly; and American society is demanding a unprecedented level of accountability for educational results.

TQM provides philosophies, methods, and technologies to address these issues in new, productive ways. Universities are adopting these methods not only to acquire new subjects for teaching but also to improve their own operations—in the classroom as well as across the campus.

Interestingly, the TQM approach has been developed as a "home-grown" methodology by United States business firms, with little or no involvement from the academic community. As recently as 1989 Xerox—a Malcolm Baldrige National Quality Award winner—attempted to hold a joint industry-academic conference on TQM and experienced an acceptance rate of less than 20 percent of the invited business-school deans and faculty members.

Now, however, that situation has changed. Industry executives are in the unusual position of teaching TQM principles to their academic friends who are working hard to acquire the knowledge and put it to use on campus. For example, attendance from universities and colleges at Westinghouse's public TQM seminars increased from one in 1988, to more than 150 in 1992.

Westinghouse is one of the "founding father" companies of American TQM, having established a Productivity and Quality Center in our headquarters town of Pittsburgh in 1980. For over 12 years the Center has been developing TQM techniques, applying improvement methods, and transferring technology to Westinghouse and other companies. Among other successes, Westinghouse operations have captured national quality awards in three countries including winning the first Malcolm Baldrige National Quality Award in 1988.

Melissaratos and Arendt

In this chapter, lessons we have learned which can be applied to the jobs of managers of academic institutions are discussed. My experience includes over 25 years as a senior line executive of Westinghouse operations with successful TQM processes, as well as three years involvement with the University of Maryland as planned and implemented a TQM initiative.

Back to Basics

There are five basic principles that guide industrial TQM processes according to Rep. Newt Gingrich (R-GA) who advocates applying these principles to government operations. The five are:

1) Ask customers what they want.
2) Set zero defects as the standard.
3) Arrange the shortest possible cycle time.
4) Improve the system, rather than personal behavior.
5) All employees must see themselves as stakeholders in improving quality.

My experience is that every one of the TQM principles we use in industry can be appropriated and usefully applied in a college or university. Vocabularies and emphases change, but this approach to management works well in any sort of organization. The Westinghouse Productivity and Quality Center has even applied TQM successfully to non-profit social agencies and health-care providers, in addition to academic institutions.

The experience of the University of Maryland at College Park (UMCP) provides a good example of the kinds of adaptation required. In developing a TQM plan, the Planning Committee first recognized that the institution has always been conscious of the need for quality. They also recognized that the goal of zero defects is much easier to measure for industrial goods than it is in the more variable product of "knowledge and understanding" of college students. Accordingly, the Committee focused on the element of creating a culture of continuous improvement as the most useful entry point for TQM at UMCP. They defined it as a "systematic process that encourages students, faculty, and staff to identify problems and achieve increasingly effective solutions for these problems."

Their definition provides an excellent starting point for any TQM effort whether it be in an industrial organization, social or government agency. The techniques of TQM can be successfully applied to this goal as well as to any of the other TQM principles.

The Customer Comes First

While recognizing that the notion of students as "customers" is a sensitive issue on campus, I do not know of a better or more descriptive word to express the concept that the goal of TQM is to "delight the customer." This does not mean that "the customer is always right." The relationship is considerably more complex, in that the very nature of education may involve pointing out areas where the student is wrong and offering corrective advice. Nonetheless, success is determined by customer (student) reactions and perceptions of quality.

Of course, there are a number of other customer constituencies who are important to the collegiate community—for example, parents, alumni, staff and faculty, their peers at other institutions, sponsors of funded research, and the general public. For state-aided schools, the taxpayers and government must be added to the list.

It cannot be overemphasized that successful TQM initiatives begin by recognizing the needs of customers and then finding effective ways to satisfy those needs. The culture of continuous improvement is focused on becoming increasingly expert at satisfying customers in increasingly efficient ways.

The Westinghouse Quality Journey

Continuous improvement of our performance has been the goal at Westinghouse since 1980. We call our version of TQM "Total Quality."

In essence, we view Total Quality as a leadership philosophy and management model for running a world-class enterprise. It collects and focuses the current "best practices" to obtain the finest possible performance from an organization. Its four imperatives are:

- **Customer Orientation: a relentless customer focus.** Customers are both internal and external to the organization. TQ methods include defining customer value structures, relating customer needs to strategic and operational issues, and measuring customer satisfaction.
- **Human Resource Excellence: involvement and empowerment of the workforce.** Participation, development, and motivation of our people is crucial. TQ activity is typically performed by employee teams that include representatives of each function and level involved in a business process, plus key customer and supplier representatives.
- **Product/Process Leadership: continuous improvement of business processes.** World-class results of TQ come from continuously improving work processes in offices, factories, and the field. Improvements generally impact both productivity and quality—reducing cost and cycle time and boosting defect-free performance.
- **Management Leadership: creating a culture of success.** TQ leadership creates a culture committed to

excellence through continuous improvement. Sponsoring, advocating, planning, and recognizing the effort are key leadership functions critical to success.

Performance standards for each of these four imperatives are summarized in Figure 1.

Figure 1

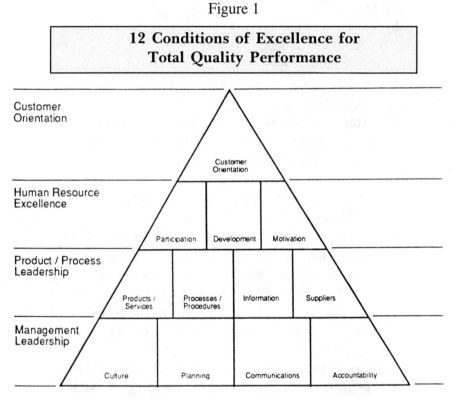

12 Conditions of Excellence for Total Quality Performance

Customer Orientation

Human Resource Excellence

Product / Process Leadership

Management Leadership

Customer Orientation

Participation | Development | Motivation

Products / Services | Processes / Procedures | Information | Suppliers

Culture | Planning | Communications | Accountability

These conditions form the basis for assessing progress in Total Quality performance, for diagnosing gaps which need to be filled, and for awarding prizes and recognition for outstanding achievement.

The formal definition of Total Quality at Westinghouse is "performance leadership in meeting customer requirements by doing the right things right the first time."

Melissaratos and Arendt

While this definition embodies the idea of continuous improvement within the notion of "leadership," the Westinghouse TQM journey has focused primarily on improving our processes—the activities our people perform to get the work done. The "right things" are those processes which delight our customers; doing them "right the first time" means performing the processes repetitively within allowable variations. That is the true meaning of zero defects, and we reach those world-class levels of performance by continuously improving our processes.

One key to success in process improvement for Westinghouse has been to focus on reducing cycle time—the elapsed time required to perform the process. Getting the same results in half the time or less requires ingenuity, innovation, and dedication, and significantly boosts the quality of the result.

This same focus works on campus. Cycle-time projects at the University of Maryland have included such efforts as reducing time to obtain emergency financial approvals from 24 hours to 20 minutes. Athletic services have cut down waiting time for season ticket holders by empowering telephone operators to make a variety of decisions which previously required managerial approval. These are both examples of process innovation which improves cycle time and provides better quality of service.

Process is the Key

In industry we work on processes ranging from entering orders and engineering the product to issuing invoices and collecting receivables. We measure improvement by reductions in process cycle time and cost and cash investment, along with quality and reliability increases.

The Westinghouse Productivity and Quality Center has developed a six-step method which enables interdisciplinary teams—at virtually any skill level—to be successful at process improvement. This technique has been used throughout Westinghouse to improve processes ranging from producing the 11 p.m. television news to designing a radar set. Average improvements include increasing customer satisfaction by 58 percent, reducing cycle time 56 percent, and lowering costs by one-third.

The six process-improvement steps are:

1) Management must commit to improvement. Senior management must believe it, live it, and communicate it to employees. In my experience, this makes a tremendous difference. Visible, ongoing management

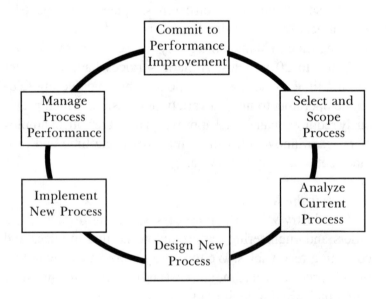

Figure 2

Melissaratos and Arendt

involvement may well be the most critically important element in creating a successful TQM effort.

2) Select and scope the process. Pick the processes which truly will make a difference to the success of the enterprise. A significant part of our work involves developing and applying methods to determine the key issues and critical processes which an organization should address. The main principle here is that no one has enough resources to work on everything that needs to be done; so, we must focus on the "critical few" things which will leverage the greatest improvement. Selecting and scoping the most important processes is at the heart of TQM planning.

3) Analyze the current process. Employee teams take over from management at this point. The teams are composed of people who actually perform the process we are reviewing. Team membership usually crosses disciplines, departments, and levels. The team starts by making a critical examination of the current process, with special attention to problem areas or areas where customer complaints are frequent.

4) Design a new process. The team then simplifies, streamlines, adds new technology, and innovates methods to get results in less time, at less cost, with higher quality.

We use a large tool kit of methods to work on new process design. The kit includes:

- Brainstorming
- Process flow charting
- Cost-time profiling
- Pareto analysis
- Functional diagramming
- Root cause analysis
- Benchmarking

- Computer simulation
- Just-in-Time procedures

There are many other techniques and technologies available to our teams. Some of these are proprietary to Westinghouse, but most of them are in the public domain and widely used in the United States. The key to success is using what the team is comfortable with.

5) Implement the new process. Following management approval, the team implements their recommended new process. This is a critical requirement: the people who develop the new process must also implement it. This requirement leads to strong feelings of ownership and involvement by our people, greatly reducing implementation time and strengthening the chances for success of the new process.

6) Manage the improved process. In particular, use statistical tools to control process variability and keep the new process on track. Verify performance and make corrections as required, all in the spirit of continuous improvement. This is the step which leads to Zero Defects and Error Free Performance. It applies just as much to white-collar and service processes as to processes in the factory. Many industrial companies have found widespread education in basic statistics is a valuable skill for their workforce to perform this step.

This step also underlines a very important aspect of TQM—"management by data." Whether in industry or in academia, all TQM activities are measurable because they are process-based. Improvement decisions should always be made by examining measurements—data—rather than by feel or intuition. A characteristic activity of TQM cultures is "keeping score."

What Do You Do First?

How do you get started on implementing TQM on campus? One good starting point is to establish a center of expertise to facilitate the process and provide training in the particular skills needed to make the initiative a success. At Westinghouse we provided a Productivity and Quality Center from the beginning of our efforts. The university equivalent might be a program office for TQM.

Next we formed a senior management sponsorship group, called a "Total Quality Council." The group's responsibilities included planning the effort (selecting the critical processes), providing resources as needed, sponsoring, encouraging, and recognizing employee participation.

From an operational point of view, selecting the right processes for improvement is the critical activity. At the beginning, we find that "early successes" are very important to establish momentum and encourage participation by our workforce. For this reason, university efforts often begin with administrative processes, which are relatively easy to measure and which make a noticeable and rapid impact on campus life. These initial successes often invite more widespread activities, and the process grows rapidly. At the University of Pennsylvania, for instance, dramatic improvements in mail delivery and garbage removal not only have saved some $160,000 a year, but by being highly visible have also encouraged many faculty members to try a TQM project in their own spheres of activity.

The Total Quality Council has another critical role, demonstrating and communicating leadership commitment to the TQM effort. In my experience, this senior level advocacy is a critical element of success. It first requires senior managers to learn about TQM and thoroughly understand it; then it requires them to become involved in improvement processes on a continuing basis. Finally, it requires taking firm action to be sure employee accomplishments are recognized and celebrated. This leadership commitment is by far the most important element of successful TQM implementation in any organization.

A final observation about management leadership: the key activities for senior managers to focus on throughout the TQM initiative are continuous communications, training, and performance recognition. These, along with widespread employee participation (60 percent participation is world class), are the key ingredients of leadership success.

How Long Before Results Happen?

Once a self-propelling initiative is achieved, what results can we expect and how soon? The best public information available at present is a 1991 report by the United States Government's General Accounting Office, prepared at the request of Representative Donald Ritter (R-PA). Titled "Management Practices. U.S. Companies Improve Performance Through Quality Efforts (GAO/NSIAD-91190)," the report examines 20 private sector companies who were winners and finalists in the Malcolm Baldrige National Quality Award competition from 1988 to 1990. Two Westinghouse divisions (one winner and one finalist) are included in the data.

This report showed that after adopting continuous improvement initiatives, these companies experienced an annual average:
- employee turnover decline of 6 percent
- product reliability improvement of 11.3 percent
- on-time delivery improvement of 4.7 percent
- reduction in errors of 10.3 percent
- product lead-time (development cycle time) reduction of 5.8 percent

- inventory turnover rate improvement of 7.2 percent
- costs of quality reduction (from lost profits, rework, and scrap) of 9 percent
- customer complaint reduction of 11.6 percent
- market share increase of 13.7 percent
- sales per employee improvement of 8.6 percent
- return on assets increase of 1.3 percent

Clearly, the TQM initiative is closely linked with excellent performance in many of the standard business measurements.

A weakness of the GAO report is that it provides no benchmarking data for comparison with other companies in the surveyed companies' industries. At Westinghouse, however, we have a database of Total Quality self-assessment scores dating back to 1981. When we correlate these scores—measuring improvements in individual units' Total Quality performance—with various results measures, we find a strong correlation (in excess of 0.9) with product reliability, total cost, complaints and returns, and operating profit margins. In other words, improvement in TQM performance is demonstrably linked with improvement in measurable performance of the organization.

In addition, our results compare almost identically to another GAO finding. In their report, the average cycle time from initiation of a TQM process to experiencing significant results was 2.4 years. In Westinghouse, the average time for an individual organization to begin reaping significant ongoing rewards from its efforts is between two and three years—a good match.

Similar results can be expected at academic institutions that adopt TQM initiatives. Early returns are encouraging in this respect, with measurable improvements in costs, customer satisfaction, and even classroom procedures reported at such campuses as the University of Pennsylvania, Oregon

State University, and the University of Wisconsin.

Many other institutions are starting TQM initiatives right now. Based on more than a decade of experience at Westinghouse, I confidently predict that the academic community will find this method very helpful in its competition for students, in controlling spiraling costs of education, and in providing the accountability it needs.

ARIS
MELISSARATOS

Aris Melissaratos is responsible for the development and performance of Total Quality and productivity activities throughout the global Westinghouse organization.

He has 25 years experience in manufacturing engineering, program and general management. He has served as manager of manufacturing systems and technology, responsible for industrial, manufacturing, process, and test engineering as well as the management of a manufacturing research and development program focusing on productivity improvement through automation and robotics. In 1980 he was appointed operations manager for the Westinghouse Aerospace Divisions. In that position, he was responsible for the manufacturing cycle of all aerospace products.

Melissaratos holds a bachelor of science degree in electrical engineering from Johns Hopkins University and a master's degree in engineering management from George Washington University. He completed course work for a doctorate in international affairs at The Catholic University of America and attended the Harvard Business School program for management development.

The Westinghouse Experience   31

CARL ARENDT

Carl Arendt's 35-year career with Westinghouse has included responsibilities in communications and marketing in a variety of businesses including electronic components, aerospace systems, and construction products. He also served as world promotion manager for Westinghouse International just prior to taking on his present position as communications manager at the Westinghouse Productivity and Quality Center (WPQC) in 1985. Arendt has a bachelor of science degree in physics from Carnegie Mellon University.

Arendt is responsible for Total Quality communications throughout the global Westinghouse organization. His particular interest for the past seven years has been the management of change processes in organizations.

Arendt's recent audiences have included senior management from Chevron, CSR Ltd. (Australia), Digital Equipment Corp., Livermore National Laboratory, Mellon Bank, Mobil, Rohm & Haas, Saline Water Conversion Corporation (Saudi Arabia), Scottish Nuclear Ltd., TVA, U.K. Royal Mail, United Way, and conferences sponsored by the American Marketing Association, The Conference Board (United States and Canada), and the United States Department of Commerce.

CHAPTER THREE:

A JOURNEY TO EXCELLENCE

Dennis P. Grahn

"All this stuff sounds good, it even looks good on paper, but I've heard it all before. My question is: How do we do it?" (Mike, the fork lift operator.)

Mike does not like too much conceptual "stuff." He is a pragmatic guy. But before we can answer his "how to" question, a bit of conceptual talk may be necessary. We need to understand "what and why" before we can understand "how."

When we begin our journey toward excellence, we may or may not see that there are major obstacles of our own making—a herd of elephants in the room, so to speak, that are blocking our ability to see our way. These "invisible elephants" are a serious, fascinating, and sometimes almost insurmountable barrier to our progress. It also turns out that they can be a powerful force which can help us on our journey if we can learn to "see" them and tame them to our will.

These elephants have a name: not pachyderms, but paradigms. They are our "invisible mental models" or "mind maps" of how the whole world "out there" **is** and how we relate to it.

This chapter is first about examining some of our mental models about ourselves and our work, and how they can either block or assist us in our journey towards excellence. These involve what we want to accomplish, why, and our general approach. Then we will discuss Mike's more pragmatic question of exactly and specifically "how."

The Roots of Excellence

Another way to look at our mental models is that they are the roots (or foundation) of who we are and how we relate to the world. They are also blueprints or maps that we use to help shape how we respond to all of life's various situations. Since they have such a powerful, governing influence on all of us, it is important for us to understand them and use them to move our progress forward. We must also be ready to adapt, modify, or even completely change our mental models if better ones come along. Professor George Box of the University of Wisconsin–Madison says, "All Models are wrong, some are useful." This is true of all models, but particularly true of our "mental models." Keep this in mind as we proceed, because we will introduce a number of different paradigm models. Realize each one is wrong (at least incomplete), but ask yourself "is it useful?"

The trend in science has been toward reductionism, a constant breaking things down into little bitty pieces. What people are finally realizing is that this process has a dead end to it. Scientists are now becoming much more interested in the idea that the whole can be greater than the sum of its parts. (Doyne Farmer)

Holism Versus Reductionism

Reductionism. There are two different ways of seeing the world that can have a profound influence on how we approach everything we do. Reductionism is the Isaac Newton, Frederick Taylor, clockwork, machine mental model of "how the world is." Reductionism says that "The whole is equal to the sum of its parts," and the way to improve any process or system is to understand and improve some or all of the "parts." This was the dominant scientific paradigm of the 17th, 18th, 19th, and the first half of the 20th centuries. Many scientific advances in everything from physics to medicine to the dynamics of business can be attributed to this mental model. It is a very viable and useful model in some situations, particularly when dealing with issues (processes and systems) of low to moderate complexity that have limited and well-defined interactions.

The reductionistic model has some significant limitations, however, and these limitations become more important as the issues (processes and systems) we want to deal with become more complex and interrelated. The reductionist approach becomes a serious liability when our "fix" to improve one part of a complex system actually does harm to the larger whole. Usually this harm takes time to play out and we may not even realize it when our fix eventually contributes to a failure of the whole system.

The Reductionist way of seeing the world is also closely related to a preoccupation with winning and individual performance that is common in our society. Over-emphasizing the performance of a single individual or team in an interrelated situation practically guarantees poorer performance of the larger system over time.

A Journey to Excellence 35

It is a scientifically proven axiom of General Systems Theory that "maximizing the performance of any individual or sub-elements in an interrelated system will prevent maximum performance of the whole system." Unfortunately, there is often a time delay in this effect which may prevent us from realizing what is happening until it is too late. Examples of the effects of this axiom are common. A few follow:

- In an attempt to increase on-time shipments, a company put in place a measurement which held the production and shipping department strongly accountable. The pressure was so high that they began sending more and more partial shipments (already an occasional practice) which significantly improved the measurement. After some time the increased "partials" caused many customers to become angry and request credit for additional freight charges, multiple handling, etc.
- The Purchasing Department is held accountable for the cost of raw materials. They buy from the cheapest source or buy bargain basement, off-specification materials on sale. The eventual result is higher waste and poor productivity in production. The Purchasing Department looks like a hero and production takes it on the chin.
- Sales people in a large furniture and appliance retail store were paid individual incentives based on their weekly sales volume. When a customer came in, each salesperson would guard "their customers" with a vengeance. Some sales people were more knowledgeable than others in appliances, some in TVs, others in stereos, still others in living room furniture. But it did not matter who could best serve that particular customer. The individual sales incentive caused each salesperson to feel a customer "is **mine!**" The sales

group talked a lot about teamwork, but did not function as a team (quite the opposite). A new sales manager with a different paradigm changed the sales compensation to a group incentive. Now, sales people gladly hand off customers to another sales person who may serve a particular customer's needs better. Sales increased significantly.

• Millions of people are starving in Africa, so we send food. This apparently helps the situation, but we are surprised when a few years later the problem is worse then ever. We send even more food, which again seems to help, but somehow a few years later the famine is far worse than it has ever been. What we do not realize is that our "help" for the immediate situation becomes like a perpetual "social welfare system" which creates dependency on our aid and does nothing to address the real causes of the problem. We may want to send food, but that is not enough. Part of our aid must be to teach people self-sufficiency and how to control their population, or else the vicious cycle will continue getting worse.

• Quality, productivity, and safety are three major concerns of any business in day-to-day operations. Is it possible to over-emphasize any one of these to the detriment of the others? It is fashionable to say "focus on quality and you will get productivity." It is also fashionable to say "safety is our number one concern." Is this reality? Would productivity suffer if we focused only on quality? Would productivity suffer if we are obsessed with safety to the point of guarding every move we made? Is not reality the fact that we must consider all of these factors (and others) together as a system, to find the best way to balance them all effectively?

Reductionist View: "I have specific job skills developed over many years of experience. I will not share them with anyone because it is part of my own personal job security; they cannot lay me off because I am the only one who can do the job."

Holistic View: "I have specific job skills developed over many years. I must share them, because if we all do, it will strengthen the whole company and increase everybody's job security."

These are just a few of many situations where our mental models of the world influence our behavior. How we deal with each of these situations is profoundly influenced by them. Reductionism is a successful paradigm for some situations, but has serious and even potentially disastrous limitations for many others. What is the alternative?

Holism. Another way to view the world is as an interconnected web where every activity and every situation is related to, has influence on, and is influenced by, many other activities and situations. Holism says that "The whole is greater than the sum of its parts" because these interactions can produce unique and unpredictable outcomes. This mental model of "how the world is" is at least as old, perhaps older, than reductionism (the ancient Greeks had this dialogue).

New scientific insights and tools such as computer simulations have shifted the scales to Holism because it represents how the world really is better than reductionism. We might begin with Albert Einstein's Relativity Theory (everything is relative to the observer) and Werner Heisenberg's Principle of Uncertainty (no measurement can be absolutely precise because all are affected by the act of measurement), which were originally applied to physics, but seem to apply to human organizational situations as well. We could continue with the discoveries of E.H. Lorenz in 1963, and many others since, who have increased our understanding of how dynamic systems interact in ways that amplify Heisenberg's tiny uncertainties in our measurements (or data or understanding) through the process of feedback and iteration, to produce very large effects very quickly on what we observe. This becomes more and more representative of what really happens in our businesses and other institutions as the situation (or system) in question becomes more complex and interrelated.

One way to apply this new paradigm in business is by using General Systems Theory to understand and improve business systems. A lot of work by scientists such as J. Canfield, J. D. Farmer, M. J. Feigenbaum, J. Gleick, I. Prigogine, M. J. Radzicui, and a host of others has prepared the conceptual and experimental basis for this application. Margaret Wheatley's best selling book *Leadership and The New Science* has set the stage and the challenge.

Some of the best and most practical work has been done over the last two decades at M.I.T.'s Sloan School of Management. This work is called "Systems Thinking" and is described in Peter Senge's best selling book *The Fifth Discipline*. Systems Thinking is the Fifth Discipline. It is a way to operationalize the holistic paradigm so that it can be used in practical ways to improve business systems and organizational dynamics. Senge (1990) explains his views on how Systems Thinking can be used to successfully integrate his other four disciplines—Personal Mastery, Mental Models, Shared Vision, and Team Learning—into a highly successful organization. All of the concepts, methods and tools of Systems Thinking have their basic roots in the holistic paradigm and General Systems Theory.

In the works mentioned above, there are many experimental and practical examples of applying the holistic paradigm and the concepts, methods and tools of Systems Thinking, to real business situations. They could be applied to any of the real life examples mentioned earlier or virtually any situation.

Some examples we have found practical and useful are as follows:

- The Beer Game is a game designed to teach Systems Thinking by experience and self discovery, rather than by conceptual discussion. A modified version of it can be used to teach first line supervisors, production workers, and office workers the purpose, value and skills needed to apply statistical tools (SPC) and statistical thinking to improve work systems. The principle involved is "visibility works." These tools help make what is happening more visible. It teaches what is expected of them, and why, in a way that is fun and easier to understand and to translate into a new behavior than conceptual discussions or going through practical examples (no matter how relevant those examples my be).

- Management Flight Simulators are computer programs that simulate many of the interactive dynamics involved in a particular business. You "manage" the simulations by getting feedback on performance for many dimensions such as profit, growth, ROA, ROE, sales volume, turnover, inventory, training, market share, receivable, payable, cash flow, and many others. You then use this information to make decisions on asset purchases, hiring, training, market strategy, new products, or any of a number of other business decisions. You can watch your vision, strategy, and various decisions play out over years (or decades).

Some people argue that you can never get a computer program to simulate all of the dynamics of a real business. This is true of course, but they can be surprisingly realistic in their behavior. An analogy can help explain:

- Football scrimmage practice during the week is never an exact simulation of the game coming up on Sunday. Even so, most people would agree that scrimmage is useful, even necessary to properly prepare for the game. It doesn't guarantee that you will win, but it certainly increases your odds.

Where do business managers get to practice? To hone their decision-making skills? The answer is usually by making mistakes in real situations. Until now, business managers had no "practice field" other than their real jobs. Management flight simulators provide a very realistic practice field (or scrimmage if you prefer) to use information, make decisions, and watch them play out. It is not reality, but it is close enough to get realistic practice. Used properly, you can get the equivalent of ten years experience in just a few hours.

- Logistics Simulators are cousins of management flight simulators. They are computer programs that allow you to visualize the dynamics of product and information "flow" in a complex business system. You can simulate an existing system and run it in accelerated "real time." The visual display allows you to "see" the whole system operating at once. Discontinuous flow, bottlenecks, inventory buildups, and other logistic opportunities become visible. You can play realistic "what if" scenarios by adding equipment or people, changing the layout, restructure to cellular instead of departmental production, etc. Running the program in these new configurations gives you an idea of how they will work, where problems may occur (so you can deal with them up front), and what the benefits of various approaches will be. The ability of these simulators to visualize complex interactions helps us locate the real "systems leverage points," where small changes may produce dramatic improvements. These methods and tools all help us think more systemically in our quest to continually improve our business and organizational systems.

There are a host of other Systems Thinking tools that have been developed. It is the tools, and the skills to use them, which translate concepts into real world activities that produce progress.

The holistic paradigm, and the practical application of General Systems Theory by using Systems Thinking, is a different way to approach continuous improvement than traditional reductionistic scientific methods. Each offers a way to explore and improve business and organizational processes and systems, but the approach, the methods and the tools are different. We need to understand both, so we can apply the most appropriate approach to whatever situations we are faced with.

Holistic system improvements try to define the "underlying structure" so that when we apply our fix, it is not to the symptom but to the actual underlying cause. This is difficult because these structures, and the interactions between sub-elements, are often very complex and difficult to define. The tools of Systems Thinking are designed to help us do a better job (never a perfect one) of understanding and improving complex systems.

A very important conclusion that comes from using the Holistic Paradigm and General Systems Theory is that the best systemic solutions are often not very obvious and sometimes quite simple. In complex systems, a small amount of effort in just the right place can cause a tremendous improvement (or a tremendous problem) because of the amplifying effect of repeated iterations in a non-linear relationship. This may seem like a difficult concept, but it is really quite simple and we see it every day. An example is when an unintentional wrong word or deed can cause a rebellion (or strike) which is way out of proportion to the original word or deed. Complex systems are "sensitive" like this to certain things at certain times. If we can discover these sensitivities, and time our action(s) properly, we can avoid problems and sometimes cause major improvements with small effort.

One last point about complex, interactive systems in that they tend to be "self-organizing." This is a property of systems described by non-linear dynamics or "Deterministic Chaos Theory."

At this point, Mike the forklift operator would be quite sure we have lost our marbles, but this insight has some very important ramifications about our general approach towards excellence. The Reductionist paradigm suggests breaking a system into pieces or sub-elements. The next steps are to examine these sub-elements and eliminate any non-value added steps, then improve the accuracy and efficiency of what remains. The Holistic Paradigm suggests that we try to understand the whole system (how all of the sub-elements interrelate) and how it fits with our purpose, then devise our improvement strategy based on this understanding. It may involve a small "tweak" to a sensitive node or a complete system redesign, or anything in between.

Many real life systems are so complex we could never fully understand them. Even if we could, we could never predict them because, like the weather, they are very sensitive to initial conditions—initial conditions that Werner Heisenberg proved we can never know precisely. Perhaps there is another approach which is more viable when it comes to the issue of leadership in a business organization.

Margaret Wheatley suggests an alternative to an "engineered approach" to leading change in an organization. Our typical approach would be either a reductionistic "bits and pieces" analysis or a whole system "causal loop" analysis or some other form of scientific analysis by a team of experts. This analysis would lead to a comprehensive "re-engineering" proposal with an implementation plan, resources, timetable, responsibility, accountability, and all the other solid, pragmatic business activities that make us feel real progress is happening.

This approach does work, but is it the best way to adapt to our rapidly changing world? A very high percentage of reengineering projects fail in the long term (same is true of SPC programs, TQM programs, MBO programs and many other attempts of this nature). Might there be a better way to organize our general approach?

Margaret Wheatley suggests that Deterministic Chaos and the Theory of Self Organizing Systems offers an alternative. We can still use the methods and tools of either Reductionistic or Holistic science when they are appropriate to a given situation, but our general approach to leadership would not be to initiate a detailed, structural analysis leading to an imposed, reengineered solution. Rather, we would focus on just two principles that underlie self-organizing systems as follows:

1) Establish a shared purpose: Provide meaning, clear values and a mission. Why do we exist as an organization? What do we want to accomplish, be, or become? Peter Senge (1990) describes it as "shared vision." Somehow make this clear and strong, even inspirational if you can, because **it is the principle around which you organize.**

2) Self-Referential Information: Establish an information system that gives real time, accurate and usable feedback to the organization on how it is performing **in reference to its purpose.** This information also compares the internal status of the organization to the external environment continuously. The model looks something like this:

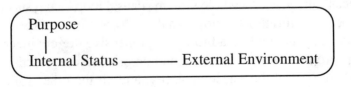

The idea is that an organization with a clear and strongly shared purpose which also has good self-referential information will "self-organize" to achieve that purpose. Theoretically, it would not be necessary to "engineer" and impose an external structure on the organization. It would also not be necessary to impose any "re-engineered" changes on the organization as time passes, because it would be constantly adapting or **re-engineering itself** to changes in the external world.

It would seem that this model must also be supported by people of high ability (the motivation is supplied by the shared purpose or vision) and a resource rich environment. These resources could include financial and other physical assets, but more importantly the necessary skills which include both Reductionist and Holistic Scientific Methods (use whatever is situationally appropriate).

This could be considered a "generic model" (or new paradigm?) of how to lead a highly adaptive organization. Perhaps this model of organizational leadership would be more effective in certain highly competitive, rapidly changing businesses. We will examine some practical ways to bring these ideas to life in real situations later on in the chapter. First we will discuss a closely related paradigm which can support or undermine our ability to adapt and change. This is our mental model of leadership.

Leader As Servant or Leader as Steward Versus Leader as Master

The Holistic Systems view of the world not only suggests a different approach to scientific process improvement; it also strongly supports a different "role" for those of us in formal leadership positions (who influence others in a directional sort of way). Reductionism suggests rigid hierarchical structures, information given only to a few, lots of formalized policies, procedures and instructions, and very tight, hands-on "control" by a leader. Holism would suggest looser structures which are guidelines only, widely shared information, formality (of policies, procedures and instructions) kept to a minimum, and "control" placed to a large degree in the hands of whoever is doing the work. "Control" in the Holistic paradigm is not achieved by authoritarian dictum (orders and instructions), but rather by the power of people with a "shared purpose" who have good "self-referential information."

The role of the leader within a self-organizing systems model of leadership becomes more one of keeping the vision alive in people. It also involves helping them focus on the mission, helping them get the information they need to do their job, and most importantly, to continually develop their skills, habits, and other abilities so they can become progressively more self-sufficient, more self-directed, and more self-managing.

The "Leader as Master" paradigm of leadership is very common, particularly with first line supervisors. This is the "heroic" leader who mainly uses a directive style, keeps information to him/herself, gives orders and controls what is going on (at least she thinks so). She is the boss, the chief firefighter/problem solver and the disciplinarian who controls her people mainly by fear of punishment or job security. Her scope of influence is narrow and very focused on the short term ("here and now"). She may not possess all of these characteristics, but may have a number of them and they tend to dominate her style of leadership.

It is very unlikely that a holistic systems approach to organizational leadership, as previously suggested by Margaret Wheatley, could work where this sort of leadership is prevalent. It is too rigid and limiting to allow the flexibility and information sharing necessary. Such a leader would strongly resist the new approach because in his mind it would erode traditional authority and control (in actuality, authority is not undermined and control is much greater because it is in the hands of the do-er).

A different model for leadership is required to allow the Holistic, Self-Organizing Systems Paradigm to function. This leader is a servant to her people rather than a master of them. She is constantly articulating the vision of the organization in a passionate way. She **helps people** understand their mission and how they are doing in their achievement. She is a developer of people and a master of "situational leadership," who knows when to be directive, when to encourage and support, when to delegate, and has the skill to do all of them effectively. She shares information with everyone and **helps** them make sure they have all of the information necessary to do their jobs. She knows how to **help people** get resources of all kinds (money, equipment, ideas, information, scientific methods, etc.) to continually improve the effectiveness and efficiency of their work to achieve their mission. She is a "Postheroic Leader" who leads by principles and values. People **choose** to follow her from a sense of trust, respect, and common purpose.

You could sum up the two opposing leadership models as illustrated in Figure 1.

Figure 1

Leader as Master (Heroic)	Leader as Servant or Steward (Postheroic)

• Authoritarian
• Focused mainly on the short term
• The Boss
• In charge of everything
• Keeps information himself
• Executes the plans of Upper Mgmt.
• Mainly a directive style
• Gives orders
• Is "in control" (at least he thinks so)
• Disciplinarian
• Chief Firefighter/ Problem Solver
• People follow out of fear of punishment and job security
	• Principle Centered
	• Focused both on short and long term
	• The Visionary
	• Missionary
	• Shares info widely
	• Plans and helps others plan how to achieve the organizational mission
	• Uses "situational leadership" effectively (whatever "style" is appropriate to the particular situation)
	  • Directive Style
	  • Coaching Style
	  • Encouragement/Support Style
	  • Delegator Style
	• Focuses on developing others
	• Helps others learn to solve their own problems
	• Delegates authority and responsibility to others as they develop
	• Enforces discipline through punishment only as a last resort
	• People choose to follow out of respect, trust and common purpose

No one has all of the characteristics on the left or all of the characteristics on the right. It is sort of a continuum with most people having a "tendency" towards one or the other. There is a very close relationship between this model and Douglas MacGregor's model of Theory "X" vs. Theory "Y" leaders developed decades ago (Figure 2).

Theory X (Assumptions about People)	Theory Y (Assumptions about People)
• Do not like to exert themselves and try hard to work as little as possible	• Work hard toward objectives to which they are committed
• Avoid responsibility	• Assume responsibility within these commitments
• Are not interested in achievement	• Are capable of directing their own behavior
• Are incapable of directing their own behavior	• Want their organizations to succeed
• Are indifferent to organizational needs	• Are not passive and submissive and prefer to make decisions about their own work
• Prefer to be directed by others	• Will make decisions within their commitments
• Avoid making decisions whenever possible	• If trusted and depended on, do not disappoint
• Need to be closely supervised and controlled	• Need general support and help at work
• Are motivated at work by money and other gains	• Are motivated at work by interesting and challenging tasks
• When they mature, they do not change	• Are able to change and develop

Figure 2

You can see that "X" relates more to Leader as Master and "Y" to Leader as Servant. MacGregor was careful to point out that a Theory "Y" leader realizes that Theory "X" assumptions are sometime true (in a sense Theory "Y" includes Theory "X"). In the same way, a Postheroic, servant leader recognizes that a heroic, directive style is sometimes necessary. The effective servant leader is sensitive to the needs of a particular situation and has the flexibility of style to adopt appropriately. Regardless of the leadership style being used in a particular situation, the servant leader is always developing the ability, motivation, and self-esteem of others so they can become progressively more self-sufficient and more self-managing. The idea is to delegate more authority and responsibility incrementally as peoples' ability and motivation are ready for it.

Adopting the servant leader model may be a requirement to achieving the highly adaptable, business "learning organization" described by Senge (1990), or to effectively use the "new science" ideas described by Wheatley. We need to have this dialogue with our leaders and help them acquire the understanding, self-insight, and personal strength to be "servants to" and developers of their people.

Now that we have discussed some of the "invisible elephants" in the room, we need to figure out how to use them to our advantage in practical, real life situations. It is obvious that these invisible pachyderms, or rather paradigms, could block our progress. Now that we can "see" them, how can we harness their power to help us on our journey towards sustained excellence?

But How Do We Do It?

Real business systems, and particularly the human dynamics/organizational systems that control them, may often be too complex to "figure out." Traditional Reductionist

Scientific Methods may have serious limitations in this regard, and even the "new science" tools and methods of "Systems Thinking" may at times be inadequate to understand and "control" real life systems. Of course we can understand and influence systems using these tools to some varying degrees (depending upon the situation), but is there an approach that can turn the fundamentally unfathomable, unpredictable nature of complex systems to our advantage?

Perhaps there is, and it is not a new idea at all. Steven Covey (1989) calls it "Principle Centered Leadership." To become truly excellent, we must have a solid, basic foundation of principles and values which help define our purpose and give meaning to our vision of what we want to become. This is true at the level of the individual person, the team or department, and the business organization (and society for that matter). It is like a hologram, or self-similar fractal pattern generated by a non-linear, dynamic, determinisically chaotic system, i.e., "The whole is in every part" (Kim 1990).

What does this look like in a real business? It can take an infinite variety of forms, but one model could be something like this:

- Establish <u>Purpose</u>—Containing meaning, values, principles, mission, and inspirational vision. (What we want to accomplish, be, and become).
- Establish <u>Feedback</u>—Containing information, measurements, a "balanced scoreboard" to measure your real time progress (provide meaningful, self-referential information) on the internal status of your businesses with respect to the external environment, (markets, customers, government, community, etc.) and your purpose.
- Establish <u>Means</u>—Containing methods, models, skills, tools, abilities, processes, systems, maps, resources, or whatever you need to accomplish your purposes.

The Menasha Corporation Excellence Process

A Real Example: As a business organization, journeying towards excellence is not at simple as one-two-three, but it may be as simple as three-four-five: 3-wins, 4-goals, 5-drivers. The three wins are the **Purpose** for which the organization exists (or vision if you prefer). The four goals are the necessary prerequisites to effective self-management and self- organization. The five drivers are the **Means** by which we accomplish our purpose. (Or, said another way, we accomplish our purpose by focusing on the five drivers). This is an incomplete—and therefore "wrong," but potentially useful—model that can help us communicate our vision and the means we use to move towards it, in an understandable way to all 5000 of our people.

We will explain each of these elements in a little detail. As you will see, the necessary "self-referential information is built into both the four goals (goal #2) and the five drivers (driver three and within the driver model itself). Notice also that very specific tools, methods, and skills are associated with each of the drivers.

One final point: to journey towards sustained excellence, you cannot be satisfied until **all** three wins are synergistically achieved. Compromising any one of them will derail the process in the long run.

Three Wins
Win #1—"WIN FOR OUR CUSTOMERS"

Win #1 is creating a "win for the customer." Our customers are at the center of what we do, but they are certainly not "always right"—are you? Customers are people too, so first and foremost we must establish a relationship of trust by being trustworthy. Then we must constantly work to really understand in depth their constantly changing needs.

It is a commonly repeated cliché that we must strive for

"customer satisfaction." Actually, this is a very unsatisfactory and insufficient goal. Customer delight is a much better goal! Some examples:

- A fortune 100 company is a customer of one of our packaging plants supplying them corrugated boxes. They produce personal hygiene consumer products on high speed, automatic case packing production lines. Our boxes must be very high quality (color graphics, erect, and fill with no jam-ups, etc). They were very "satisfied" with our boxes and service.

  One day this customer calls us and says, "We will soon be introducing a new product with some difficult and very important packaging requirements. Will you help us?" We said yes, and three of our people met with five of theirs, including two of their production workers. We taught them how to use Quality Function Deployment (QFD) by using an affinity diagram and a House of Quality Matrix, etc., which worked very well; they thoroughly enjoyed the process.

  A few days later we received a letter saying "you are truly an unusual supplier. Not only do you give us high quality products and services, you also teach our people how to use the newest quality methods and tools as a bonus. We would never have expected this from a corrugated box supplier." Is this giving a customer what is expected (meeting expectations), or going beyond to unexpected value? Is this satisfaction or delight?

- Certain customers we have are unhappy if we send them two or three bad boxes in a truckload of 15,000 (that equals a 0.023 percent defective). Why? Because it could mean three jam-ups on the packing line and 30 to 45 minutes downtime in one shift.

One time our designer made an error, and we sent them a whole truckload of defects that would not run. What could have been a disaster actually became an opportunity. The lady that runs their packaging line knows us (and likes us). Instead of calling her boss, she called us, and we had a team on sight within a half-hour. We found the problem, helped her adjust her machine so the boxes would run (with permission from their packaging engineer), fixed the next truckload, and came back to help her adjust back to standard. No production was lost (I suspect she may have speeded up the line a bit to catch up). Then she told her boss about the problem.

A few days later we received a letter from their purchasing department that said, "You truly are an unusual supplier! You are the only one that sends us a major problem and corrects it before we even know we have one." Satisfaction or delight?

- Last example: You go to a restaurant and you are completely satisfied with their food quality, service, and price. You go to their competitor across the street and are also completely satisfied with food quality, service, and price. But, at the second restaurant you were impressed by the unexpected fresh flowers on the table and the songs the owner played on his violin. When your out-of-town relatives come to visit, which restaurant will you take them to? Is this satisfaction or delight?

"Delight" always wins over "satisfaction." You satisfy a customer by giving them what they want. You delight them by understanding their real needs and providing them unexpected value whenever you can. This produces a long-term, trust-based relationship (and many customers are even willing to pay a bit more for this).

A big part of this sort of relationship is product reliability, dependability, controlled variation, and service quality, but it is even more important to be innovative and responsive to changing needs. Achieving this sort of "win" for your customers (either external or internal) produces the potential for a sustaining, mutually beneficial relationship.

Win #2—"WIN FOR OUR PEOPLE"

Win #2 is creating a "win for our people," the people who work with us in our company. Our people control all of our assets and the relationships inside and outside of our company.

Official leaders and managers have influence, but do not "control" much of what goes on in any business. Control is actually in the hands of the production worker using the machine, the sales or customer service person talking to the customer, the maintenance person doing the maintenance, etc. Ultimately, each person controls his own quality, productivity, safety, and other aspects of his job (such as how well he works in a team). This is reality!

Our people have needs and can be "delighted" to work here) just like our customers. People are much more likely to "delight" external customers if they themselves are delighted, but how is this accomplished? We must challenge and stimulate the whole person. (Holistic paradigm?) People are task do-ers, but they are also minds, hearts, and spirits. Unless we can engage people on all levels, they will not be delighted in the long run.

Stephen Covey (1989) has a model that begins to explain this. He says people need "to live, to love, to learn, and to leave a legacy." We all have these needs, though some of them may be buried deeply in a cynical world view in some of us.

If we can engage people in these four ways, we can begin to tap into their full measure of loyalty, trust, dedication, innovation, and the myriad kinds of potential that each of us brings to our work. An important point is that we cannot <u>cause</u> this to happen for other people. Each of us must do this for ourselves. But we can be a model, a positive influence, and we can help establish an environment where it is more likely to happen. "To live" means the basics: food, shelter, clothing, a feeling of security, support in times of trouble, and the ability to provide for my family. These are the basic resources companies provide in the form of wages, benefits, a safe working environment, job security, etc. "To live" also includes my physical health and fitness. Physical health and fitness is a basic foundation for all other contributions. It sharpens our mental abilities, enhances our social/emotional well-being, and energizes our spirit.

"To love" means our social/emotional health: Healthy relationships at work, good friends, and a supportive and loving family. We can love our work, but there is a difference between healthy love and obsession in any relationship—work or personal. Without an interconnected web (holistic view?) of social/emotional support, we can become brittle and shallow. Ultimately our work, our mental health, and our life will suffer.

"To learn" means growing and developing our potential for contribution by continually learning new skills. These include technical skills to accomplish our work and other tasks, interpersonal skills to effectively work with others individually and as a team, leadership skills for our own personal life and how we influence others. "To learn" also includes our mental health (which is strongly influenced by "to live" and "to love"). As we continue to grow and develop, our confidence and self-esteem will grow accordingly. A person with true wisdom knows how much they do not know and realizes that everybody knows more about something than they do. Confidence, self-esteem, and the humbling nature of true wisdom (how can we be pompous, self-important or self-righteous if we truly begin to understand our limitations?) is a strong defense against mental disease.

"**To leave a legacy**" is having meaning in our lives. It means to have a purpose, a mission, an inspirational vision that fuels our motivation. If we have a compelling vision of what we want to be or become, this vision pulls us towards it with great power. If we can share this vision or purpose with others and we can honestly assess our "current reality," the "gap" between the two becomes a powerful motivator to work together (Wheatley 1992). This gap also helps us define what kinds of results or "result areas" are most important to accomplish, what kinds of "performance indicators" we need to measure our progress, and what are the most important specific actions we can focus on to achieve our mission and move towards our vision. "To leave a legacy" means engaging the spirit of people and is driven by a sense of values, meaning and purpose. It means participating in, contributing to, and having ownership in what our purpose is and how we will achieve it. Achieving win #2 is ultimately up to each of us as "proactive" individuals to accomplish. No business organization can make or cause these things to happen, but a business organization can have strong influence on them in a number of ways.

Win #2 and win #1 are strongly and intimately related to the servant leader paradigm. If we can effectively teach people the philosophy, roles, and behaviors associated with the servant leader model, it is my belief that both of these wins would be much easier to achieve and sustain. The practical steps we might take to achieve this vision of leadership are discussed in more detail later under **"means—the five drivers"** (Driver #1—People Quality).

Win #3—"WIN FOR THE BUSINESS"
A "for profit business" has needs too. Long term profit above a certain level is necessary to justify the investment of capitol. Certain performance levels of Return on Assets, Return on Investment, and (or) Return on Shareholders Equity need to be met or the business will not survive and grow. These needs vary considerably from small, privately owned companies to large publicly traded companies, but the need is still there.

Closely related to sustaining profit and growth is the maintenance of customer and supplier relationships, identifying potential new customers, new markets, and innovative new products and services. Building and maintaining a reputation for quality products and service is also critical. If the needs of the business are not met in the long term, the other two wins are not possible. Everyone concerned with a particular business should understand what these needs are, get feedback on how well they are being met and work constantly to see that they are achieved.

Purpose, Vision, Mission
The vision of "win-win-win" is a way to create a mental image of what we ultimately want to achieve. Delighting customers with unexpected value, providing people the opportunity for contribution and personal growth, and meeting the financial survival and growth needs of the business should all be achieved together and in balance. If we compromise any one of the three wins by focusing too hard on any one of the others, we will harm our long term performance and not sustain our journey to excellence.

One of the absolutely essential keys to keeping a proper balance between these three wins is a constant flow of accurate, meaningful, and real time information on each. The three wins themselves form a sort of interrelated system because each strongly influences the others. How to set up such an information system and the tools and methods available to help, is discussed in more detail later under "**means—the 5 drivers**" (Driver #3—Information Quality).

Goals Of Excellence —The Four Excellence Goals

If achieving the three wins is our vision of excellence, how do we go about moving towards this vision? In a business organization, excellence can only be achieved by, with, and through people.

Human organizations are "self-organizing systems" (Wheatley 1992) in the sense that they form relationships and structures that use resources to achieve a purpose. The Reductionist Scientific Paradigm tends to lead us to impose external structure (e.g., management hierarchies, departmental structures, etc.) by breaking down and analyzing the parts of the system, then fitting them together like a jigsaw puzzle. This structure is often engineered (or reengineered) by an outside expert or group of experts such as Industrial Engineers or Consultants. This is the Frederick Taylor, Henry Ford approach and it works! It is very useful, even necessary, in some situations.

The Holistic Scientific paradigm, or Systems Thinking if you prefer, suggests another approach. This is not to say that Systems Thinking rules out the "analysis by component" approach, but it does say that this approach has serious limitations in many situations, particularly when dealing with the complex and highly interactive systems that make up a business.

The Systems approach would suggest that you allow the structure to form or emerge from the "inside out," rather than imposing the structure from the "outside in." It is related to the Servant Leader paradigm because you **delegate** responsibility to all of the members of the organization, rather then **direct** them in the way that they are going to organize. How much delegation is given and in which areas, versus how much encouragement, coaching, or direction depends on the level of ability and motivation present in the organization. This leads us back again to the servant leader paradigm which is at it is foundation a "people development" focused model.

We know that a self-organizing system needs a meaningful purpose or vision to organize around, in this case "win-win-win." We also know it needs good self-referential information on its current status with respect to each "win." The four excellence goals represent specific goals that help us move progressively more towards this self-organizing potential. The more we can tap into this potential, the more flexible and adaptable our organization becomes to a rapidly changing business environment.

Another important result of this approach is high motivation, commitment, ownership, responsibility and accountability for all people in the organization (people **own things they participate in helping to create** or recreate). As we achieve the four Excellence Goals, we enable the individual members of the organization to participate more effectively in the self-organizing potential of human dynamic systems.

The Four Excellence Goals are as follows:
1) We understand our business.
2) We know what is expected and how we are doing.
3) We have the skills to perform.
4) We are involved in business, progress and change.

These goals allow each of our business units to focus on specific actions that enable the self-organization potential to

Grahn

emerge without needing to deal with, or fully understand (does anybody?) all of the conceptual underpinnings of Holism and Self-Organizing Systems Theory. We can take specific actions to achieve each of these goals and this will enable a natural evolution towards more and more self-management, self-direction and self-organization.

Goal #1—We Understand Our Business

This means that we work at having <u>all</u> of our people understand the particular business they are in. For example:

UNDERSTAND:
- Who is the customer?
    - External or ultimate customers
    - Internal or intermediate customers
- How does the customer use the product/service?
    - What are the **customer's needs**?
- Suppliers
    - Capabilities and constraints
- Where things are going
    - Business plans, strategies and progress
    - Competitive pressures and industry trends
- How my processes fit
    - The impact of my performance on customers
        (internal and external)

WHICH RESULTS IN/LEADS TO:
- Sense of team, partnership, ownership (we and us, not them and they); a sense of access, feeling "in the know"
- I am important; what I do makes a difference
    - Self-esteem
    - Pride of workmanship
- A sense of **meaning** in my job
- Better decisions
- More concern for performance and improvement

A Journey to Excellence   61

Goal #2—People Know What Is Expected, And How They Are Doing

For example:

EXPECTED OF: BY:

• Division

                                Management/Employees
• Department/Team   Customers (internal & external)
                                Suppliers (internal & external)

• Individual

DEVELOPMENT OF EXPECTATIONS:
- • Interactive process to build understanding between parties
- • Collaborative where possible

KNOW HOW YOU ARE DOING:
- • Building systems and processes to get feedback
  - Natural and direct when possible

WHICH RESULTS IN/LEADS TO:
- • Early warning—to proactively anticipate problems/ opportunities
- • Automatic course correction (Process Control)
- • Recognition and building "Pride of Workmanship"
  - Internal and intrinsic
  - External

Goal #3—People Have The Skills To Perform

For example:

SKILLS, KNOWLEDGE AND WAYS OF THINKING:
- • Basic skills
- • Conceptual skills
  - Critical thinking skills
- • Technical skills

- Understanding my process
- What it is capable of
- How to control
• Process improvement skills
  - Scientific Methods
  - Inductive/deductive reasoning/theory
  development
• Growth skills
• Managerial skills
      (**all performers** need to plan, organize and control)
• Interpersonal/relationship skills
      (group dynamics, team leadership, meeting leading,
      etc.)

WHICH RESULTS IN/LEADS TO:
      • Enabling/empowering people to meet and exceed their expec-
tations of themselves and of others

Note: Quality of "fit" (selecting and positioning people) and personal
      responsibility for our own growth and development are founda-
      tion elements.

Goal #4—People Are Involved In Business, Progress, And Changes
There are four levels of Involvement:
          1. Awareness/understanding
          2. Input
          3. Joint decision making
          4. Direct responsibility

Understanding that involvement can take any of these four
levels can prevent some serious misunderstanding and unful-
filled expectations. We must be clear and up front about
which level we are at in a given situation. Then people will not
be disappointed and angry if decisions are made that they did

A Journey to Excellence   63

not directly participate in. People understand they cannot be involved in everything, and clarifying this helps us not to create unrealistic expectations.

We use collaboration and two-way interaction to:
- Develop understanding (Goal No. 1)
- Make and accept expectations (Goal No. 2)
- Get feedback (Goal No. 2)
- Build skills (Goal No. 3)

The team process is a basic vehicle to make never ending improvement in the above areas which results in/leads to:
- Synergy
- Motivation
- Partnership ("we" and "us")
- All one team

When we achieve these four goals in a meaningful way, people become more self-managed and self-directed, both as individuals and teams. This enables our business organization to become progressively more self-organizing, which in turn makes it more flexible and adaptable to change. The result is that we can achieve our purpose and move towards our vision—the three wins.

The Means —Five Drivers

People need many different kinds of resources to help them on their Journey to Excellence. We want to provide a resource rich environment with physical assets, financial assets, and human assets to use them. In addition to physical and financial resources, people need skills, information, concepts, plans, methods, systems, and processes to achieve their purpose. How can we organize the various developmental resources we have so people can get a feeling for the "big picture" and see how each of these "tools" fits in the overall scheme?

A "mental map" we have found useful is a model called "The Five Drivers of Quality." This model is used in conjunction with the three wins "vision" and the Four Excellence goals to help explain and guide our journey. People need to see both how things are interrelated and how individual types of training, skills, tools, and other resources help support achieving our purpose. It helps answer both the questions of "why?" and "how?"

Systems Theory explains why you cannot create the best systems performance by focusing on sub-elements. A better approach in a complex, dynamic system is to locate areas that have organizational "leverage." We cannot focus effectively on all of the drivers at once, but we can use the model to try to see the "whole" picture. Then we may be able to locate where a change would do the most good, while continuing to maintain the rest.

The leverage points in a particular business organization change with time and circumstances. The driver model is sometimes useful to help us visualize the whole system so we can identify and focus in the right place at any given point in time. We want to address all five of the drivers in a properly balanced way; we need to consider the particular systems structure, the current status, how each element influences all of the rest, and how the system is performing in response to both its purpose (vision) and external environment (markets, customers, competition, etc). As one driver is effectively addressed or if business conditions change, the leverage points change also.

The Five Driver Model is a systemic influence model, with each driver (and the results or outcomes) influencing each other through feedback loops of various kinds. The flow of information ties them all together. Still, certain drivers have more "influence" on others, so their order is significant. Driver #1 has the most influence, #5 the least, and so on.

Outcomes or results have a strong influence on all of the drivers too, but not as much as the drivers have on them.

We should again remember Professor George Box's basic principle: "All models (maps, paradigms, ways of thinking) are wrong; some are useful." This model is a simplification and only shows some of the systemic interrelationships.

People Quality Is #1

This type of quality influences all of the rest. It is always a high leverage in any organization, yet it is frequently neglected from the standpoint of developing the whole person. People must always be responsible for their own development, but organizations provide opportunities for this to happen. (Or sometimes, to obstruct it.)

The methods for focusing on "People Quality" are the selection and development processes in use. This also requires an effective and humane "deselection" process for people who do not fit in.

People are selected based on organizational needs to serve customers. Then they need opportunities to help them continuously improve their own development based on information about changing customer needs, their needs, and the company's needs.

Two areas of selection and development we focus on are "soft" skills and habits—which include personal leadership and interpersonal/teamwork—and "hard" skills, which include job related technical skills. We have specific methods and tools to define what is needed for a particular job, assess an individual's current level, and further develop these skills and habits.

One of the foundational models we use for people quality selection and development is Steve Covey's *7 Habits of Highly Effective People* (1989). The *7 Habits* model and training materials provide us with a method to teach the

66   **Grahn**

principles, assess people's abilities, and build upon their competency in practicing these basic habits.

Seven Habits Summary

Habit #1—Be Proactive. Learn that each of us is capable of choosing how we respond to any circumstances, not based on emotional reaction (reactive—anger, fear, sadness, etc.) but based on what we value, believe in, and want to accomplish (our visions, mission, direction in life). One measurement of this is the "language" we use:

Reactive	Proactive
• He/she <u>makes me</u> so mad!	• I <u>choose</u> to be angry (based on a violated principle or value).
• We've always done it that way!	• There is always a better way.
• It's not my job, man!	• I <u>choose</u> not to do that job.
• She doesn't know what she's doing!	• I disagree with what you are doing (to her face).

Habit #2—Begin With The End In Mind. Identify and clarify what you value, believe in, and want to accomplish. Have a "vision" for ourselves that inspires you. The key to leadership for each of us is integrity of action on those things we value, believe in, and want to achieve. The measurement of this is having a "vision and mission statement" that clearly states—in writing!—our values, beliefs, and what we want to be or become.

Habit #3—Do First Things First. Have a plan! Plan your time around achieving your personal vision and mission. Spend time planning what you will do the following week to accomplish what you want to do. Spend some time every day doing something in your plan, focused on achieving your mission in a step-by-step way. Measurement—Have a written plan to follow and an effective time management tool to help you execute it!

Habit #4—Think Win-Win. Know when to be competitive (think win/lose) and when not to be. Do not compete against people you need to maintain a lasting relationship with. This does not mean that you give in! It means you go for a win for everyone. Nobody has to lose if you can find a solution (or conflict resolution) which satisfies and delights all concerned. This habit is the foundation or "root" of effective interpersonal relationships. Measurement —competing only when appropriate, and not against people you must live or work with.

Habit #5—Seek First To Understand, And Then To Be Understood. In any important encounter, but particularly in a conflict or an emotional situation, seek first to understand the other person's perspective. Try to understand her point of view as thoroughly as you can (not just what she thinks, but how she feels about it). Let her know you understand by reflecting back both the content and the feelings of her perspective.

When she feels you really understand her, ask for the same courtesy. Carefully explain your point of view and your feelings. It is this deep understanding of each other that is the way to finding a win/win resolution. Measurement—Letting other people speak first and truly listening to them, both on their point of view and feelings.

Habit #6—Synergy. Conflict and disagreement can be very bad if it causes people to fight and become angry, defensive, etc. It can also be very good if it results in a solution (or resolution) that not only satisfies but delights both parties. Synergy is the potential result of habits four and five. It is not compromise! The idea is to believe there is an answer which will delight all of us, then to find that answer together by deeply understanding each other and constructing the solution from everyone's needs. True breakthroughs (new paradigms) can result from Habit six. Measurement—Willing to really try to work with someone until the issues are resolved with solutions that delight both!

Habit #7—Sharpen The Saw. We must have four kinds of health to be truly effective people: 1) physical, 2) mental, 3) social/emotional, and 4) spiritual. It is up to each one of us to develop ourselves in each of these areas. Value physical fitness/health! Believe social life and emotional health are important! Believe in something that inspires and uplifts your spirit! Measurement —Proactive people take action focused on their values, beliefs and personal mission. Exercise and eat regular, nutritious meals. Work to develop your mental skills by reading, education, and training. Develop close and rewarding social/emotional relationships. Have a personal vision you believe in that uplifts your spirit, and a mission to make it happen.

The Seven Habits are as appropriate for teams of people and organizations as they are for individuals. Our vision, mission and Performance Planning and Coaching process corresponds to Habits one, two, and three. Training tools such as Zenger Miller, Interact and Team Interact help develop organizational Habits four, five, and six. Our Managing Personal Growth training seminar corresponds to Habit seven, etc. Our success as an organization will depend upon how well we learn to practice these habits, as individuals, as a team, and as a company.

Since each individual person is like a link in the chain of our organization, how well they understand and practice the Seven Habits is critical to our success. While this is ultimately up to each person to do, the organization can assist them by providing training and tools to help.

We can also provide a list of other methods and tools to build leadership and interpersonal skills that align with and support the Seven Habits and Principle Centered Leadership. Teaching concepts is one thing, but actually changing behavior is something else again. This takes practice and feedback for enough repetition until the skill is learned or the habit is ingrained. Some of the tools we use are:

Zenger-Miller—Sixty plus behavior modeling type training modules for all sorts of situations, e.g., Leading Effective Meetings, Problem Solving, Motivation, etc.

Interact I-II-III—Interpersonal Problem Solving, Teamwork, and Handling Difficult People.

Managing Personal Growth—How to manage your own development towards a personal vision.

The other major arena of selection and development for us to achieve "people quality" is **technical job skills**. We must match the skills to the task and each of us must continually sharpen and broaden our existing skills and develop new ones. We employ job task analysis, skill assessment, and skill development tools to continually build essential capabilities (or core competencies). An additional benefit we receive from having people with a high degree of technical competency is self-esteem. When high self-esteem, technical ability, interpersonal skills, and principle centered leadership habits are blended together properly, "People Quality" is the result.

Personal Leadership and Interpersonal and Technical Skill Development is not just for a selected group of people in an organization. Everyone is a manager and a leader in many aspects of their contribution. The more we can encourage and support this, the quicker we will move towards our vision of win-win-win.

Driver #2 —Innovation Quality

Innovation in the form of new ideas must happen at all levels of an organization and on many different kinds of issues. Some of these issues are to develop new products and services, ways to solve a problem, ways to improve product quality and service quality, ways to reduce waste of materials and time, ways to improve productivity, ways to manage information, etc. The challenge is how to promote and encourage this, because innovation is how to get change to work for us rather then against us!

There are a number of methods, tools and other types of actions a business organization can do to promote innovation from all of its members. The most basic is establishing the expectation and providing everyone the time to be creative (make it part of your cultural expectations).

The key is to create an environment where it is okay and even encouraged to play with ideas. We need to have settings where we can experiment, take risks, try new ideas, and learn from our mistakes. This is a strength we have in our culture and to stifle this with a lot of talk about "zero defects" and "do it right the first time" may do more harm than good in some situations. Trying to adopt Japanese methods and quality philosophies is playing to their strengths, not ours. We should learn from other cultures, but it is important to structure our approaches to fit our culture.

Beyond the basic tool of brainstorming, many ways exist to enhance and promote innovations. One of the ironic twists to innovation is that we often strive for it in team situations using various team processes, but innovative ideas come from individuals even more often than in team settings. A strong "team feeling" in a work environment can help motivate individuals to want to help the team. Therefore employee involvement teams which are effective also help promote individual innovative ideas.

Using technology and other methods to enhance innovation are discussed in Michael Schrage's book *Shared Minds* and Bryan Mattimore's book *99% Inspiration*. One of the best "how to" books on creativity and innovation is *Serious Creativity: Using the Power of Lateral Thinking to Create New Ideas* by Edward DeBono. We need to use these "Tools, Tips and Techniques" when appropriate in all of our attempts to improve, regardless of what the focus of the improvement may be.

In our organization we focus on "conveyance and synergy." This means promoting synergy, which is a form of creative innovation, between various functions by conveying technology, markets and customer information, capabilities, and knowledge between all of our diverse businesses. We do this with both information technology and cross divisional conferences specifically designed to achieve this goal. The objective is to promote both adaptive (learning to cope within existing paradigms) and generative (seeing truly different paradigms) types of learning.

Peter Senge (1990) talks about mental models and team learning as two of five essential disciplines. Our ability to learn from each other and to break out of our mental models (create synergy) in today's rapidly changing world, is necessary to make change work for us. Companies who can do this greatly increase their survival potential; those who do not will survive only by luck.

Information Quality Is Driver #3

Self-referential information, feedback, knowing how you are doing; no matter how you describe it, quality information is essential for all progress. One way to think about it is that you need a continuous stream of feedback on your current status (individuals, team, and business organization) as this status relates to achieving your purpose and the external environment.

Many of us feel overwhelmed with information. There is a paper and electronic information blizzard of data which constantly tries to get our attention. The question is: How can we effectively see through this blizzard and focus on gaining the knowledge and wisdom we need to achieve our purpose? The first key to this potential quagmire is having a clear purpose in the first place. The clearer our vision of what we want to accomplish is in our mind, the better our mission can be used as a way to screen the flow of data we receive from the "information super highway." We can then begin to welcome the information blizzard—we even hunger for it—but we only use and explore that portion which helps us in our journey to achieving our vision and mission. Like everything, this is a balance. We censor information using our purpose but it is also desirable to explore knowledge in other areas for its own sake. Learning is fun and we need to keep a broad perspective, but a clear purpose can help us a great deal in deciding how to acquire and use information.

A model developed by Senge (1990) is useful to help understand what we are dealing with. He separates what we know into five areas as follows:

Data—This is the continuous stream of events or individual inputs that constantly bombard us.

Information—This is data organized in a useful way. For example, data could be a page full of numbers or written text on individual observations. Information could be a chart, graph, or picture showing a pattern the numbers or observations may produce. Once we have decided what data we need, then we must process it into a form of information that is potentially useful. An ounce of information is worth a pound of data.

Understanding—Understanding comes from digesting information and beginning to see the patterns of change (or trends) which exist. We have reached understanding when we develop a hypothesis through inductive/deductive reasoning that can begin to predict, with some relative degree of certainty, what the system may do next. An ounce of understanding is worth ten pounds of information.

Knowledge—We have achieved knowledge when our understanding has reached a point where we can take action on a system with a reasonable chance of producing a predicted or desired outcome. We achieve knowledge through testing, experimenting, and using other scientific methods (or other means) to verify our hypothesis. We can use scientific methods, such as Design of Experiments, to gain a knowledge of the underlying relationships in a system and use this knowledge to effect desired change. An ounce of knowledge is worth a hundred pounds of understanding, but it is often hard work to get.

Wisdom—We achieve wisdom when we know how our actions will play out in the long term. This requires us to know the underlying structure operating in a system. It is the "systemic structure" that determines how any change will play out over time. Wisdom helps us apply "systemic solutions" that sustain, rather then "symptomatic solutions" which may temporarily relieve the symptoms, but often make the situation worse in the long run. Only experience produces wisdom, and this may take many years or even decades (and many painful mistakes) to learn. Still, an ounce of wisdom is worth a ton of knowledge, so it is worth the effort to strive for.

Senge (1990) suggests that we must look beyond events and patterns of change or trends to get at the underlying system structure. This understanding, taken in conjunction with a foundation of basic principles, can help us make wiser and more enduring positive changes. The tools of Systems Thinking and systems archetype were developed to help us begin understanding systems structure.

The use of SystemsThinking tools is a different way to use information. Statistical tools can give us some insight into variation and patterns of change, but fall short of helping us define how system structure produces variation. Systems Thinking tools and experimental designs can both be used to define underlying structure.

What type of information does a business need to keep the organization informed and able to adapt effectively? First, the information must be self-referencing in such a way as to compare an accurate assessment of the organization's current status, in reference to its purpose and the outside environment concurrently. In other words, we must be able to gain knowledge (and wisdom) about all three relative to each other: current status to purpose to outside environment. Some of the areas a majority of businesses need knowledge about are:

- Changes in existing or emerging new potential markets.
- Locate new potential customers.
- Changes in existing customer needs.
- Existing customers' perceptions of product, service, and information quality they currently receive.
- The capabilities, strategy, tactics and likely future direction of the competition.
- The needs of our people in how well they are being served as internal customers in their daily work.
- The needs of our people and how well they are served for personal growth, fulfillment, recognition, and development towards "personal mastery" (Senge 1990). (Core Competency or skills development.)
- The needs of the business and how well it is being served for future survival, growth, and return on investment to the owners.
- The business status with respect to government regulations, demographics, and other global changes.

- The needs of our neighbors in the communities where we operate, how well we serve them, and how we are perceived.
- Changes in technology so we can remain state-of-the-art in our target markets.
- How well we are fulfilling the stewardship of our planetary environment.

We use a number of methods and tools to gather and analyze the kind of information mentioned above. Focus groups, phone surveys, interviews, and Quality Function Deployment matrices are a few common examples.

Probably the most unique way we gather information and generate knowledge (wisdom) is by a process we call "Excellence Process Visits." These visits resemble "audits," in a way, but they are very different in certain fundamental respects. Excellence Process Visit teams spend a number of days at a particular business unit (or our corporate headquarters) doing interviews, observing team meetings, looking at information systems, etc. They use the three wins, four goals, and five drivers models as a guide to assess current status, progress, opportunities, and make recommendations for improvements.

The "visit" teams consist of people from our corporate headquarters and other business units. The objective is to give the visited business feedback in the form of self-referential information from an outside perspective. This process differs from traditional audits in a number of significant ways, but the main one is that it is not a "scoreboard" where anyone is competing for a "prize," a "certification," or a "favorable report back at headquarters." The information and learning is shared only with the business unit being visited and they can choose to use it any way they want. (We do expect them to inform their vice-president—who is never on the team—what actions they plan as a result of the visit, and to share the results and planned actions in some way with all of their people.)

Grahn

This process has gained so much credibility within our company that the business units do not try to "hide their dirty laundry." On the contrary, they tell the visit team where to look for the dirty laundry and ask for ideas on how to get it clean. There is no need for the window dressing, non-value added bureaucracy, cover-ups, ritual deception and falsification which often accompanies ISO 9000 audits, customer quality audits, and Malcolm Baldrige audits, in some (many?) companies.

The way Excellence Process Visits are positioned defeats the anxiety, fear, and pressure of competitive or punitive "police type" audits. We have also found that they are terrific growth and development opportunities for the visit team members, who often gain as much value as the business unit being visited.

Information coupled with trust is the glue that holds our organization together, enables progress, sparks creativity, and helps us attempt to change. It links the three wins, promotes the four goals, and connects the other four drivers together. That is why we feel there is so much organizational leverage in developing effective and efficient information systems.

Driver #4—Planning And Decision Making Quality

High quality people using innovation and creativity who have high quality information need ways to <u>plan</u> how to use the knowledge and wisdom they are gaining to achieve their purpose. Effective and efficient planning should occur at five levels: individual, team, department, business unit, and corporation.

These plans should have the characteristic of "self-similarity" at each level. Department plans reflect and support the organizational plan, the team plan supports the department plan, and the individual plan supports the team plan. All of them are aligned with and support the organizational purpose as defined by the corporate vision and mission.

The planning process begins with establishing the alignment of purpose. This means creating a vision and mission at the business unit, department, team, and individual levels which are aligned with and supportive of, but not identical to, the organization purpose. Creating this is not a top down process, it must be done by the people themselves in the department or team. We have a participative workshop that uses the "three wins" to help each team, department, and business unit formulate their own vision and mission together, so understanding and ownership is maximized. This process is supported by personal missions.

Development of the personal mission of each individual is assisted by our basic Seven Habits training process. Habit two, "Begin With the End in Mind," is called "the habit of personal vision." During the training process on Habit two, we help all participants develop a personal mission. Next in Habit three, "Do First Things First," we help them develop a planning process and use a time management tool (personal organizer) that focuses their time on achieving their mission. We strongly believe that this is the key to effective time management.

This individual mission is a very personal area and we do not intrude in it, but we do recommend that if a person's personal mission is not aligned with his or her team, department, and organizational mission in certain ways (particularly the base values and beliefs) then the "fit" is questionable; a proactive person should seek work elsewhere. Poor fit in this area can do much harm to an organization, and what is worse, years of working where you do not want to be can ruin a person's life.

Once the alignment of purpose is begun (this is an ongoing, dynamic process, not a one-time exercise) then the actual development of plans can begin. We have a process called "Performance, Planning, and Coaching for individual contributions (PPC) which establishes our philosophy and gives us methods and tools to develop plans.

We use our basic PPC process for each team member which involves establishing four to seven "result areas" for each person. These performance plans also include defining what needs to be done in each area, establishing performance indicators to judge progress, and defining what action steps (with needed resources and timing) will be taken to address this result area. These result areas are developed by the performer to achieve both his personal mission and the team's mission (which supports the department and organizational mission). Once the result areas are developed, the performer has a dialogue with his "coach" about the plan.

Your coach is your department or team coordinator. (Could be a supervisor or area manager, but with roles different than a traditional boss.) The coach helps the performer align her result areas and action plans with the team mission, determine if sufficient resources are available to execute the plans, and cover any blind spots or areas of need the performer may have missed. When mutual agreement on the plan is reached, the performer now "owns" the implementation and the consequences of success or failure.

PPC is also used in a modified format called "Organizational Performance Planning and Implementation." OPPI is used at the team, department, business unit, and corporate levels. OPPI is a very participatory, team-centered planning process which is a customized version of "Hosin Kanri." This planning and implementation process uses "The Seven Management and Planning tools" and a host of other data gathering, information processing, plan structuring and implementation tools as needed to help guide the process. The steps are shown in Figure 3.

Figure 3

FOUNDATION ELEMENTS

VALUES
- Pre-eminent: All forms of integrity and honesty which lead to credibility and trust.
- Continuous growth in knowledge, ways of thinking, awareness, and skills; continuous education and training for all employees.
- Constancy of purpose toward never ending improvement.
- All one team.
    - Treating all people with dignity, respect and fairness.
    - An effective, open communication system.
    - Non-punishing interpersonal environment.
    (Does not mean free from consequences.)
- An environment that fosters creativity and innovation.
    - Leads to responsible risk taking and individual expression.
- People are valued and rewarded for their contribution which results from their knowledge, expertise, and performance.

BELIEFS/PARADIGMS
- Business is a process (systems theory).
    - We must understand the underlying system structure to implement change with wisdom.
    - Systems decay without energy focused on growth and maintenance.
- Quality is first.
    - Customers (both internal and external) are the focus of everything we do.
    - Product and service quality results from design and process quality.
- People are responsible for their own growth and development. Managers and organizational processes help focus and actively support individual efforts.

- Organization structures often create communication barriers unless people work at being approachable.
- Aligning people strengths with organizational needs are the most important decisions managers make (quality of fit).
- There is a need to keep important long term issues clearly in focus or they will tend to get lost in the press of short range urgent items (P/PC balance).

Figure 4

Seven Management Planning Tools

	Tools Used
1. **Flush out and organize all of the issues** into result areas that need to be addressed to achieve our mission.	• Driver #3 - Lots of current information about our external environments and current internal status. • Affinity Diagramming.
2. **Prioritize result areas** by influence, action ability, organizational impact, etc.	• Inter-relationaship digraph. • Prioritization matrix. • Driver #3: Information.
3. **Develop and prioritize specific action plans.**	• Tree Diagramming. • Driver #3: Information. • Prioritization Matrix.
4. **Determine Ownership** with specific accountability and responsibility for actions and timing. (This becomes someone's personal PPC "result area.")	• Responsibility Matrix.
5. **Define Implementation** sequence, timing, and resources needed (and contingency plans through potential problem analysis if needed).	• Activity Network Diagram. (critical path method) • Process Decision Program Chart. (potential problem analysis) • Gant chart.

A Journey to Excellence

6. **Implement Plans.**	• Activity Nework Diagram. (critical path method)
	• Process Decison Program Chart (potential problem analysis)
	• Gant chart.
7. **Follow up on Progress.**	• Activity Nework Diagram. (critical path method)
	• Process Decison Program Chart (potential problem analysis.)
	• Gant chart
	• Report to coach and/or steering committee.

Progress is monitored on a regular basis by the "owner" and discussed with his or her coach or steering committee at least quarterly (sometimes more often depending upon the situation). The complete planning process is revisited annually for progress reports. Plan changes due to new information can occur at any time and are reported to the steering committee immediately.

Ownership is always taken by one person who has agreed, after a team dialogue, to be responsible and accountable for a specific action or result area. At the same time in step four, one or more co-owners and resource persons are determined (if necessary) who have agreed to assist the owner with implementation. We have found that the process of team dialogue on the issues, priorities, what actions to take, and who is accountable (using these tools) can produce shared understanding and clear linkage in people's minds between specific actions and our mission (strategic alignment). We also see strong ownership of specific actions steps, more clear understanding of what each action step requires, and a lot of team support for each action, even though one person is the coordinator for each specific result area. Ultimate responsibility (and the consequences) for any result area rests both with the coordinator (owner) and his team (co-owners).

Ghandi said, "People who plan always do better than people who don't, even if they don't follow their plan." In the same vein Winston Churchill said, "The plan is nothing; planning is everything!" Perhaps overstated, but the point is valid. The planning process of discussion and dialogue, of digesting the information on your current internal status versus the outside environment and your mission, mutual understanding, and shared direction are more important than the final plan. The plan itself may change—will change— with new information coming in. The plan itself must be flexible, adaptable, and changeable, not cast in concrete.

The plan itself and the planning process are both "tools" we use to accomplish our purpose. Someone once said, "He who only knows how to use a hammer, thinks everything is a nail." The principle is to never let a tool become your master! We use them; they do not use us. This is a very common and deadly mistake.

Keeping this one caution in mind, effective and efficient planning is essential to sustained progress and achieving our mission. We have found PPC and OPPI to be very useful tools to help us achieve "Planning and Decision Making Quality."

Driver #5 —Process Quality

"Process Quality" is essential because the best plans and decisions (made with the highest quality information, by the highest quality, most innovative people) do not mean much without an effective and efficient process to implement them. We have also learned that the way we go about this is critical. Focusing merely on "process improvement," with the mindset that we can produce overall improvement by working on one or several processes (which are subsets or sub-elements of our whole system) can be fundamentally wrong. Systems theory plainly states that we harm the whole system if we optimize the performance of any one (or several) processes that make it up out of context with the whole.

We still want "process improvement," but the whole system context changes our approach in many ways. For example, would it be an improvement to reduce the efficiency of any process? In our old way of thinking, the answer would obviously be "no"; but in a whole-system context, if reducing the efficiency of one work process or department improved the overall system, the answer might be "yes."

Examples of problems caused by focusing on improving certain aspects of a business systems without considering the impact on the whole are frequent. For example:

- Purchasing Department buys cheaper raw materials to make their performance look good, but the impact on production or product quality is negative.
- Customer Service Department cuts back on training or personnel to reduce costs, and customer service errors and delays get worse.
- Maintenance Department cuts back on preventive/pre-dictive maintenance actions to make their budget look good, and unplanned machine downtime goes up.
- On-time delivery becomes such a high focus that product quality suffers (or vice versa).
- Production Department extends production runs to im-prove productivity and machine efficiency, and fin-ished goods inventory goes up.
- Sales Department pushes for sales volume, and margins go down.
- Materials and Logistics manager reduces both raw materials and finished goods inventories to meet his/

her ambitious goals, and production is slammed with numerous "hot" short run customer orders and raw material "stock outs."

We have all experienced the effects of some of these "errors in judgment," but were they errors? In each case people were trying to improve their local process, which is what we want everybody to do, but in many cases the way we do it comes back to bite us in the long run. In some of the cases mentioned above it might have been a better decisions to buy more expensive raw materials, do more training, more preventive maintenance, shorter production runs, less sales volume, or more raw material and finished good inventory. How can we know what the right decision is?

Unfortunately, the bottom line is that we can never be sure. Real life systems are too complex and interactive to figure out with certainty. Fortunately for most of us, these systems are often very "resistant" to bad decisions, which means the effects of our bad decisions do not do immediate or obvious harm, or the system "heals itself." Unfortunately this also means we may not get feedback on our mistakes (which is often the only way we learn).

We can't "figure out" what a system will do with certainty, but we can improve our odds of making correct decisions. There are two actions we can take to improve the odds:

1) Base our decisions on sound fundamental principles— This is the first and foremost consideration.

2) Try to see the whole system before we take action to improve any problem that is a part of a larger whole.

Resources and tools are available to help with both of these strategies. Some of them are:

Strategy one
• *Principle Centered Leadership* by Steven Covey.
• *Stewardship* by Peter Block.
• *The Fifth Discipline* by Peter Senge.
• *Leadership and The New Science* by Margaret Wheatley.

Strategy two

- The tools of Systems Thinking can help (causal loop diagrams, behavior over time diagrams, systems archetypes, management flight simulators, or learning labs). Peter Senge (1990) defines Systems Thinking as "The discipline of seeing wholes." This is what we must try to do.
- Quality Function Deployment and some of the seven management and planning tools are also helpful.
- Doing experiments! Trying different things and taking some risks. Making mistakes is how we all learn anyway. If we do them in an experimental context we can maximize learning and minimize damage (there is no guarantee the experimental results will duplicate in a larger "real" system, but it does improve your odds).

Once we have considered our situation in light of fundamental principles and "seeing the whole," then many of the tools of Quality Management can begin to be useful. If we are working on the right things in the right context, then working to improve a process or a component of a system may make sense, as long as we realize that the definition of improvement may not be to maximize or optimize the performance of the component process. Our new definition of improvement might be "to adjust the performance of the process to whatever level maximizes the performance of the whole system." If we find the proper "leverage points," a great deal of improvement is possible with this approach.

TOOLS OF QUALITY MANAGEMENT

BASIC
- Process Flow diagram
- Cause/Effect Diagram
- Histogram

- Pareto Chart
- Scatter Diagram
- Check sheet
- Charts and graphs (SPC)
- Force field diagram

ADVANCED
- Quality Function Deployment
- Seven Management and Planning Tools
- Design of experiments
- Analysis of variance
- Linear and non-lineal correlation
- Response surface methods

A lot of improvement is possible by the process described above, but it is still often only incremental. The whole system context and tools of systems thinking suggest another approach: Complete System Reconfiguration.

This process of complete reconfiguration (some call re-engineering) might be necessary if the incremental improvements and leverage adjustments did not produce enough of the right kinds of system changes to keep the business on target and viable. The process could resemble chaotic self-organization (a property of contain systems) in the form old order -> chaos-> new order. Many examples of this sort of transformation are commonplace. [Examples: Tyranny (old form of government)->Revolution (chaos)->Democracy (new form); and old building (old order) -> Tear it down and rebuild (chaotic?) -> New building]

Margaret Wheatley asserts "you can't get to a truly creative or transformative solution unless you are willing to walk through chaos." If, as she also believes, business organizations act like living organisms in some ways, they may resist such a change with great vigor. If we wanted to make such changes, how could we pave the way?

It is true that people resist change, but it is just as true that they accept or encourage change. People respond to change in one of five ways:

1) Resist —If they do not understand the change, feel it will do them harm, do not understand why it is needed, or if the new way is a lot different than what they are accustomed to.

2) Ignore —People may be indifferent to changes that they feel will not affect them or have little effect. (Note: This can be interpreted as "resistance" by someone who has a vested interest in the particular change being ignored.)

3) Accept—If they understand the need or think it will affect them positively. (Note: Acceptance does not necessarily mean people will become actively involved in making it work!)

4) Encourage—People will assist changes if they feel strongly that it is needed, understand why it is in their best interest, and particularly if they have some ownership (participated in setting the direction for change, for example).

5) Demand—If things people care about are perceived as "going down the tubes."

All types of improvement are changes of some sort and we can get all of the above responses. One of the important keys to changes that produce sustained improvements is to get as much understanding and ownership as we can among the people affected. The best way, perhaps the only way in some situations, is to get them involved in the change process itself.

A way to sum up what is takes to produce sustained improvement is to ask three questions:

1) Is the current way we do it (process or method) effective? This means: Is the process or method focused on the "right things?" Does it help us achieve our mission and move towards our vision? Does the process or method have real value when seen in the context of the whole system?

2) Is the process or method efficient, in other words does it achieve its purpose with minimal waste of materials, time, and information? Is there a way to help the process support the whole system better? If the answer to either is "no," we have an opportunity. Then we ask:

3) Are the right people involved in a meaningful way to improve it? Do they have the knowledge and ability necessary? Are they sufficiently motivated by the task (relationship to the mission)? Do they have the means? (Proactive people who are motivated by a mission or inspirational vision usually find the resources they need, otherwise we may need to help provide them.) If the answer to this is "yes," we are ready to proceed using whatever set of methods and tools fits the situation. Many tools are available. Some have already been mentioned, such as System Thinking and Quality Management Tools. Whatever tools we use, it helps to have a step-by-step process to guide us. Two related examples are Seven Step Scientific Process Improvement or Problem Solving (using iterative generating and evaluating steps):

Process Improvement Example

The product we will improve is a material used in internal medical applications, where purity is critical to assure there is no rejection response. The standard for purity is XX particles per square inch maximum, none larger than XXX microns. The standard test is to examine a prepared cross section under a high powered stereo-optical microscope with a crosshatch grid, counting the number of particles and measuring their size.

Our vision is to be the industry leader in producing this material with a mission to double our market share within two years without sacrificing profit margins. We will only do this in a way that produces a win for our customers, a win for our people, and a win for the business. We will not compromise this balance.

We took a look at the whole system that produces and markets this product. Was the system effective? The answer from our customer was "yes, but . . . "; purity was always an

Figure 5

7 Step "Process Improvement"	7 Step "Problem Solving"
1. Establish an improvement goal (generate possible goals to achive, evaluate down to most important one.)	1. Identify the problem (generate potential problems, evaluate down to most important one)
2.Establish a measurement (generate possible measurements, evaluate down to best ones.)	2. Gather data and information (generate and evaluate)
3. Define the current situation (generate and evaluate.)	3. Define the system (generate and evaluate)
4. Define opportunities to improve (generate ways to achieve the goal – use both lateral and vertical thinning!)	4. Brainstorm solutions (generate solutions using both lateral and vertical thinning)
5. Select best solutions and implement (evaluate.)	5. Select best solutions and implement (evaluate)
6. Check Results (generate.)	6. Check Results (generate)
7. Follow up to assure sustained improvement (evaluate.)	7. Follow up to assure sustained correction of the problem (evaluate)

Note: It is very important to use both lateral thinking and vertical thinking analytical skills in each one of these steps. Interact Teamwork Training and DeBono's book *Serious Creativity* explain how.

issue. Industry suppliers always tended to push near the (XX) particle (XXX) micron limit. Other problems sometimes occurred, but this was the chronic issue on their mind.

Was the system efficient? The answer to this was "no." We had to produce about 120 lbs. for every 100 lbs. shipped, because 15 to 20 percent of production was typically rejected. The biggest reason was "purity problems."

We concluded, after a whole system analysis, that purity was a high leverage issue. If we could produce a significant breakthrough on this point, we could increase the market value of our product, gain substantial market share, and reduce our manufacturing costs simultaneously. First we assembled a team which included a sales/marketing person, a process engineer, a quality lab technician, one production supervisor, and four production workers. Then we used the Seven Step problem solving process to begin a breakthrough. The steps were as follows:

1) **Set a Goal**—Our goal was a 200 percent improvement in purity, from the industry standard of XX particles to X particles maximum.

2) **Define a measurement**—We had an industry standard measurement, determined by observing a polished cross section of known surface size, then counting and sizing the particles. We decided this measurement was inadequate for our purposes. It did not allow us to qualitatively categorize the types of particle inclusions present (e.g., burnt resin particles, metal shavings from mold, pieces of sieve mesh nets, paint from the walls). After some discussion, several team members took on a project to do volumetric particle size measurements in a thin, highly illuminated cross section, rather than just a two dimensional/surface count. They devised a way to do a 3-D particle count which gave us the even more important ability to determine the kind of particles with some accuracy.

3) **Define the current situation**—The team did a flow chart of the whole manufacturing system (including raw material production) and began gathering data on the nature of the particle inclusions, both at the same time. They put together a Pareto chart on the types of particles identified and their frequency. The data indicated burnt resin, metal shavings, and a few other types of particles were the most prevalent. Next, an affinity diagram was constructed to help define

possible sources or causes for each type of inclusion. Then an inter-relationship digraph was used to help define the patterns of potential interrelated causal influence.

Several weeks of investigation and data collection were performed, most of it by individual team members or groups of two. Almost all of this work was done while they were performing their regular job tasks, but one investigation did include a visit to the resin suppliers. If they needed any help or specific analytical tools, the engineering and (or) quality specialist on the team was available to help.

Finally the data was organized into information by using a relationship matrix and priority matrix, accompanied by some graphs and SPC charts so it could be easily "visualized." The next task was the most difficult: transforming the information into knowledge—by analysis, critical thinking, reasoning, and experimentation.

4) **Define Opportunities to Improve**—The information we gathered over a several week period was much easier to understand and use in the "matrix plus graphs" format. The team had a very good understanding of the "total system," as a result of the tools we used plus the discussions and the dialogue they helped structure. Now the task was to figure out innovative ways to change or improve various aspects of the process, in the right places and in the right ways, to dramatically improve the overall system.

We used tree diagramming focused on our "influence priorities" to help structure a focused brainstorming session on possible ideas for process improvement. (This method keeps us focused on the "highest leverage" issues first without losing the "whole system context" necessary for wisdom based changes.) We proceeded to outline possible solutions based on our new information and past knowledge.

Past experimentation had shown that "burnt resin" particles were caused by buildup inside the mold. The current way to control this problem was to stop the press (usually when finished product was rejected), disassemble the mold, clean it thoroughly, then reassemble and resume production. This expensive and time consuming process could happen quite frequently, almost daily in some situations. We also suspected that burnt resin buildup could tighten up clearances built into the mold (which has moving parts) and cause metal particles to shave off.

In a focused brainstorming session, we came up with a radical idea. What if we could periodically "purge" the mold by sending through a substance other than the resin itself? This substance could be designed to remove burnt resin buildup before it became so firmly embedded that the mold would need to be disassembled and cleaned. We would also gain the benefit of less downtime for cleaning, and if our suspicions were correct, less metal particle inclusions and possibly even longer mold component life.

A series of experiments was proposed using different kinds of purge materials with varying characteristics such as solidity, abrasion, or residue removal. Experiments were performed and analyzed using our new volumetric measuring method. It was found that this measuring method could be used to predict or anticipate when a purge should be performed to keep burnt resin and metal particles to a near zero level.

Over a period of several months, ideas were generated and appropriate experiments performed on all of the suspected high leverage processes in the system. Data was gathered and transformed into information using appropriate diagrams, matrixes, graphs, and charts.

5) **Select the best solutions and implement**—The information and results of various experiments were analyzed and compiled into a proposal which was presented to the local business unit's steering committee. The costs associated with implementation, timing, and estimated payback were included.

The implementation plan was laid out using an "Activity Network Diagram," which illustrated the sequential timing of each proposed improvement. We also used a "Process Decision Program Chart" to anticipate potential problems in one area where we were proceeding into some unknown territory.

The steering committee gave approval to a modified version of our proposal. They suggested that we hold several ideas in reserve, but authorized the rest to be implemented immediately.

Implementation began according to the steps outline in the "Activity Network Diagram." The team also used a "Responsibility Matrix" to make specific assignments of accountability and responsibility. Data was gathered on the progress of implementation and the impact on the final product as each step proceeded. This was updated weekly by one of the team members and posted on a project bulletin board so everyone in the plant was aware of their progress. Other departments affected—such as the logistics/materials department, our resin supplier, etc.—were informed and involved as necessary.

6) **Check Results**—Implementation took about four months, which put the entire project into an eight to nine month time frame. Finished product improvements were noticed as early as one month into implementation. Several other beneficial effects, such as reduced waste and improved manufacturing cycle time, were also being noticed.

7) **Follow up to Assure Sustained Improvement**—We continued to monitor the impact of each process change on the performance of the whole system. System status was continually monitored and feedback to everyone involved. The following results have sustained over a several year time period:

- We exceeded our goal of 200 percent reduction in particle inclusion.
- Material waste has been reduced by a significant amount.
- Manufacturing cycle times were also reduced by quite a

bit because it was no longer necessary to mold a lot more material for each order to cover the anticipated waste.

The results of these improvements had an impact on this total line of products as follows:

• The improved purity increased the market value of the product, so customers were willing to pay a bit more.

• Customers were delighted with the new level of purity, so they rewrote their specifications to coincide with our new capabilities. This effectively doubled our worldwide market share within a year.

• Total manufacturing costs were significantly reduced.

• Total manufacturing cycle times were significantly reduced, so we had more capacity and could be much more responsive to customers' JIT delivery needs.

Obviously the results were worth celebrating, and we did. Our philosophy of sharing success with our people also means that every person at this operation has benefited from these improvements over the last several years.

Conclusion

Can you imagine the potential impact of hundreds of teams of the sort described above? This was a breakthrough, and although all teams do not produce results as dramatic as this, all sorts of improvements are necessary to continuously adapt a business organization to face a rapidly changing world. These improvements can be either evolutionary (in-cremental) in nature or revolutionary breakthroughs. The process described can produce both types of improvements sometimes even at the same time, due to the "whole system" perspective that is taken from the beginning. It is possible for us to find that a whole process or even a whole system is not effective and/or efficient. That is why our company is no longer the highest quality and most efficient wooden tub and barrel manufacturer in the world, as we were in the 1800s. We no longer make these products at all.

How does a company guard against becoming the best "buggy whip" manufacturer in the world? The whole system approach can be a big part of the solution if you are willing to do it properly. "Properly" in this case means that we have teams focusing on this issue all of the time.

All of our teams need to operate with a "whole system perspective" as much as possible and at this level nothing is sacred except our core foundation. We have our purpose, our vision of the future, our mission, and our operating principles based upon our values. Everything else must continuously be questioned in the light of information about our current status and changes external to our company as they relate to this foundation.

Teams look at our whole portfolio of businesses this way. They work at realigning each business towards value added niche markets rather than high volume, low margin production (or vice versa if it makes sense to the whole system). They work on developing innovative new products and whole new markets associated with them. At this level of thinking we focus on identifying potential markets and then developing the capabilities to serve them (market driven) rather than selling the products we currently have the capacity to produce (capability driven). Both are important and must be kept in balance, but being "market driven" is a long term survival issue and strategy.

The point is that the process of doing improvements at all of these levels is very similar. The tools of Quality Management and Systems Thinking can be effectively applied to all of these issues when selected and modified appropriately. These methods and tools can help structure the process, keep it on track, transform data into information by visualizing and organizing, etc. They can also help transform information into knowledge by promoting critical thinking, analysis and deductive/inductive reasoning (hypothesis development), and experimentation (hypothesis verification).

Most importantly these tools can help promote real dialogue about the issues in a whole systems context. This has the potential to increase our wisdom when we are making decisions and changes to a sensitive system. The ultimate benefit of a true dialogue is that shared meaning (inspirational purpose) can emerge from it.

The Recap

Our basic Paradigms, or mental models, strongly influence everything we do. They can be a major barrier to communications, learning and progress in our Journey Towards Excellence. However these same mental models can be powerful servants to us if we can learn to see them, share them effectively with others, combine them, and use these "synergistic combinations" to build better ways to operate our business organizations.

The Holistic, or Systems Thinking, mental model is a superior way to view complex systems. The reductionist, or clockwork machine, mental model (which has been the dominant paradigm for almost four centuries) has value and works in many situations, but also has fundamental and sometimes dangerous limitations.

New developments in science and the application of Systems Thinking concepts, methods, and tools to business organization systems is beginning to open a new frontier of possibilities. The areas where this has had the most impact to date is in logistics management (materials and information flow), strategic planning (scenario planning), and learning (with management flight simulators and learning laboratories). This is the beginning of the practical applications of Systems Thinking and it will rapidly expand into other areas such as organizational/human dynamics, financial management, compensation and benefits, product design, environmental, etc. (The impact in these areas has already been felt, but it will grow rapidly.)

Closely related to the Holistic paradigm is the Servant Leader or Stewardship model of leadership. The Servant leader mental model fundamentally changes the traditional hierarchy structure. It either flips it upside down or moves the structure more towards an interconnected, networking matrix form. Departmental barriers and "turf war" issues diminish as the objective becomes to achieve our mission and move towards our vision (purpose and meaning) rather than preserving the hierarchical structure and individual, bureaucratic fiefdoms. Developing the new roles and skills of people to understand and foster this model of leadership is critical to success.

The servant leader model rests upon the premise that most people are capable of self-motivation and self-management. The organizing force necessary to promote this capability is meaning. Meaning comes from a clear purpose defined by a vision and mission rooted in our values. Once this organizing force is in place, then people need self-referential information or meaningful feedback on the current status of their organization and the external environment.

The two self-organizing concepts, purpose and information, in the presence of sufficient means or resources (financial, physical, human skills, and abilities) are capable of producing a highly adaptable business organization. Such an organization should be capable of whatever levels of improvement—from incremental fine tuning to total systems-wide restructuring—are necessary to adapt and balance both short term performance and long term survival.

The purpose can be summed up as a synergistic win for our customers, our people and the business (win-win-win). The "medical grade material" story was a real life example of achieving this vision. If people truly understand and believe in this purpose, it provides the context and motivation for continuous improvement to occur.

A model which describes the means to achieve the win-win-win vision is the five driver model. We can focus on "People Quality" by using effective selection and development in Personal Leadership and Interpersonal and Technical ability. We focus on "Innovation Quality" by teaching "Lateral Thinking" and by providing time in our environment to encourage risk taking, playing with ideas, and experimentation. We focus on "Information Quality" by defining the types of data we need and how to use the tools of Quality Management and Systems Thinking to transform this data into accurate, real time, and meaningful information. We focus on planning and decision-making quality at both the individual and team levels by using the appropriate systems thinking tools, the Seven Management and Planning Tools, reasoning/ critical thinking skills, discussion, and dialogue to help translate information into knowledge (and wisdom) by understanding the underlying structure. Then we can construct our plans and make our decisions based first on principles, then on a clear purpose, and finally on a more thorough understanding of the system by the people involved.

We achieve "Process Quality" by implementing our plans effectively and efficiently. The methods, tools, and resources necessary are many and varied. They will be different for different needs. Continuous Process Improvement is a common quality "buzz phrase," but this is in fact what we want to accomplish in this driver. The difference is that we now understand that a myopic focus on improving our own local process often does overall harm to the whole system. We need to exercise the discipline of "seeing wholes" (Senge 1990) by using the tools of Systems Thinking first, then make changes based on this perspective using other tools.

Improvements in general are accomplished in one of four ways (Figure 6).

All of these ways are useful depending upon the needs of the situation. The key is to know in advance which one you are using. This will help your strategy and the expectations people have of the results.

If we suspect we are getting "Temporary Effect," we will not be as disappointed when the improvement does not sustain. We will be less likely to get "bilked" by a slick consultant. We will realize this is only a short term fix and will apply it when we want short term results. We will know that if we want to sustain we must add more Temporary Effect again and again and again.

If we are focusing on "Training" and building needed skills/habits, we will understand that we must carefully examine the situation and provide a careful focus on what is needed (not training for training's sake). We will try to provide a proper balance between personal leadership, interpersonal teamwork, and technical skills and habits. We will realize that this method takes time, money, and requires maintenance over time.

If we are focusing on "hard wired changes" to the system, we will understand that this may require experimentation, risk taking, and capitol investments. We will realize that these kind of changes require the understanding, and better yet the "ownership" of the people who will use them in order to get the most benefit. We will involve people in these changes.

If we are attempting a "culture change," we will know how hard this is to do. We will understand that it requires a paradigm shift, a whole new set of "mental models" about work and how we relate to work and that these shifts must occur in a critical mass of our people. We will realize that training and hard wired changes are necessary, but not enough. We will understand how necessary and difficult it is to create meaningful work for people by having a common purpose, an

100   **Grahn**

Figure 6

Ways to Make Improvements

METHOD	CHARACTERISTICS	COMMENTS
Temporary Focus Effect	• Sometime large effects but usually temporary (may not sustain) • Sometimes called the Hawthorne effect, but this is a bad name since the Hawthorne studies were very controversial and did not produce verifiable conclusions.	• When we make any change that people think will help (maybe related to the placebo effect.) • Hoopla, slogan, wave the flag. • Focus people on trying to achieve someone elses goals (what I want you to do.) • Consultants sometimes depend on this effect to produce significant, short term improvement (which may go away after they leave. • Downside – may create high expectations that get discouraged when performance doesn't sustain. Creates jaded feelings, "paradigm" mentality, etc. • Safety Related Example: banner and flag waving safety campaign. Monetary safety incentives, etc.

Figure 6 continued

Training	• Sometimes performance gets worse before better due to effort and resources needed. • Takes time to produce improvements but can produce dramatic and sustaining sucess if done right. • Takes time to produce improvements but can produce dramatic and sustaining success if done right.	• Must be carefully focused on the right and necessary general and specific skills. • Needs balance between technical, personal leadership and interpersonal skills. • Downside – if done right none, if done wrong, much wasted time and effort. Training does not require constant maintainence over time. • Safety related example: Specific training on how to operate a particular machine safely.
Hardwired Changes	Immediate and sustaining improvement (if new way is followed and maintained.)	• Changes to a process such as completely eliminating a step. • Changes to a machine such as a new, automatic system. • Downside - may require significant investigation time and capitol. • Safety Related examples: Put a guard on a machine pinch point. Initiate lockout/tagout procedures.

Culture Change	• Takes a long time (unless a paradigm shift occures among people due to a crisis, etc.) • If you can do it, this produces the most dramatic and sustaining change of all. • Flexibility, adaptibility and long term survival may come along as a side benefit.	• Requires a heart felt sense of meaning and purpose among majority. • Requires an inspirational vision and mission shared by many (e.g. put man on moon by 1970). • Requires a rich information system, people of high ability and access to resources. • Downside – very hard to do (perhaps in reality, virtually impossible in many situations.) • Examples: Apollo Moon Program Any company or team truely inspired by their purpose. • An environment where everyone is totally concerned about the personal safety and the safety of others.

inspirational vision of the future, and a clear mission to accomplish.

Like all models, the distinction between these four ways to improve is artificial. In reality they are all interrelated and inseparable; but if it can help us to think, plan, and execute better, the model has some value.

In the end, we must always return to our purpose, our vision, and our mission. The results we want to accomplish refer back to the basic purpose of our company, which is to serve our customers, our people, and our business. This can be summarized as creating a synergistic "win-win-win" together:

Win For Our Customers—by meeting their needs, both defined and undefined. Addressing the five drivers properly will result in truly understanding customer needs and translating them into reliable, high quality products, services, and information. Forming this intimate partnership with our customers allows us to go beyond satisfaction to "customer delight!"

Win For Our People—by helping them meet their needs for security, fair pay, good benefits, and recognition. People also have a strong need for personal respect and the opportunity to participate on a winning team. We must help each other achieve personal growth and a meaningful contribution we can be proud of. When service to people in these ways is our goal, we help them become more committed, energetic, and creative contributors. This is the purpose of the Four Excellence Goals.

Win For Our Business—by providing business survival, growth, and outstanding financial results over the long term. This is necessary for the other two wins to happen, and they are necessary for this win to happen.

Our customers are the central focus of our business, but we must have a balanced "win-win-win" for long term success. We will not accept anything less because our ultimate goal is to enrich the lives of all the people we serve—our customers, our owners, our workers and our communities. We believe sharing our vision with everyone and then executing around the "Five Drivers" will achieve this goal.

References

Box, G. University of Wisconsin.

Bradford, D. L. and A. R. Cohen. 1984. "The Postheroic Leader." *Training and Development Journal* (January).

Brassard, M. 1989. *The Memory Jogger Plus*. Methuen, MA: Goal/QPC.

Covey, S. 1989. *The Seven Habits of Highly Effective People*. New York: Simon and Schuster.

Crandall, L. *Team Up For Excellence: A Guide To the Excellence Process*. Neenah, WI: Menasha Corporation.

Feigenbaum, M. J. 1983 "Universal Behavior in Non Linear Systems." *Physica* (May).

Greenleaf, R. K. 1970. The Servant as Leader. Unpublished essay.

Kim, D. H. 1990. *Toward Learning Organizations: Integrating Total Quality Control and Systems Thinking*. Cambridge: MIT Sloan School of Management.

Lee, C. and R. Zemke. 1993. "The Search for Spirit in the Workplace." *Training* (June).

Mattimore, B. W. *99% Inspirational, Tips, Tales and Techniques for Liberating Your Business Creativity*. New York: AMACOM.

Priesmeyer, H. R. 1989. "Discovering the Patterns of Chaos: A Potential New Business Planning Tool." *Planning Review* (Nov./Dec.).

Prigogine, I. and I. Stenger. 1984. *Order out of Chaos: Man's New Dialog with Nature*. New York: Bantam Books.

Radzicki, M. J. 1990. "Institutional Dynamics, Deterministic Chaos and Self Organizing Systems." *Journal of Economic Issues* 24 (March).

Schrage, M. *Shared Minds: The New Technologies of Collaboration*. New York: Random House.

Senge, P. 1990. *The Fifth Discipline*. New York: Bantam, Doubleday, Dell Publishing Group, Inc.

Wheatley, M. *Leadership and The New Science: Learning about Organizations From an Orderly Universe*. Berrett-Koehler.

—. 1992. "Making Friends with Confusion and Chaos." *At Work* (May/June).

DENNIS P. GRAHN

Dennis Grahn has been the director of quality management at the Menasha Corporation for the past ten years where he is responsible for teaching principle-centered leadership and effective small group/team leadership, building sponsorship for the excellence process, helping establish corporate strategy, development, and special project management. Grahn has a background in math and statistics from the Univerisity of Illinois, and in business management from Lake Forest College's Advanced Management Institute.

Grahn has 19 years of manufacuturing and quality engineering mangement experience in electro-mechanical, high tech plastics, printing, precision machining, and paper packing industries. He is a member of the American Society of Quality Control (ASQC) and the Technical Association of the Pulp and Paper Industry (TAPPI). Grahn is also a member of the board of directors of the D. J. Bordini Technical Innovation Center at Fox Valley Technical College.

CHAPTER FOUR:

ORGANIZATIONAL CULTURE—QUALITY SERVICE: THE RITZ-CARLTON APPROACH

Tami J. Gilbert

It is easy to think of quality when thinking of The Ritz-Carlton Hotel Company. The term "ritzy" is described in the dictionary as "swanky or elegant (after Ritz hotels, founded by Cesar Ritz, Swiss businessman)." The intention of the founders of the company was to develop and operate luxury hotels, and the acquisition of this name was ideal.

Relationship Management

Quality at The Ritz-Carlton was recognized at the genesis of the company in 1983. There was an astute understanding of the term "service" and customer satisfaction.

"Service is like anything else; it has a beginning, a middle and an end." (Horst Schulze, Chief Operating Officer, The Ritz-Carlton)

"Service," the business of The Ritz-Carlton, required definition in order to create culture. Therefore, it was determined that when an employee has an interaction with a guest, service is produced. This interaction consists of three steps: 1) a warm welcome, 2) anticipate and comply with guests' wishes, and 3) a fond farewell.

Applying this to the hotel business, one might think of the Three Steps of Service in terms of a big picture of the guest experience: 1) welcoming the guest to the hotel as they arrive, 2) during their stay anticipating and complying with their wishes, and 3) at departure offering a fond farewell.

While this is not entirely incorrect, the essence of the Three Steps of Service is to control quality each time the employee is face to face with a customer (guest). Alas, "born at birth" quality control.

The beginning of an encounter should start on a positive note: "Welcome to The Ritz-Carlton," "Welcome back," "Welcome to The Cafe," "Good morning." It would not seem right if the first words to the guest from the valet parker were, "Will you be staying overnight?" or from the cafe server, "What would you like to order?" or if the guest has dined at the Seafood Buffet every Friday night for the past two months and was greeted as if he had never been there before.

With the encounter off to a good start, the second step of service can be rendered, but normally is not as facile. Complying with guests' wishes, much less anticipating them, requires (sufficient) and (efficient) processes. In the case of the encounter with the valet parker, the second step of service involves issuing and labeling the proper ticket, offering hotel information, parking the car without damaging it, and filing the key correctly for future retrieval. Anticipation might include removing a gentlemen's suit coat from the back seat and helping him on with it as he exits the car; or, sending a dirty car to be washed; or, overhearing a family upset because they are late enroute to their dinner reservation and calling the restaurant on their behalf to secure it for them.

Finally, the encounter is drawing to a close, and should do so on a positive note. The Fond Farewell, or third step of service, could include "Thank you for staying at The Ritz-Carlton"; "Thank you for dining with us"; "Enjoy your stay"; "Enjoy your meal"; "Please come back soon." To personalize the product, we use the guest's name whenever possible.

Defining service for employees has given substance to an otherwise abstract product. It is designed with a critical control point built-in. If the guest is dissatisfied, usually during the second step of service, the employee is empowered to "break away" from routine duties to "move heaven and earth" to satisfy the guest. A portion of the gold standards states, "Any employee who receives a customer complaint 'owns' the complaint."

For example, the valet parker overhears a departing guest state that the Seafood Buffet was not satisfactory. In this case, the valet is compelled to probe and learn exactly how the experience was dissatisfying, and apologize to the guest as if he had sabotaged the meal himself. "Please forgive me," and follow up with something which will satisfy the guest, perhaps a complimentary invitation to return.

"We are ladies and gentlemen serving ladies and gentlemen." (Horst Schulze, Chief Operating Officer)

A highly scientific selection process is used in order to choose genuinely caring, highly responsive staff for the hotels. The Ritz-Carlton partnered with an external supplier to develop character trait recruiting. An applicant's strengths of 11 character traits are quantified and charted to indicate the alignment of personal values with The Ritz-Carlton values. For example, we look for individuals high in service orientation and empathy, whose "highest mission" is the "the genuine care and comfort of our guest," as our Credo states.

The motto of The Ritz-Carlton, "Ladies and Gentlemen Serving Ladies and Gentlemen" is part of the Gold Standards, or values, explained to all employees during a two-day orientation. All new "ladies and gentlemen" must participate in this training prior to working in any position, and are issued a Gold Standard pocket card to be carried at all times. During orientation they watch a video featuring Horst Schulze who dramatizes the Three Steps of Service, instills the gold standards, and even humorously empathizes with employees' plight of satisfying all the customers.

For several years, relationship management served the state of quality for The Ritz-Carlton very well—so well that overall satisfaction with their products and services was measured at 94 percent. By 1989 even with extraordinary customer satisfaction, Horst Schulze shocked the company by stating that on a scale of 1 to 10, The Ritz-Carlton is a lucky 6. The competition, at the moment, is a 5 1/2.

While the company was growing in terms of number of hotels (from 3 in 1983 to 12 in 1989), profitability wavered, as did turnover and repeat patronage. Horst visited Baldrige winning companies like Motorola and learned of their success with six sigma initiatives. He learned of the concept of systems which promoted employee involvement, leading to improved efficiency, customer satisfaction, and competitiveness. Companies visited by Schulze empowered employees to make decisions based on their own study of their own ideas. This "good idea" system caught his attention as it was consistent with the company's original philosophy of employees "owning" guest satisfaction. Clearly, The Ritz-Carlton Hotel Company was well poised culturally for a system of this nature.

Quality Vision

November 1990 brought "Quality Vision" to The Ritz-Carlton. This became synonymous with "Good Idea Boards." During the initiation, a corporate team visited each site to explain to employees that their ideas to improve guest, employee, and owner satisfaction would now be requested. They explained to managers that they should listen and coach employees through the process until the idea was either adopted or not adopted. A new position was created at each hotel: Quality Vision Leader. This person was appointed the ninth member of the Executive Committee to help leadership focus on quality and facilitate the adoption of "good" ideas. The management style was about to take a 180-degree turn. Instead of information flowing down to the ranks, it was flowing upward. The floodgates had opened.

By the end of 1991, thousands of ideas had been conceived and adopted. Morale soared as hotels buzzed with innovation and recognition. Idea maintenance software was installed at each site to provide access of all good ideas to all hotels. The quality movement was "Good Idea Boards."

Malcolm Baldrige National Quality Award

The arduous task of completing the Malcolm Baldrige application, for the first time in 1991, made clear what The Ritz-Carlton needed to improve in order to have a fully integrated quality system. Soon after submission we were notified that, while our application passed the first phase of the examination process, we would not receive a site visit which would have advanced us to the next stage of the process. Our chance to win the award in 1991 was eliminated, but the feedback report provided invaluable insights for improvement.

The senior leaders devoured the feedback, and appointed Patrick Mene, Corporate Director of Quality, to make the necessary changes. Mene recognized the need for eliminating inefficiencies in the complex operations of 100-year old hotel procedures. "Good Ideas" served to improve communication and satisfaction, but did little to identify the causes of problems and promote teamwork. He determined that while quantities of ideas could be accounted for, we were not able to express them and their effects qualitatively.

Quality Assurance

Enter *Managing Quality Services* (later known internally as "The Black Book"), a textbook case study on quality assurance in the hospitality industry published by the American Hotel and Motel Association. From this we learned how to create strategic quality plans at each site, with employees from every work area. Teams were assembled and trained to write mission statements, collect data regarding internal and external customer requirements and dissatisfaction, and write action plans for deployment of quality improvement.

Further, the study explained industry-specific examples of problem-solving teams. Once the annual strategic quality plan was complete, functional work area teams were formed and met one hour per week to identify and solve problems. Team members soon realized that many problems surfacing in their work areas were the result of problems in other work areas. This forced the team to recruit members from other departments to help them identify causes; thus, the discovery of "cross-functional" teams.

Other feedback from the 1991 Baldrige application included a need to improve the type of data being collected and used to make decisions.

Quality Engineers

In 1991 an estimated $72 million in waste was ravaging the way work gets done company-wide. No more could the employees act as just Ladies or Gentlemen; they needed to be Quality Engineers as well. Service is thought to be intangible, so how can it be measured? If every interaction between a guest and employee is service, how many interactions are defective? We needed the employees to document both guest and employee dissatisfaction, and the complexities found in the way they work. Ladies and Gentlemen were trained to detect complexity which was described as:

- MISTAKES—when someone makes a mistake, extra steps are added to correct the mistake or dispose of the damaged item.
- REWORK—doing the work over; it was not done right the first time.
- BREAKDOWNS—communication or machinery breaks down, causing (real) work to be put on hold.
- INEFFICIENCY—more time, movement, or materials are used than are absolutely essential.
- VARIATION—inconsistent products and services causes customer dissatisfaction, and others in the organization are forced to deal with rework.

Quality Engineers created an easy-to-remember acronym for the five components of complexity: "Mr. Biv." Taking it a step further, another employee created a mischievous-looking cartoon character to personify Mr. Biv. Today, all Ritz-Carltonians commonly refer to complexity as Mr. Biv. They report "his" existence in their work processes throughout the company on Internal Defect Reports.

Simultaneously, the Daily Quality Production Report was developed. This has nothing to do with revenue, costs, or occupancy. It deals strictly with dissatisfaction. From 14 sources, including the Internal Defect Report, complaints are aggregated to express the number of defective interactions and products experienced by internal and external customers daily. Periodically, trends are identified and causal analysis applied to eliminate the waste forever.

Process Improvement —Quality Theory Comes to Life
Since receiving 72 areas for improvement in the feedback from the winning 1992 Baldrige application, we have devised a fully integrated business management system. Critical processes identified through customer research have been assigned to various hotels for cycle time reduction and defect elimination. Measuring and improving work in progress is a new challenge to the service industry. Statistical process control, pioneered in manufacturing environments, has been accepted as a viable tool to improve The Ritz-Carlton. The goals of these improvement efforts are:
- **50 percent cycle time reduction** (the total time it takes to complete a critical process from beginning to end)
- **six sigma** defects or errors per million units (a very high level of quality, expressed statistically as 3.4 defects or errors per million units of product or service)
- **100 percent customer retention** (100 percent satisfied customers who continue to loyally use and recommend The Ritz-Carlton. Basically, we want to never lose a single customer.)

One of Deming's 14 points, "Eliminate numerical quotas for the work force and numerical goals for management" makes the aforementioned "goals" seem inconsistent with quality theory. Therefore, the leadership of The Ritz-Carlton maintains that these goals are the vision of the future, and the magnitude of improvement anticipated from use of TQM methods.

114   **Gilbert**

Only eight months into these three-year projects, teams were brought together at corporate headquarters in Atlanta to share lessons learned to date. The Ritz-Carlton, Rancho Mirage, had made some significant findings in the "reception" process. First, we looked at the process through the eyes of the customer, not through the eyes of the operation, in order to identify the boundaries and key requirements. Customer survey data was used for this, and showed us how traditional divisional and departmental organization, by design, create defects. Work flows across an organization, while divisions and departments tend to communicate up and down the hierarchy. The reception process includes reservation agent, housekeeper, doorman, bellman, and front desk agent. Representatives from these work phases were recruited to serve one year on the Quality Improvement Team. They were trained on the scope of the Business Management System and the group process, engaged in team-building exercises, and wrote a mission statement. Each team member was involved in collecting and analyzing baseline data to determine direction of the team.

We found that the original process contained 40,000 defects per million (remember the goal—six sigma, or 3.4 per million) and consumed 2.05 hours (cycle time).

Theory had taught us that most defects occur at the interface of two departments, where we must pass products, services, or information from one area to the next. We found a sizable bottleneck where customer requirements of room type and arrival time are given to the "manufacturer" (housekeeping). It first had to pass through the "distributor/middle man" (the front desk), and was then reworked by the housekeeping supervisor into individual work assignments for housekeepers. We were able to fix an obvious problem by better utilizing the computer technology already available for room assignments, which resulted in reduced cycle time of 37

The Ritz-Carlton Approach   115 percent. This method also provided better quality of information given to the housekeepers, since it included the guest's name.

The next lesson learned was that a major cause of unsuitable room assignment was smoke odor. Causal analysis was conducted by housekeepers, and solutions implemented. This resulted in a 30 percent improvement of defects in the reception process, and illustrated the need for just-in-time manufacturing of clean rooms the first time. Housekeepers created their own team to better understand the defects in their own processes, which led them to the laundry department. Why laundry? They found that they were rushing through the rooms at times, due to wasted time at the start of each shift gathering towels and linens. Why? Yet another study done in the laundry identified lengthy downtime while loads waited to be processed. Ultimately it was determined that 75 percent of the manpower processed 44 percent of the daily workload; 25 percent of the manpower processed 56 percent of the workload. Here we were able to change the scheduling methods and achieve a 30 percent reduction in cycle time.

Most projects in the company have learned that the root cause of problems lie "upstream," as many teams have ended up in the laundry department. This we proved at our hotel by plotting time saved in laundry with time saved in housekeeping on a scatter diagram. A clear relationship exists; an average of 30 minutes saved in laundry, saves an average of 9 hours in housekeeping.

The front-of-the-house reception team must rely on the quality of products and services from the heart-of-the-house laundry and housekeeping team.

The world-class processes resulting from these efforts will be benchmarked throughout the company, realizing the ultimate purpose of Total Quality Management—i.e., competitiveness.

Economics of Quality Improvement

While it is one thing to quantify the number of defects in a process, or cycle time of a process, it is quite another to determine the costs of a process. Refer to Deming's Deadly Disease: "Use of visible figures only for management, with little or no consideration of figures that are unknown or unknowable." We will never see a line item on the profit and loss statement indicating costs incurred by rework or customer defection. In fact, we could never truly know what that amount is. But to ignore these figures causes us to take actions which impact the known (profit and loss) financial numbers in the short term. This usually results in cutting value-added products and services, creating internal and external customer dissatisfaction.

The Ritz-Carlton uses Cost of Quality calculations to estimate the unknown and unknowable revenue opportunities lost when guests are dissatisfied and do not return. To do this, we look at each hotel site and identify number of customers each year, average amount spent by each customer, and percentage of dissatisfied customers per year (only 6 percent). This amount came to just under $1 million.

Similarly, we learned that when dissatisfied employees become a statistic of turnover, there is a price for it. At The Ritz-Carlton, recruitment, selection, and training averages approximately $4,000 per employee. When multiplied by the number of employee terminations, the annual losses total well over $2 million. Again, this is just one site. When repeated for all 30 hotels, the losses become so large that they simply cannot be ignored or discounted.

Another method for calculating the cost of poor quality includes a "Cost of Error." We learned of an effective format from Stephen Hall Associates that identifies the negative effects, probability of occurrence, and cost amount of each effect. These costs can be categorized as either hard, soft, or opportunity costs.

We looked at common errors in our organization and calculated average costs for each one. When these amounts are used with the Quality Production Report, they create a whole new financial picture for management to consider. For example, a reservation made for the wrong day costs approximately $255 each time it occurs, and an inflexible employee attitude costs about $303. On an annual basis, however, the reservation error costs each site an average of $285,953. Due to a scientific selection and values training system, the infrequency of inflexible employee attitude costs only $612. When considering cause and effect, the costs of errors and defecting customers are the cause of weak profitability. Therefore, trying to manage the known numbers on a profit and loss report is like trying to make a dog happy by forcibly wagging its tail.

TAMI J. GILBERT

As quality leader for The Ritz-Carlton–Rancho Mirage, Tami Gilbert is a member of the team of quality leaders nationwide responsible for improving management practices throughout the company. She has been at the forefront of the TQM movement at The Ritz-Carlton since 1989. Gilbert's primary responsibility is to focus management practices on quality goals and ensure that all employees are trained and certified in TQM and job tasks.

Gilbert's expertise and passion for an ever-evolving and complex approach culminated in 1992 when The Ritz-Carlton Hotel Company was awarded the Malcolm Baldrige National Quality Award, the highest accolade bestowed on a business by the United States Department of Commerce. Her role in preparing the staff to meet the criteria set forth in the Malcolm Baldrige application and to prepare for the examiners' site visit was a most arduous one. She was responsible for creating and expediting a total and comprehensive program that would validate the hotel company's claims made in the application.

CHAPTER FIVE:

LESSONS LEARNED: VIRGINIA'S QUALITY INITIATIVE IN PUBLIC EDUCATION

Yvonne V. Thayer

In 1989, no one in Virginia's public schools was talking about quality, TQM, or Deming. By 1993, one-third of the districts had begun implementing quality with the assistance of either local businesses, universities, or the military, or a unique corporate, state and federal government partnership. That which has happened in Virginia in four short years demonstrates the power a successful business strategy can have when it is introduced in a way that is non-threatening and when it is introduced at a time when an alternative for managing an organization is needed.

Total quality came to Virginia's schools, not through a mandate, but as an option for those who had a desire to become "better" by adopting the philosophy of continuous improvement. It came at a time when the school restructuring agenda called for new governance in support of the change process, when school-based management, shared decision-making, and empowerment needed a unifying philosophy. Quality became the sought-after philosophy that so many administrators needed. School leaders, under no pressure to adopt quality, engaged boards of education and building-level administrators in a dialogue that blended organizational development with school reform issues and ended with plans for transformation using total quality as the organizer.

As universities and colleges develop plans for implementing total quality, and as departments and faculty undertake the study that is a prerequisite for successful implementation, it can be very helpful to consider the various routes other organizations have taken to begin the quality journey. Additionally, it is important to listen to the stories about what worked, what did not, and that which is advised to those just beginning this rather extensive organizational behavior change.

The purpose of this chapter is to look at some of Virginia's experiences with TQM in public education. While not an exhaustive discussion of quality in schools, the discussion focuses on three unique partnership approaches to quality implementation in schools that augment the typical school district approach of working in isolation. The initiatives include: 1) a partnership between Xerox Corporation, the Virginia Department of Education, the U. S. Department of Education, and nine school districts throughout the Commonwealth of Virginia; 2) a partnership with area businesses, the military, private consultants, and school districts in the Hampton Roads area of the state; and 3) a partnership between area business leaders and a university in the Northern Virginia area surrounding Washington, DC.

The author has been associated with each of these efforts and makes no claim to present a purely objective view of these partnerships. Rather, an attempt is made to extrapolate information about these partnerships that made them effective or ineffective in helping schools with TQM and discuss it from a viewpoint of one who learned about quality during the experience with the partnerships. The author acknowledges a bias favoring TQM as an appropriate restructuring strategy for schools, and makes three assumptions regarding the value of interpreting the K-12 experience for higher education.

First, the bureaucratic nature of schools and institutions of higher education, while not identical, are not dissimilar. Even though total quality would probably be implemented differently in each setting, the experiences of public school educators could be guide posts for those in higher education in order to prevent errors and increase the likelihood of a successful implementation.

Second, universities and colleges, like their K-12 counterparts, lack funds for staff development. Partnerships with the business community could help higher education by utilizing a successful, proven strategy that is replicable.

Third, in order to provide an education that is commensurate with world class standards for the work place and appropriate to prepare extraordinary thinkers for the environmental, socio-economical, and political problems that face the populace, institutions of higher education should join K-12 in restructuring education in this country. TQM is one strategy to consider that has been successful for bringing about change and moving organizations toward greater productivity.

Xerox Serves as Catalyst for Quality
In 1989, very few articles had been published and disseminated on quality in schools. At that time, school leaders were beginning to read about Deming, hear about the National Malcolm Baldrige Award, and see advertisements that fo-

cused on customer satisfaction. Deming seminars were not yet advertised widely to school administrators, and higher education was only beginning to talk about TQM in business courses, and not yet in educational leadership studies. In Virginia, talk centered on restructuring schools, school-based decision-making as a new form of governance, cognitive science research to improve learning, and continued use of effective schools research to improve teaching. The Virginia Department of Education housed the Virginia Center for Educational Leadership (V-CEL), a consortium of professional organizations that served administrators. V-CEL's mission was to provide leadership training opportunities to school and central office administrators throughout the Commonwealth. In an attempt to bring the business community into the V-CEL partnership, the Center director and a business executive-on-loan to the Virginia Department of Education (DOE) wrote to David Kearns, then CEO and Chairman of Xerox Corporation, asking for support.

In *Winning the Brain Race* (1989), Kearns and Dennis Doyle proposed a six-point plan for reforming American education, and called for proactive leadership in changing schools. V-CEL staff hoped that Kearns' commitment to changing schools would materialize with financial support for leadership training. Conversations that followed over the next few months developed into a truly unique school/business partnership. Kearns and Xerox leaders at the corporation's international training facility in Leesburg, Virginia, approached the Department of Education about doing much more than sponsoring a training program for superintendents or a workshop for principals. Xerox proposed to "give" Virginia educators its quality strategy—through training programs, working papers, trainers, consultants, facilities—that had only one month before won the Malcolm Baldrige National Quality

Award. DOE accepted the offer without the slightest notion of the impact TQM could have in schools. The partnership, later called "Commitment to Quality," demanded a commitment that was yet to be realized when Virginia's educational leadership responded positively to Xerox and initiated a one-of-a-kind partnership between a state agency and a corporate giant.

The DOE knew that Kearns endorsed school-based decision-making, and, therefore, premised the potential of the partnership on improving school governance. Xerox visited seven school districts that had site-based governance in place and concluded that TQM could only improve their efforts. The quality initiative began with the idea that quality would improve decision-making. No one really discussed productivity, customer satisfaction, or team work in the early discussions between Xerox and DOE.

In January of 1990, Xerox assigned one full-time employee to work with the partnership. The Department of Education utilized the V-CEL director, her secretary, and two other DOE professional associates as the team to begin working with schools. Three school divisions that represented different areas of the state were approached about joining this partnership and learning about TQM, and they accepted, each assigning an individual to become immersed in quality and certified as a trainer—a quality specialist for the district. DOE and Xerox underwrote the costs of activities from January through September of that year.

During the first year, each of the three school districts only attempted to implement quality in three of their schools. Those trained initially in the concepts of quality, the skills of teaming, and the tools of quality management represented the nine schools and central office administrators. Xerox required the superintendents and principals to participate in all training designed specifically for the project. Quality specialists from

DOE and the districts attended additional training at Xerox facilities throughout the United States.

By the end of the first six months, partners were excited and eager to continue their efforts, already proposing plans for expansion. In order to facilitate these plans, in July 1990, the V-CEL director submitted a proposal to the United States Department of Education under the new Educational Partnership Program and received multi-year funding to expand the quality partnership. This generous funding provided the three districts in the partnership with resources to plan implementation of quality to all staff members, continue training, purchase materials, travel, and study. After the federal support of the partnership was announced, participants began receiving regular inquiries about TQM, with questions ranging from "What is quality?" to "How can I become a part of this project?"

During the summer of 1991, the project called for identifying additional participants. Applications were submitted, and six school districts were chosen to join the partnership. At that time, two of the original three partner school districts left the formal partnership. One had decided to pursue quality in a way other than the Xerox model. The other original partner decided not to implement TQM at that time. The third original partner district was highly committed to quality and continued to use the Xerox model.

Today, these seven districts rely on Xerox's model to varying degrees. All utilize the training materials, but none has replicated TQM implementation in the exact way Xerox recommended. Even with the assistance of the federal grant, quality implementation is expensive—primarily because it is labor intensive—so schools have been unable to assign staff as full-time quality specialists the way Xerox recommended. Training has been slower than is seen in business, due primarily to the limited staff development time built into the teachers' work year. And not feeling the same economic pressure to restructure that CEOs like Kearns felt, school superintendents have moved more slowly with quality and not prioritized it as their single focus.

Yet quality is alive and well and growing in Virginia. Why is that? Perhaps the positive response superintendents and principals heard from project participants encouraged them to consider quality approaches. Certainly the literature on quality has grown during the last three years, and every administrator has read something about TQM. Concurrently, professional organizations such as the American Association of School Administrators (AASA) and the Association for Supervision and Curriculum Development (ASCD) have offered workshops and publications on total quality that entice the local school leader.

One other reason is given by superintendents who inquire about TQM. Leaders know that schools must change to meet the needs of today's student, and quality emphasizes treating students, parents, and community members as customers. School leaders believe that we should rethink schooling using the child as the center of thinking. Looking at him as a customer helps us move away from thinking of the child as merely a consumer of the services we offer. Quality helps us rethink the purpose of education by examining what our customers want.

Other Partnerships Support Quality

Local school districts in Virginia have accessed quality programs through several channels. In addition to being a formal member of the partnership with Xerox, schools have been able to offer training by borrowing trainers from the cadre of quality specialists that now exists throughout the state. These trainers can provide the Xerox "New Employee Quality Training," a four-day program, to any school district in the state, with the Department of Education providing training materials for the first group of participants from a district. Many districts have taken advantage of this opportunity and use Xerox's materials as the foundation for their quality initiative.

Some superintendents have chosen to help employees learn about quality through the traditional route of private consultants. These consultants come from the business viewpoint and adapt materials for school implementation. Still other school leaders have accessed community-based businesses to help with training. Businesses that have taken the message of quality seriously are usually very quick to respond positively to a request from a school for assistance.

A second unique partnership that has emerged to support quality is the Education Focus Group of the Hampton Roads Quality Council. The Council is composed of business and military representatives from throughout the fast growing peninsula of Virginia that includes Newport News, Norfolk, Chesapeake, and Virginia Beach. The subgroup was formed to support the implementation of quality in the schools, both public and private. Focus group participants include business and military representatives, private consultants, university and community college staff, as well as school leaders. Activities of the group include talking with superintendents to assess the needs of schools as they implement quality, sponsoring TQM learning activities for school personnel, and learning more about quality as a learning group themselves. The Focus Group is not a group of experts, but rather, a network of people committed to quality who are interested in helping schools. They are well connected to the community and business leadership in Hampton Roads and are a great resource for an area school system.

The Focus Group is young and its impact is minimal at this point in time. However, it offers much potential as a resource for schools that need models to examine, and it can facilitate minimal support of resources in the community. The group represents the genuine interest that those outside the schools have in making the educational system better. Since the group is based on high interest rather than direct experience, the Focus Group is limited to facilitating support rather than offering services directly. This should not be viewed negatively, however, as schools need help networking and locating resources.

While some partnerships such as the Education Focus Group are designed to be responsive to customer needs and have as their primary mission to support local efforts, other partnerships develop to transform schools. One such group is at George Mason University in Fairfax, Virginia. The university houses the Institute for Educational Transformation (IET) which is composed of businesses in the geographical area surrounding Washington, D.C. IET does a number of things to support school change, and about two years ago formed a subgroup called the Total Quality Education Taskforce. Chaired by the CEO of a major corporation, the group includes business leaders from companies such as IBM, private consultants who work with TQM, representatives from professional organizations, and educators who have worked with quality, including higher education faculty. This group is very knowledgeable about TQM and speaks from experience about the components of quality and how they work in an organization.

This group has targeted their work to teachers who are participating in a new master's program at George Mason. The university requires teams of teachers from area schools to be enrolled in the program, so the taskforce seized the opportunity to access functional work teams to promote quality. The taskforce used two experienced quality trainers from the Xerox project who were members of the taskforce to deliver an orientation session during July 1992 to the teachers during their first courses in the master's program. Four months later, the taskforce chose from among its member organizations experienced trainers to teach the statistical tools of quality to the teachers. The trainers worked as a team to develop the training package and materials. Follow-up to that training has included consultant support in the schools and work with principals. Future plans are dependent on teacher feedback.

The IET taskforce defined quality in terms of continuous improvement and chose to target the classroom for change. Business people in the group argued strongly that they wanted to touch individual classrooms so that students would learn about quality early and strive for continuous improvement throughout their school experience. The notion of kiazen has been the underlying concept driving the task force.

Neither the IET taskforce nor the Hampton Roads focus group has directly committed funds to schools for TQM. Members of both groups contribute their time for meetings and research, so employers are making in-kind contributions to assist schools.

Assumptions Held in the Beginning

The Xerox partnership with the Commonwealth of Virginia and the participating schools has existed for several years, and those who were in the original meetings can now reflect on the assumptions that were made as the partnership began. In order for adults to learn from an experience, it is useful for them to understand the assumptions that underlie their beliefs and perceptions (Mezirow 1991). Certainly for those considering quality programs or partnerships with business to further quality efforts, an examination of some of the assumptions and subsequent actions on those assumptions made by both the educators and the business representatives who developed this partnership should be instructive. Five such premises emerge.

When the Department of Education staff started meeting with Xerox representatives and it was clear a partnership was forming, the educators thought of this as "just another school/business partnership." They in no way demeaned the effort or expected little from it, but they did not expect a major corporate industrial leader to devote the time and ongoing support that followed. Most previous attempts to bring business into the day-to-day workings of the school system had resulted in short-term commitments, usually associated with a financial contribution for a specific project. This partnership had begun with DOE asking for financial support, so their expectation for the implementation of quality was associated with money—training materials and training facilities. They never expected the business partner to be physically present for more than a few months.

Xerox's experience with the implementation of the quality strategy over the previous seven years confirmed in their minds that any attempt to integrate quality into the life of schools would be at least a ten-year commitment, and that it would occur only with a serious local commitment to insure the human resources needed for implementation. From the beginning, Xerox planned to be a serious player in the partnership. They continued to see themselves as the suppliers and the educators as the customers for learning about total quality. They assumed a vigorous posture—initiating meetings, pushing timelines, demanding support, and challenging the commitment of the educators.

Since the assumption was made by the educators that the business partnership would behave in a passive, limited way, the serious attitude by Xerox toward quality was somewhat of a shock to DOE staff and local school leaders. Although the educators felt unease frequently with the demands being put upon them by their tough-minded business friends, the partnership forced them to take quality seriously and to continually ask themselves whether they were up to the challenge of restructuring with the quality strategy.

Another assumption that was unspoken initially and quickly challenged was that total quality was a message for management alone. Probably because the partnership invitation was made to Xerox to provide leadership training, the educators thought of quality as something for school leaders. However, as DOE staff participated in Xerox training with their employees from all areas of the corporation, it became clear that the utility of quality was not only something that everyone in the organization could use, but something required of everyone. Since empowerment of workers is a conceptual focus of quality, and the honoring of internal customers is an important part of the work, total quality relies on a common understanding of language, beliefs, and practices by everyone, from custodian to department head.

As the real commitment to quality was being understood, the educators felt a sense of panic. How could everyone in a school system be educated about this way of viewing work? How long would it take to maneuver a large district from top-down management to a participatory style? Was this within the reach of schools? As these questions were pondered, Xerox reminded the educators of the size of their organization and the success they felt after only seven years. Yet Xerox had made a commitment that the schools had not considered at this point in time. Xerox budgeted for training of employees and assigned staff as quality specialists and trainers. The schools were just beginning to do this, and the recognition of the time, people, and money required to make total quality a reality could have made quality appear to be unachievable in public funded institutions.

Another assumption had been made early on, namely, that implementing total quality would not be costly. Perhaps this occurred because discussions about TQM focused on human resources and behaviors. Additionally, Xerox was supplying materials and facilitators for meetings, so the reality of the requirements for start-up and continuation of a total quality program was not addressed. Only in the last year or so, as schools have requested assistance for beginning new programs, has the cost of quality become apparent. Partnerships are helpful for deferring initial costs, but ongoing training and support for all employees demand resources. And nothing could be more deadly than to provide training and support for some people in the organization and not for others. While no two school districts implement quality exactly the same way, successful implementation has come about in those places that looked at training as a multi-year commitment, with the intent of bringing everyone into the process.

Both the educators and the business leaders made the assumption that total quality would assist with the move to school-based or site-based management. That assumption proved to be correct. The philosophy of quality, especially the work of Deming (1986), the statistical tools taught in quality training, and the notion of teaming for collaboration—all key components of quality—have assisted in the effort to move decision-making to the school level. TQM has provided the framework for site-based management that some schools needed, especially those that provided minimal training for staff in the processes and tools of teaming, problem solving, and decision-making.

A final assumption made early in the partnership with Xerox was that the cultures of the member organizations were more alike than they proved to be. Specifically, business representatives expected to see educators moving quickly to assign staff and make budgetary commitments to the quality strategy. Their experience in their world led them to believe that if educators were committed to the quality effort, immediate prioritization of resources would occur and both people and time would be available for TQM. Business partners learned how critical the fiscal year is to educational institutions and how tied people are to specific jobs. Additionally, business learned that there was an inherent resistance by educators to anyone from the business community coming into schools, proposing to tell educators how to do anything, including how to implement TQM.

Lessons Learned About Quality, Culture, and Implementation

Recommendations from the collective experience of public school educators in Virginia who have worked with total quality mirror some of the recommendations made by business consultants who have observed TQM programs over the past several years. Business found that management had to give more than lip service to the change process if they really wanted a transformation to occur (Schmidt & Finnigan 1992); that training was a necessary component for *all* members of the organization to become involved (McCormack 1992); and that quality is not free (Burrill 1991). Baldrige applicants and winners learned that they had to maintain their commitment to the mission of the organization and not let quality per se preempt productivity and return on assets (Steinburg 1992).

Even though Virginia's schools have not experienced TQM long enough for evaluation or with the constancy of purpose Deming (1986) demands, the first few years of learning about total quality have provided descriptive data that can be useful to other educators. The following comments represent the author's synthesis of lessons learned for enhancing success with TQM. While transferable to K-12 schools, they also speak to institutions of higher education, governmental agencies, and other public service providers, all of whom experience difficulty determining the role of the customer in an organization that utilizes funds from a variety of sources.

1) The endorsement of TQM by the leader of the organization is critical to successful implementation, and that endorsement must be demonstrated by his/her participation in TQM activities. The school superintendent has to be the first person in the district to call for total quality in order for other personnel to believe that leadership is serious about change. Further, superintendents need to learn about quality along with other members of the organization. They not only model appropriate behaviors but they learn alongside their staff. Superintendents in this study most successful with a rapid implementation talked about quality frequently and saw relationships between quality and the strategic directions of their organization.

Those sites most successful with their efforts had highly enthusiastic superintendents, and those that were not successful reflected circumstances in which either outsiders or internal staff tried to persuade their leader to adopt quality. In unsuccessful situations, the superintendent never believed that TQM was right for schools, so the transformation to a customer-driven organization could not occur. The leader did not focus on his internal customers, or did not believe her problems were due to faults in the process rather than to bad people, or could not work in a system that decentralized decision-making.

2) Upper management training is necessary and should begin before other members of the organization are trained. There are several phases to training that can occur in an organization that is beginning or even is considering quality. Staff need orientation to quality, education about TQM, training in statistical tools, training in communication skills and meeting guidelines for teaming, exposure to problem solving and quality improvement processes, and training in other group dynamics as deemed appropriate by organizational behavioral specialists. In Virginia, some districts have selected teachers and other staff to receive initial training with some administrators. The strength of this approach is the inclusion early on of all roles in the organization as decisions are being made about TQM. However, there is a risk.

When staff are exposed to quality and want to implement it before management is ready, they may become impatient and lose enthusiasm, seeing it as another fad that leaders are talking about, but not truly implementing. In Virginia, this occurred in a few settings. Teachers would even look up at trainers and ask, "Why are you training us? It is the principals that need to be hearing this!" Workers know whether they are empowered; if they feel unempowered to make the changes proposed through quality, the training seems like a joke. In fact, it is not fair to managers or supervisors to expose their workers to this style of leadership if they have not collectively agreed to work this way and received the training needed to be successful.

3) The language of quality is useful to non-business people because it facilitates different thinking about the purpose of the organization. Educators have become more sophisticated in their approach to planning and leading, and have begun to think as business leaders do. Good school leaders read business management books and are able to translate the information into their particular setting. An example of how this is working is the keen interest in strategic planning. Many educational institutions are developing a vision for their future by examining their organizational mission, shared values, and goals for the next few years. The language of quality supports this effort by defining the planning process around the needs of the customer and by giving educators a language that is commonly used in the business community. For example, identifying the customer helps members of the organization create a vision that is well-focused and appropriate. The goals of the organization become the standards by which quality operates, the desired state or level of performance is the benchmark the organization wants to achieve, and the customers' requirements can be found in the environmental scans used to determine needs of the organization.

Some educational leaders have attempted to abandon the language of quality and implement the philosophy without the language. Their attempt has been to de-business the language and attach education-ese in its place. The problem with this is that most educators have not studied quality long enough to make this shift appropriately. The learning curve with quality requires several years of study and experience. The initial look at quality sometimes creates a simplistic view of the theory, and educators are quick to take a theory or model and begin tinkering with it to improve it. Those in the Virginia experience who were highly successful stayed true to the language and used training materials as they were designed for business. And they developed the added benefit of using a language that breaks down the barriers between the business culture and the culture of schools.

Commonly used terminology that should be familiar to those in higher education considering TQM is found in List A at the conclusion of this chapter.

4) Every organization has its own culture, but good training materials are transferable from business to schools. Xerox gave Virginia educators a wonderful gift when they offered exposure to their internal training programs. When they turned over their four-day New Employee Quality Training to the schools to use, they were not only offering a program with seven years of experience behind it that would have cost thousands of dollars to replicate, they were delivering a quality product! Although skeptical at first about its utility with school people, Virginians found that this program was designed with good adult education principles in mind, and that the activities and simulations used to teach skills were as appropriate for educators as for business people. Similarly, when the business representatives from IET met to design training for teachers in Northern Virginia, the materials they had used with their companies were found to be learner-friendly with teachers.

The message from both of these experiences is that organizations beginning the quality journey should not hesitate to utilize good training materials from businesses that are willing to partner and support new efforts. The key to successful training is the expertise of the trainer, and as long as that person can make the necessary translations from the business culture to the education culture, rewriting materials should not be necessary.

5) Quality was designed to enhance productivity. Some school leaders have become so intrigued with the philosophy underlying quality and the notions of empowerment, decentralized governance, finding errors in the process and not blaming people for mistakes, that they have failed to understand what quality is indeed about—productivity. Quality certainly helps educators think about serving all of its customers, not just the ones for whom learning comes easily, and it facilitates involvement by everyone in the improvement of the total educational system. But the bottom line is productivity—doing more in less time or with fewer resources, and eliminating waste. Sometimes the good feelings and positive attitude of total quality mask the purpose it serves for the organization.

6) Taking a critical posture about total quality helps you ask the right questions. Whenever an organization adopts a new philosophy, program, or simply implements a project, leaders wince when the criticisms are voiced. A TQM approach to running an organization—be it a school, a university, or a hospital—will be different and these differences will touch everyone. Hopefully they will be viewed positively, but in reality some people will feel that they are losing power and will be resistant. A skilled leader can use this resistance to build support. Adults learn by having their assumptions challenged and by thinking critically about the options before them (Brookfield 1987). To learn about quality in depth and to explore the power it offers, leadership should encourage a critical exploration of the philosophy. Thinking about what will happen in the organization if quality is not implemented, or what will happen if another approach such as the learning organization (Senge 1990) is adopted, will develop clarity about what TQM is and is not. It will facilitate thinking about the organization in a developmental way, looking at what will work in the organization now and what could be beneficial later. Of greatest value is using critical comments or questions to clarify an individual's understanding of the transformation that is needed in the workplace (i.e., the institution). A skillful teacher can use the critical comment to help the skeptic learn, as well as further the understanding of others in the organization. One school district in Virginia stated that they purposefully chose their greatest skeptics for their first quality training. They knew that convincing people who were typically "hard sells" would benefit them immediately, because these people, convinced that TQM was good, would go back to their buildings and begin garnering support.

7) Dialogue among those implementing quality is helpful. Everyone acknowledges the value of networking, but creating a dialogue about what is happening in an organization is rare. Educators in Virginia found it very helpful to talk with others who were implementing quality. They shared stories, discussed strategies, and problem-solved difficulties. A formal network of trainers for TQM in schools meets several times a year, and these persons are responsible for helping others gain certification to train. Additionally, school districts have shared training programs and given seats to outsiders in order to further implementation in new sites. The Department of Education sponsored a state-wide conference on total quality in education and participants praised the round-table discussion groups that encouraged people to talk about what they were doing.

It is not uncommon for leaders to believe they do not have time for dialogue. Yet talking with others, learning, and challenging ideas help initiatives such as TQM improve and become better.

Pitfalls to Avoid

Richard C. Whiteley, vice chairman of a Boston-based consulting firm, has cited several "red flags" that point to a failing quality program (*Why Quality Programs Fail* 1990). Among these are false starts (much fanfare and no follow-through), the quickfix syndrome (dramatic results expected in a short time), no space on the executive agenda (management fighting fires instead of concentrating on quality), and no guts at crunch time (total quality program budget suffers when revenues are low).

Observations of the programs in Virginia's schools lead to four other pitfalls to avoid when educators begin quality programs.

1) Avoid using bits and pieces of total quality programs and calling that quality. It is tempting to select from the many components of total quality, do a little training, and then believe you are implementing TQM. The complexity of total quality is not seen initially, but those who have studied it over time will see that each of the components builds to enhance productivity. Teaming alone is not quality; using the tools alone is not quality; listening to the customer alone is not quality. Quality demands commitment, so understand from the beginning that quality requires attention to every process in the organization and will have to be *the* priority for creating change.

2) Do not expect to change the culture of your organization overnight. Culture change does occur with quality, but only after years of implementation. Management guru Peter Drucker (1993) warns that corporate culture cannot be changed by implementing new programs, but can be utilized for management change. It is important to respect the culture of educational institutions and not attempt to recreate them externally. The change to total quality must occur within the organization, building by building. And it will take time.

3) Monitor how organizational members are using the language of quality, and do not let them stonewall implementation by arguing over terms. One of the ongoing debates in education centers on who the customer is. Further, Deming adds to the debate over what education's product is by asserting that students are products in the system. Educators view students as customers, but get confused when thinking about the product that is passed on from one level to another. The debate is important because it helps clarify thinking, but it should not stop progress in learning about quality and beginning to improve processes in the system.

Some people believe that TQM is owned by business because it began in manufacturing. It is important to dispel the myth that quality does not work in service-based industries, public service agencies, or education.

4) Remember that a little bit of knowledge is dangerous. It is so easy to choose the quality strategy and begin building support without an implementation plan. Leadership must plan for total quality and continue to read, dialogue, and learn. Because quality is seen as a buzz-word, everyone thinks he knows what TQM is and can talk about it. Do not make assumptions about what total quality can do for your organization until a number of people in leadership positions have become immersed in the literature, read the work of several quality writers and researchers, and looked at the experiences of others.

Improving the system of education in Virginia is a process that will take years and years. A perfect system will not be reached, but one that is more responsive to the needs of students and the wants of the community will be achieved. A system that avoids waste and maximizes resources is possible. A system that is guided by high standards and one that measures success throughout the teaching/learning process is the goal. The total quality strategy does not dictate what the products and services of an organization are, but it does help leadership focus on how work is done. The belief is that improving the processes of the system will improve the products and services.

Looking at education as one system—understanding the interdependencies that exist within the system—creates the need to take a systemic approach to change. Total quality is one very effective way to approach systemic change. It is possible to learn about quality through the experiences of others; initiating partnerships with businesses that are quality driven and networking with other education providers who are using TQM are two ways for universities and colleges to access support.

References

Brookfield, S. D. 1987. *Developing Critical Thinkers*. San Francisco: Jossey-Bass.

Burrill, C. W. 1991. "Ten Ways to Kill a Quality Program." *Quality Progress* 24 (4): 87-89.

Deming, W. E. 1986. *Out of the Crisis*. 2d ed. Cambridge: MIT Center for Advanced Engineering Study.

Drucker, P. F. 1993. *Managing for the Future*. New York: Truman Talley Books.

Kearns, D. T. and D. P. Doyle. 1989. *Winning the Brain Race*. San Francisco: ICS Press.

McCormack, S. P. 1992. "TQM: Getting It Right the First Time." *Training & Development* 46 (6): 43-46.

Mezirow, J. 1991. *Transformative Dimensions of Adult Learning*. San Francisco: Jossey-Bass.

Schmidt, W. and J. Finnigan. 1992. *The Race Without a Finish Line*. San Franciso: Jossey Bass.

Senge, P. 1990. *The Fifth Discipline: The Art & Practice of the Learning Organization*. New York: Doubleday Currency.

Steinburg, C. 1992. "The Downside of Quality." *Training & Development* 46 (3): 11-12.

"Why Quality Programs Fail." 1990. *Training* (November): 72-73.

Xerox Corporation. 1989. "New Employee Quality Training." In *Leadership Through Quality Training Program*. Stanford: Xerox Corp.

List A

14 Points: Deming's beliefs about the behaviors needed to create a quality-driven organization are described in the Points articulated here. He believes that organizations striving for quality must break down barriers that prohibit people from working together, cannot be based on fear, must focus on educating workers, and should eliminate numerical quotas and performance evaluations. In educational terms, the Points speak to breaking down barriers between institutions and departments, providing retraining for professors, and eliminating grades and groupings that put students in competitive situations.

Benchmarking: Examining the processes used by a competitor or other kind of organization that produces a product or service of the quality desired. School leaders may benchmark their technology services against another school that has been recognized as a leader in technology. They could benchmark their student services against a program in another institution or a commercial enterprise. Higher education leaders may use benchmarking as a tool for improvement, so that one day their school is the benchmark for that process.

Collaboration: The way people in a quality-driven organization work together. Inclusive, collaborative efforts in a school could include any decision-making process previously completed by one individual or one department.

Continuous Improvement: The philosophy that undergirds quality. As customer requirements continue to change, products and services must change in order to maintain quality status; continuous improvement is achieved not only by creating new products and services that conform to customer requirements, but by improving existing processes within the system of the organization. Continuous improvement in colleges may include improving

Virgina's Quality Initiative   143

the way the counseling department delivers services, revising the curriculum based on annual student performance and regular customer feedback, and maintaining high standards for students, faculty, and program outcomes.

Cost of Quality: The cost associated with creating and delivering a quality product or service. When a college develops a new program, the cost of quality includes not only initial development costs, but also the cost of piloting the program, modifying the program to meet customer requirements, and implementing the program throughout the college.

Customer: The person (or collection of people) who receives the service or product and determines if quality is achieved. An external customer is the person outside the organization who receives the end product or service. An internal customer is anyone who receives output (during the production process) directly from someone else in the organization. External customers for education are students, parents, community members, businesses, and policy makers. Internal customers include faculty, staff, administrators— anyone who is part of the process and receives output from another person during the process.

Empowerment: Sharing of power between all who work in the organization to 1) enable teams to function, and 2) create synergy for effective decision-making and problem solving. It stimulates a culture that allows those closest to the customer to make day-to-day decisions. In higher education, empowerment of teachers and students could influence decisions about curriculum and instruction as well as the utilization of resources.

Meeting Guidelines: Rules agreed upon by a team or organization to guide meetings. Guidelines may help set parameters for meeting, outline roles played by various team members, and provide structure for setting agendas and keeping minutes. School personnel may find meeting guidelines helpful with faculty meetings, university committees, and student-teacher conferences.

Problem Solving Process (PSP): A process adopted by an organization, used consistently throughout the organization by teams to facilitate problem solving. While models may vary from five to seven steps, most models include the following activities in the process: identification of the problem, analysis of the problem, generation of possible solutions, selection of one solution, plan for implementation, implementation, and evaluation of the solution. PSP is an enabling process; that is, PSP enables the users to address problems within an existing process, to improve not only that process, but the system overall.

Quality: Delivering products and services that meet and exceed customer requirements. For colleges, creating educational products and delivering an educational program that conforms to the requirements of students, parents, and the community.

Quality Improvement Process (QIP): A process adopted by an organization, used consistently throughout the organization by teams to prevent errors as new products and services are developed. QIP focuses the team on customer conformance, emphasizes planning for quality, and requires the collection of data to measure the effectiveness of the process. QIP is an enabling process; that is, QIP enables the users to prevent problems in a new process, allowing problems in the process to emerge before the process is implemented system-wide. QIP will be new to higher education leaders, and offers great potential for teams charged with implementing new ideas or programs. This step-by-step process can be used for such things as developing handbooks and curriculum guides, creating an interview guide, developing a selection procedure for a scholarship applicant, and designing a new schedule.

Statistical Tools: Techniques for managing information related to processes in the system or tools that can assist during the problem-solving process and decision-making. Common tools include flow chart, check sheet, Pareto chart, brainstorming and list reduction, nominal group technique, histogram, run chart, cause & effect diagram, scatter diagram, control chart, and force field analysis. Educators may find that they have used some tools—such as the run chart and brainstorming—extensively, but have not been previously introduced to other tools, such as the Pareto chart and control chart. The control chart is important to monitoring processes via Deming's statistical process control.

Supplier: The supplier provides the customer with raw materials to create the product or service, or with output created during the process. Suppliers of output to instructors include copier paper distributors, textbook publishers, and other faculty who taught prerequisite courses.

Teaming: Utilizing multiple talents and experiences of organizational members to share in the production of a product or service. Teams are given the responsibility to solve problems and make changes in the processes that create the product or service, and are held accountable for the end result—that is, whether the product or service is one of quality (as defined by the customer).

Total Quality Management (TQM): A strategy for managing an organization that insures quality. It is usually associated with the work of Joseph Juran and his three components for TQM: quality planning, quality control, and quality improvement.

YVONNE V. THAYER

Yvonne Thayer is assistant superintendent for instructional services in a Virginia school district. There she oversees the pre K-12 program for 6100 students. Prior to joining the school system, she worked for the Virginia Department of Education as a Regional Services Representative, where she facilitated the implementation of TQM in local schools. At DOE she directed the partnership between Xerox Corporation, the state, and several school divisions to adopt Xerox's award-winning quality initiative, and received funding from the federal government to expand the effort through the Educational Partnership Program.

She is often called upon to facilitate TQM training sessions for schools and is currently leading her school district on the quality journey. She is particularly interested in showing school leaders how quality furthers reform efforts but must be an integral part of a developmental plan for changing public institutions.

Completing her doctorate at Columbia University's Teachers College, Thayer works with colleagues interested in restructuring government utilizing the model of the learning organization.

CHAPTER SIX:

PARTNERING FOR QUALITY

Anthony W. Corso

The major premise of continuous improvement is that by involving everyone in the organization in the daily search for incremental improvements; providing everyone with the training, techniques, and authority they need to identify and fix problems; setting high performance targets and measuring results; and focusing the company's strategic vision on the needs of its customers, everything a company does—every product, service, or organizational process—can be improved. (Bowles and Hammond 1992)

The movement towards continuous quality cited in this quotation is frequently handicapped by the behavioral requirements integral to the Total Quality Management process. Embracing cooperation, participative decision-making and teamwork is not easy in organizations where competition, rugged individualism, non-cooperation, and centralized control are predominant features.

One approach to this somewhat insurmountable situation is thought to be the promotion and formation of partnerships, both within and outside an organization, among the organization's employees, divisions and groups, and in turn, with and among suppliers or vendors whose products or services heavily influence the pursuit of quality. Partnering is described by one commentator as, "encouraging alliances between and among all of the units and divisions of a corporation, inspiring them to jointly implement a process of continuous improvement in an open, committed, collegial fashion, leaving behind traditional attitudes of hostility, competitiveness, and confrontations" (Poirier and Houser 1993).

The hypothesis is that partnering can result in a permanent dedication to courses of action which can clearly benefit the organization, its various divisions and departments (internal customers), and those whose investment decisions determine the corporation's survival—the external customers. Furthermore, by extending the partnership to outside suppliers, organizations can realize increased profits from consistent quality, lower inventories, shorter cycle times, and innovative enhancements (Poirier and Houser 1993).

This chapter describes a unique application of "partnering for quality" drawn from the experiences of Pacific Bell, California's largest utility, and the University of California–Berkeley Extension. Both organizations formed a partnership to design and implement a distinctive TQM certificate program featuring "joint learning" through which a major division of Pacific Bell and its vendors and suppliers were to engage in a learning process as fellow students. The program, currently in its third reiteration, is recognized as a highly successful innovation in corporate education and has led to

Partnering for Quality 149

similar engagements. New relationships have also emerged among corporate and outside supplier participants whose relationships have historically been conflictual due to the aggressive negotiating of price and costs.

As a result of this experience, the University of California established the "Berkeley Partnership in Professional Development Program," which the President of the University recently described as playing a vital role in endeavors to help the State of California resolve its declining economy and regain its competitive edge (Peltason 1993). In this respect, successful partnering between academia and business could have broader economic benefits. This fact is increasingly recognized by both institutions.

The Challenge of Academia-Business Partnerships

A group of America's corporate leaders recently appealed for innovative partnerships between business and education arguing that both have a responsibility to learn, teach, and practice TQM. They claim that by working together, companies and institutions of higher education must accelerate the application of TQM in academe and business; a necessity if the educational system and economy are to maintain and enhance their global positions (Price 1993).

One might predict that their recommendation will not be widely nor readily seized upon, given the bureaucratic resistance to change which is commonplace in most organizations, including academia, and the reluctance of many academics to involve themselves in what they describe as "corporate training" versus what they do—"educate." Also, there is a lingering fear in some academic quarters that once education is removed from the campus, or otherwise modified, it loses its quality and legitimacy. Despite such attitudes, and others that will be discussed, a more highly educated and skilled workforce is required if American corporations are to compete in the emerging global economy.

Although many employees are contending with more complex and demanding job responsibilities and pressures for higher levels of job performance, educators are hesitant to assume increased responsibility, regardless of the ascribed benefits of TQM. Besides, there are suspicions that programs like TQM might and are being used to further trim the workforce.

For those willing to confront such attitudes and concerns, there are other and perhaps more detrimental stumbling blocks, most of which reside in the very nature and scope of TQM programming. TQM represents more than a "quick fix"; it is conceptually tricky and operationally difficult. It advocates formidable changes in deeply held corporate perspectives, values, and operating procedures—the paramount importance attached to centralized control and decision-making, adherence to hierarchical structures and managerial control, aggressive competition, and devotion to bottom-line profitability, to name a few.

Consider TQM precepts and dicta to understand its challenge to such traditional beliefs and power arrangements: "abandon the bureaucratic structure," "empower employees," "replace control with facilitation," "network and collaborate in quality ventures," "reward and advance innovation and risk taking," "give voice to customers," "continually strive for quality improvements."

Obviously, in terms of such sweeping mandates, TQM programs will not be wholeheartedly endorsed, much less understood. Moreover, few organizations have the leadership or training resources required to successfully mount such undertakings. For this reason, educational institutions like the University of California have pursued partnerships with pub-

Partnering for Quality   151

lic and private organizations in hopes of contributing to the monumental task of promoting TQM through education.

But what is to be the nature of such partnerships? And how might academic institutions and corporations, which are often suspicious of one another, begin the partnering process? And, what factors might be expected to support or impede such affiliations? Perhaps some answers can be found in the University of California Extension and Pacific Bell's partnership experience and in literature devoted to partnerships.

Partnerships From a Business Perspective

The authors of *Business Partnering for Continuous Improvement* argue convincingly for the establishment of partnerships, particularly in the initiation of TQM programs. The authors contend that many quality programs in business are launched with considerable enthusiasm and fanfare only to run into resistance from their own employees and departments, thus producing disappointing results.

They maintain that the key to achieving continuous and enduring improvements in quality is through the building of alliances throughout an organization's business network—effectively joining employees, suppliers, and customers for mutual benefit. They optimistically state

. . . partnering is a people thing, through which men and women from all parts of the organization—working with each other and with their suppliers and customers—commit themselves to honestly improve the relationships and performances that make a business system work and survive. (Poirier and Houser 1993)

Business partnering is not a legal arrangement or a way of establishing a larger identity. It is a way of working out mutual expectations and commitments, developing a process for communicating and working together, and solving problems in ways that neither party could do alone (Schmidt).

One variation of partnering gaining increased attention and application are cooperative ventures between corporations and their suppliers. A number of corporations are heavily involved in promoting and nurturing "positive supplier relationships"—relationships which, as previously noted, have historically been conflictual, adversarial, and strained largely due to arduous negotiating over issues of price and costs. With the advent of TQM, suppliers are increasingly recognized as integral to the improvement process since the quality of what they provide, whether products or services, ultimately affects the corporation's ability to satisfy customers. This has served to highlight quality and joint-ventures over a singular obsession like cost and price.

Motorola, one of the first national Baldrige award winners for quality achievements, clearly understands this fact. It sets demanding goals (virtually zero defects) in the design of its products and requires the same level of perfection among its suppliers. One supplier is quoted as saying, "If you can supply Motorola, you can supply God" (Bowles and Hammond 1992).

The Development of the PAC Bell-Berkeley Partnership

Berkeley Extension was first approached to discuss the potential development of an in-house certificate program by PAC Bell's Executive Director of the Contract and Supplier Management Department. His reasons for choosing Berkeley included the prestigious nature of the University, which he felt would impart legitimacy to the TQM program; the fact that Berkeley Extension has considerable experience in the development of certificate programs for professional groups; and an acknowledgment that the curriculum could be designed in a collaborative manner with Berkeley's staff (Reed 1993).

Partnering for Quality   153

The Dean, Associate Dean of Extension, and the Chair of the Business and Management Department, as well as the Director of the PAC Bell's Supplier Management Division, met in a spirit of cooperation and positive rapport to discuss the certificate program. This gave notice that the certificate program had priority of importance and ensured that the design of the program could proceed with a maximum degree of openness and trust. Although PAC Bell was in the forefront of corporate-wide education in TQM, such efforts were judged insufficient in terms of the operations of the Supplier Management Department; it sought more in-depth education and TQM training for its employees especially as it relates to partnerships. The objective was to achieve closer relationships with vendors and suppliers as a means of cooperatively reaching quality objectives, and thus offering more efficient service to internal as well as external customers. In this regard, the Department was dedicated to a professionalization of its employees, a redefinition of the adversarial nature of purchaser-vendor relationships, and the promotion of mutual problem-solving.

PAC Bell insisted that suppliers also be enrolled in the certificate program as a means of cementing affiliations. Smaller firms which lacked the financial resources to participate, particularly those representing minority owners, were offered corporate tuition support.

From academia's vantage point, the Extension was chiefly concerned that the program accomplish what the client expected. In particular, the Chair of the Department of Business and Management felt that the program should offer more than theoretical concepts; it needed an applied component. For this reason, he suggested that teams of employees and suppliers jointly develop and implement quality initiative projects, demonstrating the benefits of partnerships to both parties.

A series of meetings were held with members of a Pac Bell curriculum design committee further exploring the utility's educational and training requirements. A number of persons felt that the curriculum should focus exclusively upon mastering the tools and statistical techniques associated with TQM. However, faculty advisors reasoned that TQM was about more than techniques.

They asserted the necessity to understand the comprehensive theory of TQM, its behavioral implications, and the influence it could be expected to have upon decision making and customer relations, and—more importantly—upon the relationships between supplier managers and suppliers. In the end, both positions were accommodated; several courses specific to TQM techniques were integrated into the academic design as well as the more global view.

What emerged from the meetings and discussions was a certificate program entitled "Partners in Quality" emphasizing the formation of partnerships between Pac Bell and its suppliers. The agreed upon goals of the program were to: increase the level of professionalism among members of the Supplier-Manager organization; encourage close relationships among managers and their suppliers in terms of a continuous and collaborative search for quality; and provide participants with the knowledge and skills required to more fully participate in total quality management activities.

The certificate program included the following courses:
1) "Introduction to Applied Total Quality Management"
2) "Strategic Quality Planning"
3) "Methods of Applied Quality Management"
4) "Evaluating Software Quality"
5) "Human Factors in Applied Quality Management"
6) "Measuring the Results of Quality"

In addition, a practicum course, "The Quality Project"—applying concepts to the design and implementation of a quality initiative—was added, acknowledging that connecting theory to practice is a prerequisite in educating practitioners.

Managers and suppliers were assigned to project teams. The projects were expected to cover a wide range of areas, from minimizing costs while improving quality, to resolving complicated, recurring problems in the purchasing process, and exploring alternative methods of contracting for products and services—ones requiring less time, effort, and paperwork. The latter was of particular consequence since Pac Bell was recently organized into autonomous business units—separate departments possessing the authority to enter into purchasing contracts without the assistance of the Contract and Supplier Management Department. In this regard, the Department felt pressured to prove its value and worth to its affiliated departments and to Pac Bell as a whole.

A faculty-mentor from the University was assigned to the project to offer counsel and guidance throughout the teams' efforts. Teams met often to gather information, define the specific change initiatives, analyze potential benefits and costs, and to devise a successful implementation strategy. The mentor-professor, who was stationed at Pac Bell even after the other courses had ended, was expected to coach teams in the intricacies of project development and advise them when obstructions to progress arose.

This long-term involvement, exemplified by the project, was seen as a significant requirement of the educational partnership, since it magnified the commitment to an ongoing, mutually beneficial relationship and verified the advantages of "action-learning." Given the priority of attention to instigate quality initiatives that significantly contribute to partnering organizations, each of the projects demonstrated a particular regard for "return on investment."

Finally, faculty selected to instruct in the program were highly skilled in adult education and contemporary training methods, such as facilitating group discussion and problem solving, case study analysis, and the use of simulations and other experiential exercises. They also possessed the academic qualifications expected by the University's academic review committees. They also held extensive experience in organizational analysis and change, teambuilding, group behavior, and, of course, the principles and practices of total quality management.

In retrospect, one of the major issues for the University involved the need to modify academic requirements to meet the customer's needs without compromising academic standards. The University's criteria for academic programs are very specific in terms of the number of courses and contact hours required in a certificate program, the quality and contents of the program, the scope and appropriateness of written assignments, effectiveness of teaching methods and the type of evaluation strategies to be utilized.

In this regard, the "Partners in Quality" certificate program, like other proposed academic programs, underwent an elongated review process. The process involved an internal review by the Department of Business and Management as well as by a committee governing academic matters for University Extension. It was subsequently sent to the University's Business School, which holds authority over all business and management related courses. Finally, it was reviewed by the Academic Senate's Subcommittee on Extension.

As one might expect, the process of program approval and course approval can consume many weeks, and this proved somewhat irritating to the corporate clients who were under strict time and budgetary constraints. Pac Bell wished to begin the program as quickly as possible. Fortunately, the extension staff were able to expedite the review process somewhat, but this required considerable effort and time. In retrospect, academic review remains a major barrier to more effective client responsiveness.

Summarizing this experience in academic partnering, the Chair of the Department of Business and Management in a spirit of advocacy observed, "Perhaps our experience in creating a successful certificate program reflects the nature of a partnership, if we define a partnership as a coming together, a redefinition of relationships beyond traditional contractual definitions, to one requiring an abundance of trust, a voicing of concern for the success of both parties, and being able to go the extra mile when it is in the partner's benefit to do so" (Ebersole 1993).

Evaluating the Quality Partnership Program

Students' overall rating of the program indicate that 75 percent judged it "good to excellent," 20 percent rated it "satisfactory," and 5 percent rated the overall program "poor to fair." Those who evaluated it on the low side said that they were hungry for more tools and applications and had minimal patience for introductory material. In some instances, they remarked that there was excessive redundancy in some of the courses; too often instructors seemed constrained to explain TQM from the beginning before treating their particular subject.

On the positive side, there was common agreement that the program was conceptually strong, aligned well with issues of professional practice, and conferred an excellent foundation for further TQM partnerships. In particular, students cited the many benefits derived from a joint learning process with

158   **Corso**

vendors. It bestowed a common conceptual framework; clarified some of the problems experienced in previous contract and purchasing ventures and generated more amicable relations. Finally, it made participants more acutely aware of the necessity for structural and operational changes, along the lines championed by TQM. As expected, some behavioral changes were evident: adversarial "win-lose" mindsets gave way to a deepened sense of cooperation and trust among most "partners" and this was most evident in efforts expended in team projects.

As for the projects, a number were ceremoniously recognized as "notable achievements"—contributing to both Pac Bell and its supplier organizations. Some of the mutual benefits can be deduced from project titles:

- "Development of a Reporting and Measurement System to Track Improvement"
- "Validating Performance Measurements"
- "Improvements in the Effectiveness of Pac Bell Supplier Quality Report Card"
- "Improvement of Information Process to Suppliers"
- "Management of the Quality improvement Process in Periods of High Growth and Demand"
- "Vendor Performance Feedback Mechanism for Service Vendors"
- "Establishment of a Supplier Certification Process"
- "The Establishment of an Evaluation Process for Consultants"

Unfortunately, a number of projects had to be terminated as serious problems occurred within some supplier companies —complications often reflective of California's deteriorating economic climate. One supplier organization suffered bankruptcy; others experienced drastic changes in personnel; several smaller companies found it impossible to engage in projects because of shortages in staff and time.

Some suppliers discovered that they were employed in organizations privately adverse to total quality management and doubtful about the utility of "quality partnerships." In such cases, program participants had to become "missionaries," communicating what was learned in hopes of legitimizing their involvement. Their efforts were aided by the high visibility and importance granted the certificate program; it became a symbol of Pac Bell's pledge to quality. The message went out that vendors must move quickly in the direction of quality, if they expect to continue doing business with PAC Bell—an additional impetus to the future education and formation of TQM partnerships.

Finally, projects judged to be of exceptional value were presented at PAC Bell's annual "Business Partnership Day," a company-wide forum used to recognize supplier contributions to Pacific Bell's quality vision. This also reinforced the value of partnering as an important vehicle for achieving continuous quality.

From all indications, persons completing the certificate program experienced demonstrable gains in comprehending the scope and magnitude of TQM, the opportunities offered by partnerships, and the skills needed to be effective in such endeavors. Of significance to faculty, is evidence that the learning process embodied in the certificate program is continuing. Persons tell of meeting regularly their supplier-partners; the concepts and techniques which they learned invariably frame the discussion.

Lessons Learned

One of the issues previously described was the Extension's need to modify some academic requirements and procedures in order to meet customer's expectations, while not compromising quality standards. This can be a real obstacle in institutions having minimal experience in cooperative program design, needs assessment, or molding delivery systems in such a way as to offer academic programs in modules, times, and places that suit the corporate customer. Clearly, academic institutions seeking involvement in TQM programs must practice TQM—redefining their mechanisms and processes for program development, intensifying the responsiveness they exhibit to clients, and promulgating their new service vision throughout the academic institution and community.

Providing adequate faculty resources was and can be another hurdle. There remains a shortage of faculty who are interested or knowledgeable about TQM despite its apparent significance. In the case of Berkeley, only one faculty member in the on-campus Business School was identified as conducting TQM research and publication. The Extension staff had to identify, recruit, and seek university approval for an entirely new faculty, all of whom come from outside the institution. There could be positive benefits derived from a use of on-campus faculty—particularly from a public relations standpoint, especially at a time when academic budgets are being cut and questions are being raised concerning the amount of teaching done by senior faculty members.

The use of on-campus faculty is further complicated by the tendency of some instructors to volunteer their traditional on-campus courses without modification. Still others may be deficient in skills required to instruct adults, especially upper-level professional managers. Finally, departmental rewards are typically nonexistent for faculty instructing in off-campus programs. Perhaps public service should be elevated to the status of "publish or perish" in this regard.

While TQM educational partnerships are developing on some fronts, only a small number of educational institutions seem willing to offer more than a perfunctory course or two.

Partnering for Quality   161

The hope is that others, moved by civic responsibility and some sense of public purpose, will begin to display the necessary commitment, perseverance and skills required for educational partnering to become a reality.

As for Berkeley Extension, the Chair of Business and Management Programs reports, "it is indeed at the forefront of the University to partner, not only with business, but with organizations of all types and we hope to do more in the future (Ebersole 1993).

In a highly complimentary fashion, a vice-president of Pacific Bell recently stated, "Our partnership with UC Berkeley Extension has been invaluable in training our managers and employees. The combination of top caliber faculty and tailor-made curricula has produced superb results—this has definitely been our best cooperative experience with higher education" (Welch 1993).

References

Bowles, J., and J. Hammond. 1992. *Beyond Quality.* New York: Berkeley Publishing Group.

Ebersole, J. 1993. Interview by author. University of California Extension, 19 September.

Peltason, J. W. 1993. *Lifelong Learning.* University of California Extension Catalog, Fall.

Poirier, C. C., and W. F. Houser. 1993. *Business Partnering for Continuous Improvement.* San Francisco: Berrett-Koehler Publishers.

Price, R. M. 1993. "Forging Effective Business-Academia Partnerships." In *Continuous Quality Improvement*, edited by Dean L. Hubbard. Maryville, MO: Prescott Publishing Co.

Reed, J. R. 1993. Interview by author. University of California Extension, 18 September.

Schmidt, B. "Shifting to a Quality Culture." *At Work* (January/February): 23.

Welch, S. 1993. *Lifelong Learning.* University of California Extension Catalogue, Summer.

ANTHONY W. CORSO

Anthony W. Corso is an associate professor of management in the School of Extended Education at Saint Mary's College. He previously served as the chairman of the management program for 12 years. He received his doctorate from the University of Washington with specialties in organizational development and social change. During doctoral studies he was awarded a Mellon Foundation fellowship.

He was employed for over a decade in government as a city and regional planner in San Francisco, Richmond, and San Diego, California. He founded the Masters Program in City and Regional Planning at San Diego State where he also served as the director of the Public Affairs Research Center.

In addition to teaching, he has also served as a consultant in the field of Total Quality Management and co-authored and taught in the Partners in Quality program at Pacific Bell. He is currently conducting research on high performance management and spiritual leadership.

CHAPTER SEVEN:

PARTNERS FOR QUALITY IN A UNIVERSITY SETTING: CALIFORNIA STATE UNIVERSITY–DOMINGUEZ HILLS AND XEROX CORPORATION

Amer El-Ahraf, David Gray and Hussein Naquib

"Partners." The word has a reassuring ring to it when one is facing an exciting but unfamiliar and difficult journey. In the beginning, "guide" might have been more accurate. Like any wayfarer in a new land, it was good to have someone along who had been over the terrain before; someone who knew the route, the language and where the hazards were; someone who had charts of the territory. And so it was when California State University–Dominguez Hills set out to develop a Quality program, and the Xerox Corporation joined us as a partner in the enterprise. In this chapter we will trace the course of that maturing relationship.

El-Ahraf, Gray and Naguib

Universities and colleges are facing a new world, a tougher world, with less margin for error and less tolerance for ineffective operations. It is a world with higher requirements for effective systems and clear responses to customer needs and wishes. This new environment features an impending avalanche of new technology, significant budget reductions, demands for increased efficiency and effectiveness, downsized organizations, and a rising demand for better services.

California State University–Dominguez Hills was a classic case in this new world; it was beset with rising demands for service, substantial cuts in income, reductions in staffing, and an institutional structure that was resistant to change. Caught in this dilemma, the University turned to the quality movement for inspiration and instruction and to the private sector for mentoring. Both choices were fortuitous.

As we began the arduous process of designing a quality program which could be successful in the culture of our university, we discovered the well documented experience of Oregon State University. Executives involved in that program graciously granted us permission to use some of their materials and we used them in two ways: to articulate the elements of an effective program and to demonstrate that TQM approaches could be effective in an academic institution.

Concurrently, we also formed a partnership in quality management with the MicroElectronics Center of the Xerox Corporation in El Segundo, California. Our mentor there was Hussein Naguib, who is also one of the authors of this chapter. He had an ideal set of experiences which included service as a faculty member in three universities and eight years of experience in quality management as an executive in the Xerox Corporation. The great strength of business partners is that many are a decade ahead of most academic institutions in thinking through and implementing a quality approach to organization design and operations. Our Xerox relationship brought this significant benefit.

The Xerox Experience

Starting in late 1983 the senior leadership team began to develop Xerox's total quality initiative: Leadership Through Quality. This team of the 25 top operating executives developed the quality policy, strategy, and implementation plan. The foundation was laid in this policy statement:

Xerox is a quality company. Quality is the basic business principle for Xerox. Quality means providing our external and internal customers with innovative products and services that fully satisfy their requirements: Quality improvement is the job of every Xerox employee. (Kearns 1992)

There were five major change mechanisms in the Leadership Through Quality initiative to support the transformation of the company:

- Management: Commit to attainment of strategic quality goals. Serve as role models for implementation of Leadership Through Quality.
- Standards and measurements: Provide tools and techniques to quantify quality improvement. This includes a six-step problem-solving process, a nine-step quality improvement process, and benchmarking.
- Training: Educate every employee in the Leadership Through Quality process. Starting with the training of top managers, have them participate in training their subordinates.
- Recognition and reward: Ensure both individuals and groups are motivated and recognized for practicing and improving quality.

- Communications: Inform employees consistently and effectively of the corporate priorities and objectives and progress toward meeting these goals.

Together with our Xerox mentor, we began to explore the concepts of Total Quality Management as they are articulated and employed within the corporation. We reviewed some of Xerox's early experiences. The introduction began with three questions the corporation asked itself: Why do we need a new management philosophy? Why is "quality" used as the base for the new management philosophy? What is Total Quality Management?

In 1984 Xerox began to answer those questions. The first answer was there were many significant changes in the business environment. It was increasingly competitive and worldwide in its scope. Xerox was losing market share. There was low economic growth. Customers were more sophisticated and they were demanding high quality. The corporate work force was increasingly diverse. Advances in technology and information systems required more cultured and highly educated workers. All of these developments and others indicated that traditional management practices were no longer adequate in the new environment. It was also clear that products and services must be equal to the best in the market if the company was to be competitive. Customers, who in the past were mainly concerned about price, were now demanding high quality and competitive pricing. The answers to the first two questions were obvious, but the third question was more difficult.

What is Total Quality Management? They began to answer that question by exploring the concept of quality. Webster's New World Dictionary suggested quality is "the degree of excellence that a thing possesses." Further consideration revealed that within the context of the meaning under investigation there were two different types of quality: "quality of conformance" which is the extent to which a firm and its suppliers surpass the design specifications required to meet the customer's needs; and "quality of performance" which is the measure of how well products or services perform in the market place. W. Edwards Deming (1982) had made the distinction. They also found other definitions: "Fitness for Use," Juran; "Conformance to Requirements," Crosby, and "The totality of features and characteristics of a product or service that bear on its ability to satisfy stated or implied needs." Finally, the corporation adopted its own definition: "Deliver error-free competitive products and services on time to our customers that meet or exceed their expectations."

The corporation had a program of conventional quality controls for a long time. When they began to promote Total Quality Management they found it useful to distinguish Total Quality Management from quality control. They described quality control as "goodness" or "luxury"; it is a process in which the customer is the end user, the goal is to achieve an acceptable quality level using a strategy of inspection and correction of errors, the field of action is products, the effort is to produce quality at any price, and the responsible agency is the quality department.

Total quality is quite different. In TQM, quality means to meet or exceed customer expectations; the customer is the internal receiver, the quality goal is to achieve zero defects, the strategy is prevention of errors, and the field of action is the entire company and everybody in it. The process is designed to produce quality at competitive cost, and responsibility for the process is everybody's business.

In the University we found the distinctions between the sets of concepts in these two paragraphs to be highly significant. It was clear the TQM model was driven by customer

El-Ahraf, Gray and Naguib

expectations and the customer was not a remote end user; there was an internal customer at the end of every phase of the process; quality was produced by correcting the process to achieve zero defects, not by reworking errors caught by inspection; and the field of action was the entire University, so quality was everybody's responsibility. Attention to cost was an important element.

Next what does the word "total" mean in operational terms? The answer, in TQM: total means all company functions, all company activities, all employees regardless of their rank in the organization, plus all improvements in quality which come from resolution of existing problems and prevention of future problems. Total means the entire production cycle of the product or service from design to market.

Finally, the corporation asked, what does the word "management" mean in TQM? The answer: "Management is process-oriented, quality leadership striving for continuous improvement in all activities to meet or exceed customer requirements through the use of a structured, systematic and common approach to problem-solving and decision-making, with fun participation of all employees."

The corporation developed a shorter definition of TQM: "Total Quality Management is a set of principles and methods organized as a company strategy with the goal of mobilizing the entire company toward continuous improvement to achieve the greatest customer satisfaction at a competitive cost."

Explanatory statements pointed out what TQM is and what it is not: TQM is not a quick fix strategy, nor a program with a beginning, a middle, and an end or a buzz word; it is a long-term strategy, a process to change the culture and continually improve the organization, and a proven and successful methodology for managing business.

TQM and the University

As we contemplated the Xerox model of TQM, it was clear the basic components of the system were generic enough to be adapted to the University but must be adjusted to improve acceptability in the culture and traditions of the institution. We began to explore the differences between industry and academe. The first observation is obvious—the university is not a factory! We explored some of the permutations of that central fact:

    1) We have to concentrate on services;
    2) There is no top-down command structure;
    3) The language has to be changed;
    4) Participation in the program is largely voluntary;
    5) Students are not "customers" in the traditional sense;
    6) Students are not the product, their learning/education is the product, if there is one;
    7) Students need to be "co-managers" of their own education;
    8) If the system fails there is no opportunity for recall; and
    9) Resources for training and implementation of the program are very limited.

With the perspectives of this analysis ,we began to develop a TQM program for the University.

Adapting the Xerox Model

Academic institutions have always resented being told they should be more business-like. They properly maintain that if they become a business they will no longer be a university. We determined from the beginning we did not wish to be more business-like; we wished to use business experience and insight to become a better University. We knew we would need to design a program which could be embraced by the academic community.

An early perception of people steeped in academic tradition who are contemplating application of quality concepts in the academy is that there is a basic incompatibility between the quality movement and the academic culture. At the outset, if the academic community knows anything about the quality movement, it is thought to be of Japanese origin, concerned with assembly lines, created to improve automobile performance, and designed to cut manufacturing costs. Given these perceptions, it is difficult to see much connection with the University. In addition, the literature of the movement and the speech of consultants working in the field are filled with jargon foreign to academic experience. These barriers must be surmounted before communication begins.

The conceptual bases for the quality movement are not difficult to understand, but some effort is required to learn the concepts and follow the process. It is not until the values and philosophical underpinning of the quality movement are apparent that the essential work of adopting quality approaches to the University, and the University to the perceptions of the quality movement, begins.

Early Developments

The University and the Xerox Corporation began working together on a quality process in 1992. From the beginning, a number of decisions were made to make a successful transition from private industry to the University by recognizing the basic nature of academia and our tradition of shared governance. Thus, our CSUDH model is known as "campus commitment to shared governance through continuous improvement." We also emphasized the concept of quality service and quality management as a University-wide process, not limited to either administrative functions or to instruction even though our pilot projects are cross-functional and tend to be administrative in nature.

We wish to benefit from the successful experience of others, but are committed to development of a CSUDH model that is indigenous to its academic environment, its unique culture, and the strength of its human resources and infrastructure. When we go abroad we recognize that the culture of other institutions is important to the success of their programs. We decided when we started TQM officially to draw not only on the experiences of others, but also on the University's own experiences in implementing TQM in some areas of the University.

Thus, even though quality service was initiated formally in 1992, the campus had begun the process in 1990. For example, between 1990 and 1992 we finished the construction of two major buildings, a second phase of Student Housing, and the University's Student Union using TQM techniques. During the same period we initiated the process to convert our computing environment from Cyber to Digital, set a new financial management system, and began planning for the West Campus Project, a major effort which involves public/private cooperation in university-related commercial development. All of these projects used the principles of TQM. The "case history" of the construction experience is instructive:

> In the spring of 1991 the long standing dream of a student union for the members of the University community at California State University–Dominguez Hills, was not on schedule. The long and arduous process of confirming a site on the master plan for the University, finding a donor to help with the funding, passing a referendum to get student support for the increase in fees, securing approval for the revenue bonds, designing a unique building, carrying out the bidding process, hiring the successful contractor and beginning construction was over, but the building

process was beset with problems. There were many reasons. It rained heavily for several days in March requiring recompacting of the soil. The superintendent, who represented the contractor, had little experience with a building of this kind. The inspector, who represented the State, was known to be tough. There were many change orders coming through for the food service facilities.

In addition, there was a high degree of conflict within the construction crew. Disagreements infected the crew, and the sub-contractors soon involved the union; CAL-OSHA was called in, and the union and CAL-OSHA shut down the job site. A pattern of hostile relationships and finger-pointing ultimately evolved. It appeared that litigation was likely and long delays were inevitable. The Executive Vice President asked for all management personnel involved to work together as a team with three objectives: finish the building in a timely manner, provide the University with quality food service, and build a superb student union.

At this juncture a new construction engineer was assigned to represent the Physical Planning and Development Office of the Chancellor's staff on the project. He brought to this assignment experience and confidence in "partnering," a pattern of working together using quality management methods and techniques. His perspective on conditions at the work site was particularly important. He knew conditions on the job were not unique; he also knew there was a better way to work together. The problem was to make the transition, with personnel already mired in hostile relationships, to a problem solving process that would permit them to work together. He began his assessment of the situation with a 30-minute interview with each member of the work crew.

He laid down one rule: for every negative thing reported about the job each person interviewed must report a positive aspect. The result was a more balanced view of working conditions than a report of negative comments alone. At the conclusion of the interviews he charted all the strengths and weaknesses looking for congruences and formed his own opinion of where things stood. He concluded the superintendent and the inspector could not work together; he recommended that they be replaced, and they were.

During this period a major change in preparations for food service occurred. A contractual arrangement with California State University, Fullerton, resulted in a redesign from a cafeteria line to a food court concept represented by four vendors including Togo, Taco Bell, Carl's Jr. and Round Table Pizza. This change in concept required major changes in plumbing and electrical service and generated dozens of change orders when the building was about 20 percent completed. Using QM approaches management began the process of working through the necessary changes. In the background the Executive Vice President worked with concerned parties to keep emphasis on objectives, to foster good will, and help participants to come to the meetings thinking as a problem solving team and not representatives of different interests. He used the telephone and brief personal meetings effectively to make sure the group was ready for cooperative effort.

Meanwhile, a contract to construct a new student housing complex consisting of nine buildings was put out for bid and the University student union contractor was the successful bidder. There was considerable concern that a repeat of the union experience was in progress, but the construction engineer and others involved in the process were determined to avoid that possibility. Following consultation with the Executive Vice President, a management team composed of six people was convened, and each component (the Contractor, the University, and the Chancellor's staff) was given two votes in a problem-solving process. To assure final resolution of problems, the architect on the project was designated as arbitrator in case of "total breakdown" of the problem solving process, but it was never necessary to call in the architect to referee. The team went to work using Quality Management methods.

The team began its work by establishing a protocol for each meeting. Every meeting had an agenda which was open to amendment or additions at the beginning of each meeting. Members took turns volunteering as scribe and timekeeper, and the people serving in those roles provided a written record of the decisions reached and kept the meeting within agreed time limits. There was also someone serving as facilitator to help the team through process hang-ups.

The work began with a "Pareto Diagram" which was used to study cause and effect relationships. Using the University student union building experience as a source of data, the team produced a comprehensive list of potential problems and their probable causes. Then they worked backwards to seek ways of avoiding the causes of the anticipated problems. It worked, and many problems were avoided. When the project was underway they concentrated on one of the nine units and brought it up first. Then the team members undertook a comprehensive critique of the first building and used the data they collected to instruct the sub-contractors on the required standard of performance. The remaining buildings came in with much shorter "punch lists" of items which needed completion or correction.

From the beginning any member of the team could declare "breakdown" and call a meeting to seek solutions. One such incident involved sleep deprivation for residents in campus housing when dirt-moving machinery was being serviced, tested, and positioned starting at 5 a.m. The team considered the problem, and all adjustment of schedules was agreed to by all of the team members. Following the successful resolution of this problem, students realized they could get a hearing and a genuine effort to meet their needs. Other problems were brought to the team for consideration and resolution.

Meanwhile, work was going forward on the union. Replacement of the superintendent and the inspector helped; the replacements were chosen not only for their technical expertise but also for their people skills, but the reservoir of ill feelings and the problems caused by delays and changes remained. The situation was difficult to turn around and no miracles were achieved, but a working system evolved and the union was ultimately built, bringing the University and the community a new center of pride and campus life.

The team spirit continued and learning from the experience proved to be helpful in the Housing Project. It was completed six months ahead of schedule on an 18-month contract and $300,000 under budget. There were no contractor disputes, no claims, and no litigation. The University gained a summer and a fall semester of additional occupancy prior to the original opening date. The Contractor has developed a non-adversarial method of working, and the California State University is moving to use similar methods with all projects of $250,000 or more. (Clevenger)

This brief case history was used to illustrate some of the principles of Total Quality Management and to demonstrate that quality service was feasible in the academic community. The preparations for the quality service process continued.

Initiation of Quality Service

We began to lay the foundation of a formal quality program. We organized awareness seminars for executive management, deans, and directors. President Sam Schauman of El-Camino College and Hussein Naguib of the Xerox Corporation, introduced quality concepts to the Executive Committee. The University brought in personnel, from the Chancellor's staff and the State Department of Finance who were experienced in the management of quality programs, to introduce TQM concepts and methods. Over a period of several months we developed a Quality Service Policy, established a University Council on Quality, and conducted countless staff meetings where Quality Service was discussed.

We identified internal and external human resources. We looked for models and experience in other academic institutions: the library produced a literature search on TQM in colleges and universities. We continued our dialogue with Xerox, often seeking advice at critical decision points. We gained presidential approval for the program and the support of the Executive Committee.

To spread the word we organized a management orientation, a management retreat, a manager/supervisor/key personnel series of workshops. The Executive Vice President met with representatives of the Unions, the Academic Senate, and the Staff Council to hear their concerns, answer their questions, and enlist their support.

Several local publications were prepared to support workshops and training designs. Permission to use material from other institutions was solicited and received. An extensive workbook to support training of Sponsors, Team Leaders, Facilitators and Team Members was assembled with the aid of Xerox, Oregon State University, and other resources.

All of these preparations occurred during a very difficult time within the country, the state of California, and the California State University system. Caught in a combination of recession and a severe reduction in military expenditures, California suffered an unprecedented loss of tax revenue and the University was forced to curtail its expenditures and its operations. Faced with the prospect of extensive lay-offs of personnel and significant cuts in operating funds, the University organized a "Delphi process," which encouraged any member of the academic community to suggest ways of cutting costs and saving money. The process generated dozens of possibilities for savings and they were turned over to a task force appointed to review and evaluate the proposals and make recommendations to the President. During this process, the term TQM became a symbol for administrative layoff. This undesirable outcome was not conducive to an unemotional evaluation of the merits of using TQM approaches in the University.

Two strategies were adopted to cope with this condition. First, promotion of TQM was delayed for a time, and second, the name of the University program was changed to Quality Service. Upon completion of the Delphi process, planning for the introduction of Quality Service was again undertaken. Ultimately the loss of personnel and financial resources was not as severe as originally predicted and the forced linkage of lay off and quality service was avoided.

The planned project to document early experience in TQM-like projects in the University continued, and additional case histories were collected on part-time faculty appointment and part-time faculty clearance procedures. Both of these projects followed the Quality Service model closely, and both were highly successful.

This work goes forward in documentation of other projects including the West Campus Project, an ambitious cooperative venture with private enterprise in the development of 56 acres of University land, the telecommunications project which will ultimately lead to a tele-video-computing network of the entire campus, and conversion of the campus computing capability to a new computer and "Banner" software which will radically improve functioning of many administrative systems within the University.

The University-Xerox "Fit"

In a parallel development, the California State University organized and funded a system-wide benchmarking project in 13 administrative systems. The project, coordinated with 200 additional institutions throughout the nation by the National Association of College and University Business Officers, will provide benchmarking data on the 20 institutions in the California State University system and the others in the national program. This development will introduce benchmarking practices for the first time and provide a major stimulus to improvement of the 13 systems, including Accounts Payable, Admissions and Registrar, Collections and Accounts Receivables, Facilities, Financial Aid, General Accounting, Human Resources, Budget, Payroll and Purchasing. The data will help us identify the best practice and provide goals for our development of these systems.

We recognized from the beginning that Xerox was not the University and the University was not Xerox. There is much between us that is different. Some differences are obvious: public-private, education-business, traditional-high tech, service-product, state supported-for profit, and so on. But there were many similarities: both depended on the performance of people for success, both were driven by the desire to do better, to be more effective, and to respond to the perceived needs of customers. We soon discovered we would use different means to achieve similar ends. We started out by comparing concepts of quality.

For the University

- Quality Service was initiated in 1992 to provide better service at lower costs.
- Quality Service has full support of the President and the personal leadership of the Executive Vice President.
- Quality Service is adapted from industry models: estab-

El-Ahraf, Gray and Naguib

lish a process of continuous improvement; strengthen our sense of community; and improve the quality of working life.

Key initiatives for continuous improvement are: establishment of the Council on Quality Service; starting orientation and training activities; selection of processes for development; and appointment of teams.

For Xerox

- Leadership Through Quality (LTQ) was initiated in 1983.
- LTQ is personally driven by the CEO and senior management team.
- Quality is defined as "fully meeting customer requirements."
- Customer satisfaction is the number one priority.
- Key initiatives for continuous improvement are: benchmarking Xerox performance against industry leaders; total employee involvement to fully realize all of their talents to satisfy customers; and use of quality tools and processes to achieve continuous quality improvement.
- In 1989 Xerox Development and Manufacturing Group received the Malcolm Baldrige National Quality Award.

Comparison of these two statements revealed some similarities and some differences; both seek continuous improvement, have top executive support, and seek involvement of personnel. Xerox stresses "customer" satisfaction, uses benchmarking of competitors, is 10 years into the program. The University is more community-oriented, avoids use of the word "customer," seeks institutional goals (strengthen sense of community), and personal goals (quality of working life). Xerox TQM history was also instructive.

In 1983 Xerox realized it must evolve into a quality company. As planners contemplated ways of achieving that goal, they recognized six "elements" were involved:

- Element 1—the recognition and reward system had to be revised to change from an individual focused to a team focused design.
- Element 2—line management driven by senior management was the way to implement a total quality system.
- Element 3—people had to be trained differently.
- Element 4—a different approach to communicating successes was required.
- Element 5—the behavior of the management team had to change.
- Element 6—the company had to shift from an unstructured to a participative structured system for solving problems and making decisions.

Given these insights the CEO and top 25 managers met on several occasions and developed the "Green Book," which details what the quality change will be. The Green Book guides strategic planning (3-5 years out) and the annual plan.

Benchmarking became an integral part of the total quality process. Xerox pioneered development of the benchmarking process; the company identified four kinds of benchmarking:

- **Internal** —A comparison of Internal Operations (Operational Focus)
- **Competitive**—Specific Competitor to Competitor(s) (Comparison for the Product or Process Focus)
- **Functional**—Comparisons to Similar Functions Within the Same Industry or to Industry Leaders (Industry Best)
- **Generic**—Comparisons of Functions or Processes that are the Same Regardless of Industry (Process Focus)

Benchmarking has become a driving force in Xerox planning and operations.

The University-Xerox partnership had some definite objectives:

- To share Xerox QM experience with CSUDH senior executives to enhance their awareness of QM techniques and benefits.
- To help the University develop a road map for the implementation of QM suitable for the University environment.
- To identify key performance indicators and develop a process to assess QM maturity in the University.
- To assist the University in developing a QM training program for continuous improvement.
- To deliver support to the University in quality process facilitation, consultation, and training.

The awareness objective was designed to introduce TQM concepts and basic principles to the University's executive management team. It was based on a preliminary assessment of the organization's readiness and level of maturity for TQM implementation. A major goal was to gain top management commitment to support the implementation of TQM in the institution. Early efforts in this process were concentrated on the executive leadership; as the work progressed the Xerox leadership made repeated infusions of information and encouragement in other parts of the organization.

A comprehensive effort was organized to promote top management information about TQM and to involve them in the process. Several approaches were used to stimulate the recognition of need and stimulation of learning. Appropriate people were encouraged to visit organizations with effective TQM applications. Benchmark reports on TQM activities were circulated. Consultants and experts were invited to the campus and provided with opportunities to speak about TQM.

Local and national forums were attended. Top management personnel led the quality initiative and approved investments in TQM activities. The partnership with Xerox was given high visibility on the campus.

Organization

An early effort was made to create an organizational structure capable of planning, promoting, implementing and supporting TQM at all levels of the organization. Following consultation with our Xerox partners we developed the organization depicted in Figure 1. This particular design was selected to give the program an independent source of advice and support with clear access to each of the four divisions which make up the University. The Executive Council includes the President and the four vice presidents. The Quality Service Council was appointed with one or two representatives from each division and a designee from the Academic Senate. It is composed of senior people with influence in the university. The mission of the Council is to "direct, support, and participate in the development and administration of the quality policy to ensure that key decisions are made and resources are available for effective implementation of the TQM process."

Policy Statement

The basic policy is laid out in a simple statement:
To further the University's commitment to shared governance and high quality in our programs and services, it is the policy of California State University–Dominguez Hills, to conduct a process of continuous improvement under the title "Quality Service."(Council on Quality, California State University–Dominguez Hills)

El-Ahraf, Gray and Naguib

Figure 1

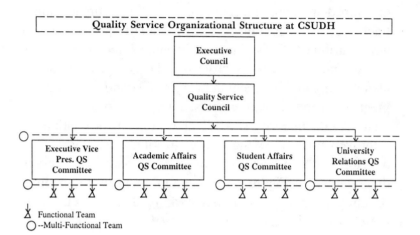

Quality Service Organizational Structure at CSUDH

Executive
Council

Quality Service
Council

| Executive Vice Pres. QS Committee | Academic Affairs QS Committee | Student Affairs QS Committee | University Relations QS Committee |

Ⅹ Functional Team
○ --Multi-Functional Team

Planning

The planning process at Xerox has been perfected over a period of more than a decade. It has a specificity and precision that is unusual in efforts of this kind. It involves all levels of management in a process to produce a plan with both process and result oriented goals and a long term time horizon. Goals are generated by customer needs and requirements and they are driven by data and supported by documentation. All goals contain a commitment to continuous quality improvement and they are made specific, actionable, and measurable. Goals are matched against the expected performance of competitors based on competitive benchmarking studies. The Pareto principle is used at each organizational level to set project priorities which are relevant to the corporate vision.

Xerox then carries out a series of planning activities for continuous improvement. An Organizational System Analysis (OSA) is conducted through competitive benchmarking. A

Partners for Quality in a University 185

long-term strategic plan over a three- to five-year time horizon is developed. From this plan an annual operational plan is developed and communicated top-down in the organization. Each organizational unit is asked to identify projects which will contribute to the attainment of planning objectives. Teams are assigned to selected projects. The company monitors results using measurement indicators and continuous assessment of customer requirements. Finally, an overall assessment of QM maturity is made and a replan for continuous improvement in achieving the organization's strategic goals is developed. The Xerox competitive benchmarking process is diagrammed in Figure 2. The commitment to competitive benchmarking is total. Benchmarking data and customer preferences drive the program.

The final phases of the Xerox process are selection and initiation of quality improvement projects, presentation of the quality educational and training program, and recognition and rewarding of team achievements.

Training

Starting with the six senior Xerox people, including the CEO, the Leadership Through Quality course cascaded down until all employees were trained. The exact training program was used throughout the entire company. This helped build the desired common vocabulary and common quality process.

Xerox has made a major commitment to training for quality. The company has published a detailed handbook on the "Problem-Solving Process." It lays out a comprehensive six-step process for solving problems, and "tools" for generating ideas and connecting information, reaching consensus, analyzing and displaying data, planning action, and preparing management presentations. A separate section describes team members' roles and responsibilities. Taken in its entirety, the

"Users Guide" is a very useful training handbook. Its purposes at Xerox are to introduce the company's new quality vision and instill a sense of mission; to provide employees with a common language, common skills, and common processes to implement the company's quality policy; and to establish a corporate culture which is customer-driven, process oriented, and based on continuous performance improvement through the prevention and solution of problems.

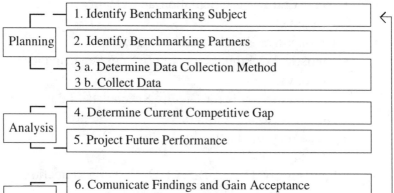

Xerox Competitive Benchmarking Process

Planning
1. Identify Benchmarking Subject
2. Identify Benchmarking Partners
3 a. Determine Data Collection Method
3 b. Collect Data

Analysis
4. Determine Current Competitive Gap
5. Project Future Performance

Integration
6. Comunicate Findings and Gain Acceptance
7. Establish Functional Goals

Action
8. Develop Action Plans
9. Implement Plans and Monitor Progress
10. Recalibrate Benchmark

Figure 2

Training for quality courses presented at Xerox (List 1) have made an enormous investment in training. Each year the corporation spends from 2.5 to 3 percent of its revenue on training. From 1984 to 1988 the company spent an additional $125 million exclusively on quality training. Every one of Xerox's more than 50,000 employees has had at least 28 hours of quality specific training.

List 1

Quality Training Program at Xerox

COURSES

- New Employee Orientation and Quality Training (5 days)
- Competitive Benchmarking (2 days)
- Statistical Methods for Improving Performance (3 days)
- Facilitation Skills for Quality Specialists (3 days)
- Managers as a Facilitator
- Managing by Fact: Work Process Improvement (3 days)
- Managing by Fact: A Delta T-Cycle Time Reduction (1 day)
- Continuous Supplier Involvement (1 day)
- Quality Function Deployment (2 1/2 days)

Given diminished resources, training in the University was much more modest than it was in Xerox. A beginning was made by developing a course for facilitators which could be administered over a two day period. Our thought was that we could recruit a cadre of facilitators from the University staff who are experienced in group process, and we would add the TQM perspectives in a short time. Before we tested this hypothesis we abandoned it because we had difficulty attracting participants with extensive group process experience and

El-Ahraf, Gray and Naguib

because we realized learning the TQM facilitative process required not only exposure to concepts but also practice in conducting the session.

Ultimately, we faced the realization that there are no short-cuts and that a more intensive and extensive training design is required. We retained the services of our Xerox partner to produce a five-day training experience, rented space in a local hotel, and identified 19 participants from several organizational segments of the University. In addition to experienced leadership, notebooks, training materials, visual aids, and a copy of *Mining Group Gold* (1990) were supplied for the participants.

The Training Design
Session I: Introduction to Total Quality Management in Higher Education

The session was designed to explore the need for TQM in higher education, learn about the evolution of quality management, review some basic concepts and the impact on an organization's culture, analyze barriers to the implementation of TQM in an academic setting, and provide some case histories of TQM in higher education. Comparisons with the academic and business experience permeated this session. The well-known "Quality Gurus" concepts were introduced, the differences between Quality Management and Quality Assurance were explained, and definitions were worked out for the words "total" and "quality." Then the discussion turned to the need for TQM in academic institutions, potential impact on the culture of the organization, barriers to implementation, and related matters. This content formed the background and conceptual base for the ensuing instruction.

Session II: Team Building

This session begins the process of quality management. It defines a team and describes its purpose; it describes multi-functional teams and functional teams and distinguishes them from task forces and Quality Circles. Then it takes up the team itself and the leadership roles including the Team Leader, Sponsor and Facilitator and describes some common stages in team development. It coaches members on how to conduct effective meetings organized in phases: preparation, organization of the agenda, roles of the scribe and the timekeeper, and the structured meeting itself. Next attention is directed to the potential behavior of individual team members during the discussion such as initiating, proposing, building, reacting, agreeing, disagreeing, clarifying, bringing others in or shutting them out, and summarizing and related actions. These insights on behavior in teams are designed to prepare leaders to recognize and handle actions which inhibit full discussion and reaching consensus on issues. Matters of this kind are also fully discussed in the textbook *Mining Group Gold.*

Session III: The Problem Solving Process

This session begins with the definition of a problem as a gap between the actual state of affairs and the way things "should be," and problem solving as closing the gap. Then participants are coached in problem-solving methods, including selecting the problem, analyzing it, generating potential solutions, selecting and planning the solution, and implementing it. Finally, the text provides the "tools" for generating ideas and connecting information, analyzing and displaying data, flow charting, cause and effect diagrams, and pert charts and other problem-solving methods.

During the final day of the instructional program, the participants were divided into two teams—one team elected to work on the recruitment, selection, and appointment process for management and staff employees, the other team to work

190   **El-Ahraf, Gray and Naguib**

Figure 3

TQM Training Design

—**Day 1**—

Session #0
Course Overview
Session #1: Introduction TQM
• Evaluation of Management
• Definition of TQM
• TQM Basic Concepts
• TQM in Education

Session #2: Team Work
• Types of Teams
• Roles and Responsibilities
• Ingredients of Effective Teams
• Stages of Team Development
• Team Building
• Basic Interactive Skills

—**Day 2**—

Session # 3: The Problem
Solving Process I
• Introduction to Problem Solving
• Overview of the Problem
Solving Process
• Identifying and Selecting the
Problem
• Tools for Generating Ideas and
Collecting Information

—**Day 3**—

Session #4: The Problem Solving
Process II
• Tools for Reaching Consensus
• Analyzing the Problem (Step 2)
• Tools for Analyzing & Display-
ing Data

Session #5: The Problem Solving
Process III
• Generating Potential Solutions
(Step 3)
• Selecting and Planning Solu-
tions (Step 4)
• Tools for Planning Action

—**Day 4**—

Session #6: The Problem Solving
Process IV
• Implementing Solutions (Step
5)
• Evaluating Solutions (Step 6)
• Tools for Monitoring Solutions

Session #7: The Problem Solving
Process V
• The New Quality Tools
• Writing the Activity Report
• Evaluating Team Performance

—**Day 5**—

Practicum
• Formation of Teams
• Commencement of Process

Partners for Quality in a University   191

on food service. During this process, the teams were challenged to use the approach described in the earlier instruction; the workshop leader alternated between the two teams, offering advice and helping them as needed. A summary of the training design is included in Figure 3.

At the conclusion of the experience, 19 members of the academic community returned to the University prepared to help with the Quality Service program, and the teams were augmented and continued to work on their chosen problems.

Conclusions

Without Xerox, the University would have achieved a Quality Service program. It probably would have started sooner; but, it would be less secure organizationally, more limited in its scope, and less sophisticated in its operations. The support and guidance provided by Xerox has strengthened the program and provided the foundation for its success.

We have reached several conclusions about our partnership with Xerox.

- We are confident that the industrial model of Quality Management can be adjusted for use in the academic setting.
- Properly selected and executed pilot projects can be used as learning vehicles and models for successful implementation of Quality Management.
- Industrial Quality Management education and training programs can be adapted for use in the University.
- An annual assessment of the Quality Management program is essential to continuous quality improvement.
- Resistance to change is a normal institutional reaction but implementation barriers can be mitigated by early recognition and careful planning.
- The aid and support of Xerox has been a major asset in program development; without their guidance and

El-Ahraf, Gray and Naguib

support, the process would have been much longer and the result much less successful.

Xerox has also identified several specific benefits of our partnership:

• Better educated college hires
• College hires with more knowledge of quality practices, e.g., benchmarking, cost of quality, teamwork, problem-solving, customer satisfaction.
• Strengthening of University-Industry ties.
• Enrichment to participating corporate executives.

Epilogue

It is too early for a credible critique of the potential contributions of Total Quality Management to the development of the University, but we have some clues where to look. The most obvious is the use of the complete repertoire of skills in the prescribed pattern to solve problems and redesign systems. None of our projects has yet come to complete fruition, but we are confident there will be major improvements in the systems under review and development. This benefit will be extended in the months and years ahead as we redesign additional systems and repeat the cycle with systems which have been redesigned.

Beyond these obvious objectives, we have begun to notice some unexpected but welcomed pay-offs from what might be thought of as "generic skills," which are parts of the detailed system design but can be used in isolation. Among these generic skills, management of meetings, networking of people previously unrelated, teamwork, and the use of such tools as brainstorming, flow charting and problem-solving are beginning to appear. Quality Service methods are becoming part of our stock of organization methods and patterns of interaction independent of the full pattern of application.

In addition, we anticipate contributions to our working environment from such concepts and skills as:
- More effective meetings
- Recognition of the value of teamwork
- Growing respect for collective intelligence
- Sophisticated critiques of existing systems
- A disciplined problem-solving process
- Tolerance for the detailed work of system development

We are not yet celebrating the demise of bureaucracy, but Quality Management with its multi-functional teams is providing a horizontal dimension to operations that is needed. Leading organization experts now envision an endlessly changing organization design; vertical integration designs tend to be slower, more rigid, more resistant to change; organization boundaries are high and it is more difficult to solve problems that cross organization boundaries; multi-functional teams that build bridges among units and solve multi-functional problems are essential components of a flexible organization. Properly staffed teams produce problem solutions that are, in part, pre-coordinated in the team itself. Thus, proposed solutions which cross organization boundaries are more apt to be successful when proposed by a multi-functional team than those negotiated by division leaders or directed from the top.

These are organization benefits, but the intended contributions are <u>improved services</u> to internal and external users of the services under development. In the months ahead it will be easier and quicker to purchase goods and services through the University purchasing system; the fund raising system will be more focused, successful, and responsive to the wishes of donors; food service will be more attuned to the preferences of customers and more profitable; and the staff and administrative recruitment and appointment process will be easier, more effective and faster. Collectively these system improvements will make the University more efficient, but even more significant is the growing realization that it will make the University more effective as it becomes more responsive to the people who are dependent on its service.

One thing is clear. Today is not like yesterday; tomorrow will not be like today.

References

Bemowski, K. 1991. "Restoring the Pillars of Higher Education." *Quality Progress* (October).

Clevenger, M. Personal Interview. The California State University.

Coate, L. E. 1990. "Implementing Total Quality Management in a University Setting." July/ Corvallis, Oregon: Oregon State University, July.

Coate, L. E. 1992. "Total Quality Management at Oregon State University." March. Corvallis, Oregon: Oregon State University.

Case History. 1993. "Application of TQM to Construction Management of the Student Union and Student Housing II." California State University-Dominguez Hills.

Council on Quality. California State University–Dominguez Hills.

Deming, W. E. 1982. *Out of Crisis.* Cambridge: Massachusetts Institute of Technology.

Deming, W. E. 1993. *The New Economics for Industry, Government, Education.* Cambridge: Massachusetts Institute of Technology.

Detweiler, R. C. 1992. "University Policy on Quality Service." California State University-Dominguez Hills.

Girifalco, A. J. 1992. "Partnerships for Quality." *Quality Progress* (February).

Horine, J. E., W. A. Hailey, and L. Rubach. 1993. "Shaping America's Future: Total Quality Management in Higher Education." *Quality Progress* (October).

Kayser, T. A. 1990. *Mining Group Gold.* El Segundo, California: Serif Publishing.

Kearns, D. and D. A. Nadler. 1992. *Prophets in the Dark.* New York: Harper Collins, p. 179.

Naguib, H. 1992. "The Implementation of Total Quality Management in a SemiConductor Manufacturing Operation." El Segundo, California: Xerox Microelectronics Center.

Osterhoff, R. J. "Xerox Corporation Business Products and Systems." The Conference Board: Baldrige Winners on World Class Quality.

AMER
EL-AHRAF

Amer El-Ahraf is presently the executive vice president and professor of environmental quality and health services at California State University–Dominguez Hills. He received his doctorate in public health from the University of California–Los Angeles in 1971, his master's in public health from UCLA in 1965, and his doctorate of veterinary medicine from Cairo Univeristy–Egypt in 1962.

El-Ahraf's position of executive vice president calls for him to advise the president on all matters pertaining to the future of the university, as well as holding the responsibility for all university-wide projects and special activities. Prior to this position, El-Ahraf was vice president for academic affairs at California State University, and before that was the associate vice president of academic resources at California State University.

El-Ahraf has written over 220 papers, presentations, book reviews, media interviews, guest editorials, and other publications dealing with public helath, environmental and health care management, zoonotic diseases, toxic and carcinogenic substances, planning, public policy and university management.

DAVID GRAY

David Gray is vice-president emeritus of California State University–Long Beach and president of David Gray and Associates, a consulting firm in the not-for-profit sector, especially higher education. He has carried out a series of consulting assignments for California State University–Dominquez Hills, where he is currently serving as a special consultant to the executive vice president on the Quality Service project. Gray received his doctorate in public administration from the University of Southern California.

HUSSEIN
NAGUIB

Hussein Naguib is the operations manager of Xerox Microelectronics Center in El Segundo, California, and holds a doctorate in materials science from McMaster University of Ontario, Canada.

Naguib has over 22 years of technical and managerial experience in research and in the development and manufacturing of silicon integrated circuits. He has over 7 years of teaching and research experience at Cairo University (Egypt), McMaster University (Canada), University of Salford (U.K.), and El Fateh University (Libya).

Naguib has been actively involved in Xerox's Total Quality Management since 1985. In addition to TQM, he is currently leading integrated continuous improvement programs at Xerox Microelectronics Center based on the concepts of total productive maintenance, cycle time management, and activity-based costing.

CHAPTER EIGHT:

IMPLEMENTING TQM IN A COMMUNITY COLLEGE: LESSONS LEARNED

Linda M. Thor and Sharon Koberna

Vertically-integrated/Cross-functional are four words that sum up the implementation of Total Quality Management (TQM) at Rio Salado Community College, one of the Maricopa Community Colleges in Phoenix, Arizona. Simple words— but people are often taken back when they hear them. At Rio, they are becoming a way of life. Vertically-integrated involves working in teams that have all levels of the organization involved. Teams are cross-functional in that they cut across departments and areas. Add to this "no rank in the room," and you have active participation and involvement from all, but this paradigm shift did not happen overnight.

Rio's TQM journey began six months after the arrival of a new president who went to each of the constituent groups separately and asked them if they would like to consider implementing Total Quality Management at Rio. Typical of how most institutions make decisions, the top administration was present at our first TQM exploration meeting. Also present, however, were associate deans, faculty, and representation from support staff. All heard the same message and participated in the decision to bring TQM to Rio. We strongly believe that this level of participation has been the bedrock for our success in implementing TQM at Rio. It is critical that there be as much participation as possible from the very beginning. People are more receptive to change and new ideas if they are part of the process from the onset.

During the first half-day session, a consultant reviewed the basic concepts of TQM and provided an overview of the commitment required. The consulting group, the Technology Exchange Center (TEC) based in southern California, explained that Total Quality Management is a commitment to excellence—excellence achieved by teamwork and a process of continuous improvement. TQM means dedication to being the best, delivering high quality programs and services which meet or exceed the expectations of our customers. The philosophy of Deming was the dominant approach studied, although other teachings were reviewed.

We learned that Total Quality Management at Rio would mean committing to:
- Quality improvement throughout the organization.
- Attacking the processes, not the employees.
- Stripping down the processes to find and eliminate problems that diminish quality.
- Identifying our internal and external customers and satisfying their requirements.
- Instilling teamwork and creating an atmosphere for innovation.

We quickly reached consensus that this was something that the College would embark on. A TQM Steering Team was formed. This team was made up of administrators, faculty, and support staff. We established our ground rules for conducting meetings which included:

- This is a safe zone.
- No rank in the room.
- Everyone participates; no one dominates.
- Help us stay on track.
- Listen as an ally.
- One speaker at a time.
- Be an active listener.
- Give freely of your experience.
- Maintain each other's self-esteem.
- Agree only if it makes sense to do so.
- Keep an open mind.
- Maintain confidentiality.
- Have fun.

All teams and meetings adopted this draft version of the ground rules. One of the first orders of business at each meeting is to review the ground rules and make changes to meet the needs of that particular group.

The Steering Team then went through self-guided awareness building sessions in which we watched videotapes describing what total quality organizations look like and completed exercises challenging our paradigms about leadership. We also had extensive training by our consulting group in the principles and philosophy of quality. During this time the Steering Team also developed an implementation plan— in other words, what does it take to have total quality at Rio Salado Community College. Our implementation covers six areas.

Roles and Responsibilities

The Steering Team guides TQM efforts by:

• Determining the philosophical approach to total quality.
• Authoring the vision, mission, and implementation strategy.
• Establishing the process for project selection, and assigning continuous improvement team members and coaches.
• Review and facilitating implementation.
• Assuring a smoothly paced integration of total quality.
• Providing direction for rewards and recognition.
• Establishing measures for assessing TQM progress.
• Applying TQM tools and techniques to its own process.

TQM Coordinator

• Responsible for the day-to-day implementation of TQM.

The Critical Process Team (CPT)

• Responsible for coordinating the assessment and implementation of strategic plans.

The TQM Coach

• Responsible for the application of TQM tools and techniques to Continuous Improvement Teams.

The Continuous Improvement Team (CIT)

• Responsible for the improvement of selected work processes through the use of the Continuous Improvement Cycle and TQM tools and techniques.
• Responsible for the actual development of project statements, clear documentation of their analysis, process improvement, standardization and documentation of the project.

As a matter of principle, everyone will be allowed sufficient work time to be involved in the TQM process.

Quality Focus

To achieve a quality focus, Rio will select areas of improvement that relate to the vision and mission.

Quality Culture

Rio's efforts to develop a quality culture will focus on these five areas:

- Reducing fear.
- Knowing employee needs.
- Rewarding and recognizing our people.
- Furthering cross-functional team work.
- Clarifying behavioral expectations.

Communications

All members of the Rio community will be provided with the opportunity and encouragement to expand their communication skills. This includes opportunities for interaction among individuals in all levels in the organization.

Improvements in internal communication will focus on:

- Developing a more college-wide awareness of Rio.
- Removing fear of change.
- Creating an appreciation of the interdependence that exists among the members of the Rio community.
- Encouraging a strong awareness of each other's needs and expectations.

Improvement in external communication will focus on:

- Enhancing Rio's public image.
- Expanding and reinforcing a positive image of Rio's faculty and programs locally, statewide, and nationally.
- Encouraging a strong awareness of our external customer's expectations and needs.
- Ensuring that all employees have sound, factual information about the College.

Education and Training

Education and training are critical elements of the TQM effort. Rio's aim is to achieve a learning environment for its students and all who work or are in contact with the College. A learning environment is a receptive one, where staff members understand and relate well to the concepts in the College's vision and mission, and share a positive awareness of internal and external customers.

The training and education process will provide skills in the following areas:
- Problem-solving and process improvement.
- Communication and meeting skills.
- Interpersonal and team building-skills.

Measurement

Measurement is an important component in the TQM effort. Rio Salado Community College will document its improvement in work processes and quality focus in three ways:
- As measured against its own levels of achievement and improvement.
- As measured against other institutions in the district.
- As measured against other institutions and or programs nationally.

In our self-study we became aware of, and began addressing, the concept of paradigms. Futurist Joel Barker (1989) tells us that a paradigm is simply a set of rules or regulations that defines our mental boundaries and guides us in our problem-solving within those boundaries. Paradigms are common and useful because they allow us to filter incoming experiences, and select data or a concept that does not fit our rules and regulations. They help us make decisions.

Sometimes our strongly held rules and regulations blind us

to new opportunities, obscure effective strategies, and block creative solutions. The problem then, as Barker (1989) tells us, is not paradigms, but paradigm paralysis. Paradigm paralysis results when we simply refuse to accept a new way of doing something. Paradigm paralysis results when our rules and regulations keep us from discovering the future.

Our first task was to recognize that we must have constancy of purpose, and the first step in achieving constancy of purpose is to create a vision. A vision, of course, is a preferred future, a desirable state, an ideal state. At Rio we worked to develop a vision that has three qualities:

- It comes from the heart.
- We, alone, can make this statement.
- It is reaching and compelling.

The vision becomes the driving force behind the institution. All other plans and activities must line up with the vision. Something this important must come from the group as a whole. One person in isolation should not be the heart of the institution. Our Steering Team wrote the first draft of the vision statement. After extensive discussion and word-smithing, we shared it with the entire College. Every employee had the opportunity to provide input into this vital document. Each person wrestled with what Rio was about and where we were headed. Again, more word-smithing was done and continued discussions were held. Our final vision is truly a shared vision:

> Rio Salado Community College is the College of choice for our students because we guarantee the opportunity for academic success through excellence in teaching, competency-based curriculum, and student shared responsibility for learning. Our responsive and responsible commitment to our students and communities is evident through accessible student

services, innovative learning design, and convenient delivery, supported by advanced technology. As leaders in total quality, we foster a supportive and collaborative academic and work environment that empowers each individual.

There is a wonderful description in *The Fifth Discipline: The Art and Practice of the Learning Organization* by Peter Senge (1990) of how a shared vision empowers employees and encourages team learning, risk-taking, and experimentation. He calls it living with the creative tension between vision and reality. He quotes the President of Herman Miller, Ed Simon: "When you are immersed in a vision, you know what needs to be done. But you often don't know how to do it. You run an experiment because you think it is going to get you there. It doesn't work. New input. New data. You change direction and run another experiment. Everything is an experiment, but there is no ambiguity at all. It's perfectly clear why you are doing it. People aren't saying 'Give me a guarantee that it will work.' Everybody knows that there is no guarantee. But the people are committed nonetheless" (Senge 1990).

Our next action was to refine our mission statement, which defines our role in society. One of the basic tenets is that individual workers cannot know what to do to contribute to the enterprise if they do not understand and give support to its purpose. Additionally, this purpose must be constant and not changing every day. It must be a purpose which attracts their hearts and minds.

Our Mission statement:
Rio Salado Community College creates convenient, high quality learning opportunities for diverse populations. We specialize in customized, unique programs and accelerated and distance delivery formats. In all that we do, we pursue continuous improvement and innovation, and we challenge the limits of tradition.

Thor and Koberna

The next step was to ensure that every employee knows and understands the vision and mission statements and can relate them to his or her job. We conducted a series of departmental meetings where the employees participated in an affinity process to develop a vision for their unit that was consistent with the overall College vision. All people can identify where they fit into the whole and how their work unit contributes to bringing us closer to our vision and living out our mission. This was the first major step in empowering all employees.

Extensive training is required to implement TQM. We began with the president and TQM Coordinator visiting each work unit and giving an overview of the philosophy and practices of TQM. This not only showed the support of senior management, but also gave employees an opportunity to talk to the president, an important step in developing a sense of inclusion and teamwork.

Building on this, our consultants conducted an initial 40-hour training for 25 volunteers from all levels of the College. The training included an overview of the philosophy of TQM, Internal and External Customers, the Plan-Do-Check-Act Cycle (P-D-C-A), the Continuous Improvement Cycle, Planning and Problem Solving Tools, Basic Statistics, Meeting Management, and Communication and Team Building Skills. These are not topics that only managers or faculty need, or that only support staff need to discuss and learn. There were managers, faculty, and support staff together at the training. The tremendous value and benefits of having a cross-functional group become a learning community cannot be stressed enough. We have found that working together on a team to improve a process builds understanding and a strong sense of group cohesiveness. Misunderstanding, competitiveness, and lack of trust quickly vanish when people are working toward a common goal.

This integrated training gives the College a common language and understanding of the philosophy and implementation of TQM. The tools can be applied to all disciplines and work environments. The perception that one group gets more of something, or another group is not quite educated enough to understand something, is dispelled. We may have different functions to perform, but we are all involved in processes that we need to continually improve.

Following this training, it was decided to customize the training specifically to Rio and conduct future training ourselves. Because it is important to model the behavior you wish others to adopt, our training was conducted by a vertically-integrated/cross-functional team. Our seven trainers included faculty, clerk-typists, program advisors, adjunct faculty, and various levels of management. All have an equal part in the training and contribute their unique strengths and talents. Participants for each training session are also from all employee groups: management, faculty, and support staff. To date, all regular full-time employees and several part-time staff have been through the 40-hour training. We have also modified the training slightly and are training adjunct faculty members as well.

At the conclusion of the first 40-hour block of training we were ready to establish our first Continuous Improvement Teams (CITs). With input from the entire staff, the steering team selected four projects to work on. A continuous improvement team is responsible for the improvement of a selected work process through the use of the Plan-Do-Check-Act and Continuous Improvement Cycle (CIC) using TQM tools and techniques.

Our Continuous Improvement Teams have between five to seven members. As with everything we do, they are vertically-

Thor and Koberna

integrated and cross-functional. Members of the team are employees who are involved in the process being looked at and someone from outside the process to offer an objective viewpoint. All teams have two trained coaches, a team leader, and the process owner. The process owner is the person who has the authority to make a change in the process.

Departments also establish teams to work on processes that are within their departments. These teams are established under the direction of the unit head and improve processes that are specific to that department. A coach from outside the department is brought in and the P-D-C-A, CIC, and quality tools are used. In this way we are tackling problems at all levels.

Clear, timely, open communication is critical in implementing TQM. Getting information out to everyone is important. To this end, we have instituted several communication vehicles. Each Monday morning the President's Bulletin comes out on electronic mail, and hard copies are made for those not on electronic mail. Upcoming meetings, governing board actions and issues, College activities and changes, and special employee recognition are some of the items covered in the President's Bulletin. There are three features of the bulletin that promote two-way communication. The first is Rumor Control. Employees can send any rumor that they hear, signed or anonymous, to the president and it will be addressed in the bulletin. One employee writes of his experience: "Having anonymously authored two rumors, I was shocked that you actually answered them." He goes on to write that he has been motivated to set up a new course for his career and to stop waiting to be noticed. He closes: "Thanks for the inspiration that led me to take charge of my destiny! P.S. I promise not to author any more anonymous 'rumors.' From now on, I'll send them direct!" Also featured are the Question Box and Suggestion Box. Again, employees are encouraged to write regarding any area, and all are addressed. These steps have opened communication and helped in reducing fear in the work place.

There are employees impaired by fear in every organization. There are people with good ideas who do not express them because they are afraid. There are people who make mistakes that cause great damage because they are afraid to ask a question about something they did not understand.

Things can not really change when fear is a controlling factor. Daniel Ostreich and Kathleen Ryan, in *Driving Fear Out of the Workplace* (1991), define fear in the workplace as "feeling threatened by possible repercussions as a result of speaking up about work-related concerns."

This fear can express itself in those silences that plague most managers and most meetings. Silence represents the absence of ideas, the lack of enthusiasm, suggestions that never go beyond the ordinary, conversations that circulate but never concentrate, unfinished business, and mediocre performance.

We distributed an anonymous survey to all employee groups to begin to identify fears. The four fears most often cited were those fears related to individual employees not being able to do the best job possible. They were:
- Work overload interfering with doing one's job well.
- Dealing with interpersonal conflict in the work place.
- Lacking information or resources to do one's job well.
- Having one's job performance adversely affected by others.

As a result of this survey and further discussion with staff members, we instituted additional training opportunities addressing the root cause of some of these fears. Two workshops were developed: "Giving and Receiving Feedback" and "The Change Process."

Another specific training request came from front-line employees—customer service. A 20-hour training segment was established covering techniques to deal with difficult, indecisive, irate, or insistent customers. We had always been rated high by our customers (our students) in the services we provide. In requesting this training, the staff was acknowledging that there is always room for improvement and their desire to be proactive, not reactive.

We must reward employees for helping us maintain this focus on customers. If we recognize that people are more committed to their own ideas than ideas foisted on them from above, then we need to reward them for their ideas. If we push decision-making down to the appropriate level, then we need to reward people for making good decisions. If we encourage every employee to be creative and dynamic, then we need to reward them for creativity and dynamism.

At Rio Salado, we surveyed all of our employees regarding rewards and recognitions. When we asked what employees should receive recognition for, the top three responses were:
- professional excellence,
- service to customers, and
- contributions to their departments.

And, when asked how they wanted to be recognized, they said they would like a letter from the president placed in their personnel file with a certificate of recognition.

They were offered banquets, flowers, plaques, mugs, seminars, books, and so forth; they chose non-material things as their most desired rewards.

When employees feel they have a part in determining the vision that they are working toward, when they feel they have the ability to voice their concerns without fear of reprisal, and when they know that they will be recognized (even in a small way) for the extra efforts they make on behalf of the organization, then, and only then, will teamwork be developed that allows quality management to work.

In October 1993, Rio Salado won the Arizona Governor's Award for Quality—1993 Pioneer Award. This award is patterned after the Malcolm Baldrige National Quality Award, and all private and public sector applicants compete on an equal basis. The feedback report, provided by the Board of Examiners, states several strengths of Rio's TQM initiative:

> Under the leadership of its president, the College has taken steps to implement quality processes throughout the organization. Efforts are devoted to TQM training, development of mission/vision statements, implementation of long-term strategies, and involvement of employees in teams to assess and improve critical processes in all areas. . . . Deployment to the full-time staff is evident, and results show improvements in many areas.

> TQM is incorporated into the everyday activities, with many operational units and Critical Improvement Teams using TQM in planning, problem-solving, decision-making, and improvement of processes.

Many ask if the time and effort necessary for TQM is worth it. We firmly believe that it is. Although not all results are tangible in dollars, there are definitely cost savings. Some of our early results have been:

- Received 10-year reaccreditation from North Central Association of Colleges and Schools (NCA) with the TQM initiative cited as a strength. The report stated that "The system of governance at the College is defined by teamwork, collaborative decision-making, and open communication."

- One of our Continuous Improvement Teams (CIT), Requisition Process CIT, reviewed and revised the methods by which supplies and materials are purchased. Their recommendations were adopted by the entire Maricopa District, saving money, reducing error, and reducing final costs.

• The Schedule CIT improved the processes in development, printing, and distribution of the semester schedule. The first semester alone they saved nearly $25,000.

• The Bad Debt CIT saved the College $6,504 in its first semester by improving the drop/add process. The team has decided to continue working on the problem and has renamed itself the Zero Debt CIT. Their continuous improvement efforts will continue until there is no bad debt incurred by students.

• The Information Process Center began utilizing a formalized internal feedback loop and made improvements based on the results. Now, when work is completed, the technician completing the job places a personal phone call to the requester to report that the job is completed. This is a direct result from internal customer feedback.

There are many other rewards and results that we have experienced. One of the most exciting is the TQM-in-the-classroom initiatives. Myron Tribus says that "students study and learn IN a system. The job of faculty is to work ON the system, to improve it continuously, with the help of the students." At Rio Salado, we are working on improving that system. In the TQM-in-the-classroom model, the faculty member and the student together identify a process that needs improvement based on data, observations, and input from both students and faculty. The class may develop a project statement such as: "To improve student note-taking skills so that they can reduce study time and increase comprehension." They then follow the cycle steps of planning, data collection, implementation, measuring effect, and standardization. During each of the steps, information is discussed and team decision-making occurs. Students actually learn to use TQM tools such as cause and effect diagrams, force field analysis, and flowcharting.

This model for TQM in the classroom is the core of Rio Salado's efforts to implement total quality in the instructional side of the College. Through these projects, our students will learn what TQM is, will learn TQM tools and techniques, can see the results of TQM activity, and can feel at home in a TQM environment. Perhaps most importantly, they take a proactive role in their education and make informed decisions on how to improve their own learning.

We are proud of our efforts to date, but we recognize that we are in a race with no finish line. At the end of one of our early training sessions, a participant summed up this understanding very nicely: "This is a process—not an answer—and we are part of the evolution of that process." One of the most far reaching elements of implementing TQM at Rio Salado has been this realization: we are all part of the process. It is up to us to work together to improve the process.

References

Barker, J. 1989. *The Business of Paradigms.* Burnsville: Charthouse Learning Corporation.
Oestreich, D., and K. Ryan. 1991. *Driving Fear Out of the Workplace.* San Francisco: Jossey-Bass, Inc.
Senge, P. 1990. *The Fifth Discipline.* New York: Doubleday Currency.

LINDA M. THOR

Linda M. Thor is president of
Rio Salado Community College in Phoenix, Arizona, which is currently provid-
ing leadership in the implementation of Total Quality Management in other community colleges. Thor received a
bachelor's degree in journalism from Pepperdine University,
a master's of public administration from California State
University, Los Angeles, and a doctorate of education degree
in community college administration from Pepperdine University.

Prior to joining Rio Salado in 1990, Thor was president of
West Los Angeles College in Culver City, California. Her
appointment as WLAC president followed a successful tenure
as the senior director of occupational and technical education
for the Los Angeles Community College District. For six
years Thor served as the director of communications services
for the nine-college district. Prior to joining the LACCD in
1974 as a public information officer, she was director of public
information for the Pepperdine University School of Continuing Education.

SHARON KOBERNA

Sharon Koberna is an adjunct faculty member in psychology at the Rio Salado Community College. She has a master's of education in counseling from Northwestern Arizona University, a bachelor of arts in adult education from Ottawa University–Phoenix Center, and an associate of arts from Rio Salado.

Koberna has had experience in many areas to expand Total Quality Management. As an adjunct faculty member at Rio Salado, her instruction is based on quality learning principles, and she has coordinated TQM activities across the college. She has been the administrative assistant to the dean of instruction, where she was responsible for coordinating all activity involved in college curriculum development. Koberna has also been program advisor where she developed promotoional material, outreach programs, and workshops, and advised students on programs of study.

Koberna has given many presentations over TQM for surrounding colleges and conferences and has co-authored various publications involving TQM.

CHAPTER NINE:

TQM IMPLEMENTATION: A PERSPECTIVE FROM 20/20 HINDSIGHT

Marvin E. Lane

Introducing TQM principles into an organization is a complete organizational transformation, and thus is a decision which should not be made lightly or without deliberation and much planning. The purpose of this chapter is to share perspectives, experiences, and lessons learned that may be helpful to others desiring to transform their organization. TQM pioneers wish their 20/20 hindsight had been available at the beginning of the journey. These seasoned veterans wish they could have begun the journey with the experience and knowledge they have at the present time. However, a pioneer begins his or her journey into the unknown understanding that somebody has to make the mistakes which allow others to enter hostile territory appropriately prepared.

Philosophical Base for TQM

TQM pioneers are captivated by possibilities the philosophy seems to hold for an organization willing to undergo a transformation process. This author, one of the early pioneers, sensed the TQM philosophy held great promise for organizational transformation and questioned whether or not the philosophy was not the final word. Despite these feelings, the author soon discovered that the principles worked, made sense, and facilitated the transformation of an organization. In the spring of 1993, the author was introduced to Margaret Wheatley's book, *Leadership in the New Science*. A reading of her book seems to indicate that Wheatley has begun the process of developing a more complete philosophy for TQM based on natural organizations. It appears that those who operate organizations on a day-to-day basis make organizational processes more complicated than necessary because they lack an understanding of causes. They end up using many words and lots of paper to make up for sound principles. Wheatley uses the physical world as a basis for her theories regarding systems and organizations, and this chapter outlines some of the principles her book discusses and how these principles may relate to a TQM organization. The reader is urged to review Wheatley's book for more in-depth information.

A Journey

Lamar Community College began its TQM exploration in 1988, when a group of 15 people attended the Quality Academy for training and returned to begin the implementation process. The Vice President for Student Services began the formation of teams in the student services department.

The Vice President formed work unit teams organized around common interests and supported by an "All Staff

Team" which included a representative from each of the work unit teams. In retrospect, five years experience indicates a need for a mechanism to provide overall coordination and continuity among work unit teams. These initial efforts, however, started the process of developing wholeness and laid the ground work for the eventual emergence of cross functional management teams.

Individual members of the All Staff Team were challenged to take responsibility for their work units, but were also reminded that they are working within a larger organization, Student Services. Departmental Management Team meetings, held on a frequent basis, reinforced the concept of wholeness at the department level. The All Staff Management Team, in conjunction with work unit teams, also provided the ground work for later formation of cross-functional teams. It also helped reinforce the concept of wholeness for individual departments and for the organization.

Discovering a Vision

Organizations have vision statements, mission statements, statements of purpose, and some even have value statements and guiding principles. In a Newtonian sense, most vision, mission, and value statements are linear because the statements attempt to create a future state for the organization. Some authors believe a powerful statement will propel an organization towards its vision because of commitment to the vision and the fact that work is organized to accomplish the stated vision.

The future-state vision of a Newtonian organization is based on the philosophy that an organization is a dissipative structure. Therefore, the organization has to be constantly propped up, regrouped, held together, and recreated or it will dissipate and cease to exist. The "New Science" paints a different picture of an organization. The "New Science" organization is a dynamic living organism that has the potential to renew and recreate itself to higher and higher levels of reality. The vision in a quantum organization is discovered. The vision is inherent within the organization and needs only be discovered by those working within the organization. Once discovered, the vision becomes a compelling force with a magnetic property that maintains the organization over time. The vision for a quantum organization is so powerful that it allows great autonomy within the organization. Individual work unit teams and cross-functional teams carry out their day-to-day functions with autonomy, but in step with the organization's vision. The quantum concept of vision is an expansive, compelling, powerful force that propels the organization into the future. The vision keeps the organization true to its basic purpose and allows the organization to constantly renew and regenerate itself in response to environmental change.

Wholeness

Newtonian Science teaches us that the sum of the parts is greater than the sum of the whole. However, anyone who has worked with people fully understands that the efforts of two people may equal less than two or more than two depending on the relationship developed between the two people. "New Science" organizations assume two people working in an appropriate environment with appropriate tools, training, information, and support will equal a sum greater than two.

Individual performance is a result of expectation. The highflying, upwardly-mobile young professional is created by those who work with that person on a day-to-day basis. Likewise, the person who can do nothing right is a product of the expectations of those who work with that individual on a day-to-day basis. Reality is created. The goal of a TQM organization is to provide each individual with appropriate tools, training, and autonomy to create new and creative solutions to organizational problems. The individual participates in a meaningful way and becomes a dynamic creative contributor to the organization.

This author's 20 plus years of experience as an educational administrator has resulted in numerous conversations exploring why individual expectations and organizational expectations do not converge. This dilemma exists because we do not approach the organization or self through the concept of wholeness. Organizations demonstrate a lack of understanding of the concept of wholeness through frequent shuffling of people, creation of new departments, deletion of departments, and restructuring of processes and systems in a continual search for the perfect organization. Each restructuring results in frustration because the desired outcomes are not accomplished. Frustration stems from the fact that those who work in organizations have not thought of the individual and the organization as a whole. Leaders assume that dissecting and rearranging parts produces a greater whole. Concepts from quantum science lead the author to believe that the whole is greater than the sum of the parts. Therefore, those who want to fully understand the functions of the parts must first fully understand the whole. All members of the organization— from the president to the janitor, from the faculty to the administrator—find their individual needs and those of the organization more fully realized when the concept of wholeness is part of day-to-day activities.

The process of discovering a vision for the organization begins the process of creating the reality of the whole being greater than the sum of the parts. The result is individuals, teams, cross-functional teams, and management team efforts

A Perspective from 20/20 Hindsight   221

being magnified. All individuals and teams understand the organization as a whole, which magnifies their individual action and supports the concept of wholeness for each individual and the organization.

Information

Organizations implementing the TQM philosophy quickly confront old paradigms in which administrators protect and hoard information because information is equated with power. Many fear that information freely shared throughout the organization will usher in a reign of chaos.

TQM requires the manager to become a facilitator and co-partner with team members in carrying out day-to-day activities of the organization. Teams cannot conduct the day-to-day business of an organization, resolve issues assigned to a project team, or work on cross-functional issues if they do not have access to timely, accurate information. Administrators, beginning with the president, must freely share organizational information and allow multiple interactions, if new and better ways of conducting the organization's business are an anticipated outcome.

The "New Science" philosophy supports the flooding of the organization with information. The flood of information, which may seem chaotic to some, results in new ways of looking at old problems, new ways of thinking, new ways of conducting day-to-day business, new relationships, and innovative solutions to problems. Teams or individuals cannot be expected to function effectively if they are not granted full access to a broad array of information. This means that the organization's computerized information system must be freely shared and access must be granted to those who need information from the organization's data banks. Those in charge of computing programs and data banks must be willing to assist teams in organizing, digesting, grasping, and interpreting information in new ways.

Information is the fuel of an organization. Those who fail to recognize this starve their organization and prevent individuals from being productive, creative employees. Those reluctant to believe that information is the life blood of an organization should listen to the coffee chatter of an organization that hoards its information. Information vacuums cause workers to create information to fill the void. Employees understand the need for information to flow freely throughout the organization. Failure to respond with appropriate information results in the creation of information, which may cause the energy of the organization to focus on the wrong issues.

Relationships

Learning to work closely with others is an individual process for each person in an organization. The American way has always emphasized the rugged individualist who takes full responsibility for him or herself. Likewise, American children are taught from an early age that rewards are given to those who are self-sufficient and get the job done. However, traditional management cultures have little concern about the number of wounded bodies left along the way.

Pioneer TQM organizations have found it difficult to implement the teaming process because little information was available about how people worked together in a team environment. Through trial and error, training programs have been developed to assist teams in becoming sophisticated work units capable of tackling tough issues and resolving interpersonal conflict. TQM organizations places great emphasis on relationships among individuals and between individual departments and the larger organization; information is a tool for improving relationships.

At Lamar we found chartering to be an effective vehicle for providing guidance to departmental teams, project teams, and cross-functional teams. The charter outlines the scope of responsibility and the autonomy granted to each team. A team is expected to develop a mission statement which provides feedback on the team's understanding of its charter. The team also develops ground rules for day-to-day operations as a part of the team's organizational activities. Ground rules become a living document that defines how the team will deal with the issues, what relationships are expected between team members, how the team will carry out its day-to-day functions, how the team process can be used to create agendas and minutes, and a clear delineation of operating procedures. Team ground rules may be changed at any time with items being deleted and added as necessary to facilitate the teaming process and the development of strong relationships.

Lamar has found ground rules and agreements to be an effective mechanism for resolving conflicts which occur within a teaming environment because teams have a mechanism for defining working relationships and procedures. Experience indicates that investments in training and delineation of ground rules and agreements leads to a cohesive team that is able to tackle difficult issues and resolve interpersonal conflict.

Control

Administrators have a tough time distinguishing between the concepts of control and order. Since the Roman Empire we have been taught that control maintains order within an organization. Control keeps processes flowing, employees functioning in a reasonable fashion, and gets the day-to-day business accomplished. However, order and control are not the same concept. Control happens when   someone has approval over a process that is not necessary for that process or system to function on a day-to-day basis. Order is order, and order is achieved when a logical, step-by-step process exists to accomplish a task without unnecessary steps in the process. A process or system is functionally ordered if it is devoid of unnecessary interference from individuals or the organization. When unnecessary steps exist in a system or process the unnecessary step is typically an attempt to assert control over the process.

Some administrators seem to believe that control is the primary vehicle for maintaining the day-to-day functions of the organizations. Plus, administrators who do not maintain control of the processes and systems are considered by some to be weak administrators. The emerging TQM organization is required to engage in new thinking about what it means to be an administrator in charge of a department, a system, or a process and what it means to work with individuals. The challenge is to develop systems and processes with built-in order. The ultimate challenge is removing the concept of control from our day-to-day language. The author understands that outside forces will always require the maintenance of control over some systems and processes. However, the organization should make every attempt to minimize the effect of control on the orderly conducting of day-to-day business.

Administrators, while supporting of changes that are taking place and comfortable with the teaming process, are frequently reluctant to give up or dispense with their tried and true ways of conducting the day-to-day business of the campus, which is based on the concept of control. These administrators are also reluctant to commit to any structure or organization that seemingly erodes control within their organization. Reluctance to change is reinforced by the fact that a traditional organization gives rank, prestige, and greater pay to those who manage large groups of people through the control processes. The New Science organization, however, will develop new heroes and new ways of defining who receives higher compensation to keep the new organizations on track. Individuals who help the organization achieve wholeness, who are able to articulate the vision of the organization in a way that empowers and creates a greater meaning attraction for individuals, plus individuals who are able to fully utilize the team concept to conduct the day-to-day business of an organization will be the ones rewarded by the new organization.

Lessons Learned

This author uses the word quality with trepidation because the mere utterance of the word carries an emotional charge. Each individual reading this chapter will reach differing interpretations of quality, just as individuals within an organization know quality when they see it. Each person has a hard time defining quality for the organization, but they are always willing to tell you when something or someone is not "quality." Senior administrators implementing quality may rightfully be skeptical of using the word quality when implementing a continuous improvement process. Much time and energy is wasted on discussions and debates about whether a process, a system, a person's action, or an organizational policy is "quality" when the real issue should be whether or not the policy, practice, or process contributes to the achievement of wholeness for individuals, teams, and the organization. Quality is the ultimate goal of an organization—which is as it should be. However, stating up front that an organization is beginning a quality movement may be setting the stage for unnecessary conflict.

Through six years of implementing TQM, we have learned that calling an initiative "quality" sets up expectations which may not be achieved immediately. It is more important to focus on the specifics of transformation as outlined by Wheatley; the same results will be produced. Whether you use the terminology of TQM or not, the focuses are the same: sensitivity to customers and their needs, general customer satisfaction, and systems and processes that focus on day-to-day improvement. Not using the word "quality" seems to be a less confrontational method for transformation.

A second lesson learned, which may surprise some, is that presidents initiating quality are held to higher standards than they were prior to the introduction of the concept to campus. The president is a visible target and everything the president does is judged against someone's standard of quality. The president has no forewarning, no standard by which he or she is to judge his or her performance, but each individual within the organization has his or her own individual standard by which to judge the president's day-to-day actions. Therefore, any president beginning or contemplating the implementation of TQM should be fully aware of this fact. Some may wonder if it is worth the stress and strain placed on the president. An easier way may exist to accomplish a transformational process, which is why the author encourages colleagues to review Wheatley's book prior to beginning implementation. The concepts in her book hold potential for constructive implementation without some of the risks the early pioneers faced.

A third realization is that the new organization will be a loosely coupled, loosely knit organization by current day standards. However, by quantum standards it will be a tightly knit, finely tuned system that is constantly renewing and reinvigorating itself as the organization responds to its environment. The rewards will go to those who have learned to work within the new organization. The author realizes this is a frightening scenario; many will be put off by the prospect and will become defensive at even the slightest hint of change. Hopefully, models will be developed that allow employees to touch, feel, and interact with a model prior to an organization beginning a transformational process.

A fourth realization is that most organizations beginning a transformation grossly underestimate the training necessary to develop the new skills needed to transform the organization. It is assumed that highly educated individuals will be able to make the transition, change their paradigm, and envision a new way of thinking and new ways of conducting business. The transformation process, however, is difficult! Therefore, just-in-time training must be available and be conducted in a way that allows individuals and the organization to gracefully undergo a transformation process.

The training should be immediate and ongoing and challenge individuals to greater heights of autonomy as the organization restructures, to allow the expression of individual creativity. A primary predictor of success for any organization is the willingness and preparation to provide ongoing training to its employees. Training must be relevant to each organization, which means that "canned" programs may need to be customized before being introduced to an organization.

Training funds need to be set aside to ensure ongoing training programs. It is interesting that educational institutions believe that everybody in the outside world should participate in ongoing self-development and renewal processes, but devote almost no funds to the ongoing development of employees within educational institutions. The lack of commitment to training by educational entities may be due to underfunding. Many educational organizations barely have enough money to manage the day-to-day affairs, much less funds to invest in upgrading individual employee skills. Somehow each administrator must find the means to overcome this deficiency. Leaders must rise to the challenge and not grossly underestimate the role training plays in the success of organizations undergoing transformation.

Conclusion

Implementation of TQM within an educational organization brings challenges and moments of triumphs. Those brave enough to chart new waters will find it a most challenging process. Resources, both human and financial, are required to move an organization from a state of status quo to a self-renewing state. Leaders will experience moments of great personal accomplishment and equal times when they will wonder if it is worth the effort being expended. The outcome is a team-based organization with a sense of wholeness and self-organizing systems that allow individual autonomy and freedom. The road to success, however, may be blocked by such obstacles as the need for constant training, resources that are lacking, and naysayers who constantly point out that the organization is headed in the wrong direction. Traditionalists have a strong stake in maintaining the status quo.

Those bold enough to engage in organizational change liken the process to a rocket ship being launched from the earth. The rocket expends most of its fuel escaping the earth's gravitational force. Once it is free from the gravitational forces of the earth, very little fuel is necessary to propel the rocket to its final destination. Organizational change is like the launching of the rocket ship. Tremendous energy and resources have to be invested in the initial stage to free the organization from its traditional paradigms and help administrators differentiate between control and order. Despite setbacks and the energy required to bring about transformation, the author has found TQM to be a powerful tool for moving an institution from past paradigms into challenging new frontiers.

References

Covey, S. R. 1991. *Principle Centered Leadership.* New York: Summit Books.

Covey, S. R. 1989. *The Seven Habits of Highly Effective People.* New York: Simon and Schuster.

Hubbard, D. L. 1993. *Continuous Quality Improvement: Making the Transition to Education.* Maryville, MO: Prescott Publishing.

Juran, J. M. 1992. *Juran on Quality by Design.* New York: The Free Press.

Gitlow, H. S. and Gitlow, S. S. 1987. *The Deming Guide to Quality and Competitive Position.* Englewood Cliffs, NJ: Prentice Hall.

Lane, M. E. 1992. *Quality in Education.* Los Angeles: ERIC Clearinghouse for Junior College, University of California.

Senge, P. M. 1990. *The Fifth Discipline: The Art & Practice of the Learning Organization.* New York: Doubleday.

Spanbauer, S. J. 1992. A *Quality System for Education.* Milwaukee, WI: Quality Press.

Walton, M. 1986. *The Deming Management Method.* New York: Perigee Books, The Putnam Publishing Group.

Wheatley, M. J. 1992. *Leadership and the New Science: Learning About Organization From an Orderly Universe.* San Francisco : Berrett-Koehler Publishers.

MARVIN E. LANE

Marvin E. Lane has been president of Lamar Community College since 1982. He holds bachelor and master of arts degrees, and a doctorate of education, all from the University of Northern Colorado. Lane's experiences range from retail experience, truck driving, elementary teaching, K-8 principal, and district superintendent supervision of student teachers.

Lamar Community College became a pioneer TQM institution under Lane's leadership which resulted in national recognition. Lane is a nationally known presenter, has written chapters for three books, and was the editor of *CQI: A View From the Trenches* (Prescott Publishing, Maryville, Missouri, 1994). He serves as national president of the Continuous Quality Improvement Network (an international network of community colleges engaged in the implementation of quality concepts) and is immediate past president of the Lamar Force to develop a plan for major corporations to become active sponsors of a pilot TQM project in the Jefferson County Public School. Lane has also worked with the Colorado Department of Education school restructuring task force.

CHAPTER TEN:

LEARNING, LEARNING ORGANIZATIONS AND TQM

John Cleveland and Peter Plastrik

The design of an educational institution implies certain answers to the following questions:

1) Why and how do people learn? (A theory of learning.)

2) How do you organize individuals around a collective purpose? (A theory of organizational behavior.)

Today we would answer these questions very differently than we would have 20 or 30 years ago. Current research is significantly changing our understanding about why and how individuals learn, and our understanding of organizational behavior has changed how we think about organizing groups of individuals around collective purpose. Unfortunately, the new answers to these questions are not reflected in the design and behavior of most educational institutions.

Total Quality Management (TQM) has recently achieved popularity as a tool for improving educational institutions. We believe that TQM's popularity and success arise from the fact that it allows groups of individuals in organizations to rapidly learn together. When it works, it is because the concepts, practices, and tools of TQM are used to support a fast and disciplined learning process. When it fails, it is because organizational leaders do not understand that learning is the core of TQM, and they seek to use the tools and practices to achieve more traditional management objectives, such as higher levels of control over what workers do, how they do it, and when they do it.

The assumptions about learning inherent in TQM are consistent with new theories of learning that are changing classroom practice. The implementation of TQM in an educational institution therefore represents a unique opportunity to unify classroom and management practice with a common theory of learning.

Educational Design Assumptions

The design of educational institutions (both K-12 and post-secondary) is based in large part on how we answer some key questions. Table one shows the design features of educational institutions that are influenced by our assumptions about learning theory and organizational behavior.

Some very new answers are now being posed for each of these questions. In each case, a significant "paradigm shift" is occurring that has significant implications for the design of educational institutions. The changing assumptions in each of these areas are discussed in Figure 1.

New Answers to The Question: Why and How Do Individuals Learn?

There has been an enormous amount of new and exciting research in the last several decades that challenges some of our

Figure 1

Our Answers to These Questions . . .	Affect these Design Features
Why and how do individuals learn?	• Pedagogy • Instruction delivery • Teacher preparation • Classroom design • Assessment • Credentialing Process • Discipline divisions
How do you organize individuals around a collective purpose?	• Authority relationships • Decision-making process • Role definitions • Reward systems • Organizational structure

traditional assumptions about individual learning. This shift in theory has in turn spawned a wide variety of new teaching practices and tools (Bonwell). Some of the key developments include:

- Research in the cognitive sciences that provides new insight into how the brain works and how we perceive, process, store, and act on information (Caine 1991).
- Theories about the nature of intelligence and how it affects how we learn (Gardner, 1983).
- Research on learning styles, and how different individuals perceive and process information in different ways (Kolb 1984; McCarthy 1987).
- Research on the link between social networks and learning (Institute for Research on Learning 1993).

Figure 2 summarizes some of the key shifts in assumptions about learning that are implied by the new research.

Figure 2

Why and How do Individuals Learn?	
Old Answers	**New Answers**
Knowledge is a "thing" that is transferred from one person to another.	Knowledge is a relationship between the knower and the known; knowledge is "created" through this relationship.
Knowledge is objective and certain.	Knowledge is subjective and provisional.
Knowledge is organized in stable, hierarchical structures that can be treated independent of one another.	Knowledge is organized "ecologically"; disciplines are integrative and interactive.
Learners receive knowledge.	Learners create knowledge.
We learn best passively, by listening and watching.	We learn best by actively doing and managing our own learning.
We learn alone, with our minds, based on our innate abilities.	We learn in social contexts, through mind, body, and emotions.
We learn in predictable sequences from simple "parts" to complex "wholes."	We learn in wholes.
We all learn the same way.	There are many different learning styles.
We learn in order to have purpose.	We learn when we have a purpose.
Our "intelligence" is based on our individual abilities.	Our intelligence is based on our learning community.
The teacher is the authority who possesses and transmits knowledge.	The teacher is an enabler who organizes learning experiences.

Learning, Learning Organizations and TQM   235

New Answers to the Question: How Do You Organize
Individuals Around a Collective Purpose?

Our assumptions about what constitutes a "good" or "well-designed" organization have changed significantly from the early part of this century. The core metaphor has gradually evolved from the "well-oiled machine" to the "healthy, growing organism." (As one colleague expressed it: "Egads, it's alive!") The rethinking of the relationship between individuals, organizations, and their environments has resulted in radical organizational restructuring in almost every sector of the economy. Some of the slowest organizations to change have been public sector and educational institutions, primarily because the extrinsic market forces tend to be weakest in those sectors.

Figure 3 summarizes the shift in thinking about organizational behavior.

How Do You Organize Individuals Around a Collective Purpose?	
Maintain strong top-down control.	Allow local control, united by purpose.
Focus on the operating unit.	Focus on the "whole system."
Organize units in a rigid hierarchical structure.	Create a flat, mobile, flexible structure.
Create competition between units.	Emphasize cooperation and teamwork.
Avoid change.	Expect change as the norm.
Control information centrally.	Create open information systems.
Divide work between those who "decide" and those who "do."	Let those who "do" decide, based on shared vision and values.
Focus on individual performance.	Focus on the system.
Use extrinsic motivation.	Use intrinsic motivation.

Figure 3

Cleveland and Plastrik

There is a correlation between "old"thinking about learning and "old" thinking about organizations. In both contexts there is: a) a hierarchical structure of top-down control; b) the reduction of work into small, separate parts; c) strong use of extrinsic motivation; d) an emphasis on working alone rather than together; and e) a focus on creating stable, unchanging structures. By contrast, both the "new" learning and the "new" organization emphasize a reduction in hierarchy; open information flow; a focus on the whole system; working together in teams; and flexible, versatile structures of knowledge and organization.

Implications for the Design of Educational Institutions
The new ways of thinking about individual learning and organizational behavior require us to rethink the design of educational institutions. Some of the potential design implications are described below:

New Assumptions About Learning Could Lead to:
- Different classroom practices, including less lecture; more "action" learning; greater variety in instructional media (voice, sound, motion, visuals, etc.); different assessment; more innovative means of demonstrating mastery; broader use of technology.
- Different preparation of teachers and faculty, including more emphasis on understanding the learning process, not just subject matter.
- New classroom design; more flexible learning environments that are conducive to group work.
- More learning outside of the classroom.
- Helping students understand, and take responsibility for, their learning process.
- Breaking down the barriers between the disciplines; more inter-disciplinary work; more focus on underlying concepts and less on detail complexity.

Learning, Learning Organizations and TQM   237

New Assumptions About Organizational Behavior Could Lead to:
- Flatter organizational structures and a reduction in the "professional managerial class" in education.
- More involvement of faculty in strategic decision-making.
- Elimination of traditional academic "departments" with more rapid forming and reforming of cross-disciplinary groups.
- More complex and rich interactions between educational institutions and their "markets."
- Restructuring of basic compensation and reward systems.

Total Quality Management as Organizational Learning for Higher Education

For institutions of higher education to respond to changes in learning and organizational theory requires accelerated organizational learning. In simplest terms, this means doing at the level of the organization what we are trying to do in the classroom—create new knowledge and new behaviors through active learning.

Learning, in its simplest form, is a cycle of :
1) perceiving new information about the world;
2) making sense of that information; and
3) acting on the information.

All learning occurs in the context of our "mental models" of the world—i.e., the underlying assumptions we have about how the world works. Joel Barker (1985) refers to these mental models as "paradigms." Our models filter the information that we perceive; we make meaning by fitting the information into our current mental models and adjusting them appropriately. Thus, we use the mental model to influence how we act.

238   **Cleveland and Plastrik**

TQM is a set of principles and practices that allows groups of individuals in an organization to learn together by: a) making explicit their mental models of the world; b) agreeing on what the information they have means; and c) acting collectively.

There are many different "schools" of TQM thinking. W. Edwards Deming, Joseph Juran, Kaoru Ishikawa, Phil Crosby, and the other quality "gurus" each tend to emphasize a different dimension of the discipline (Deming 1982; Juran 1989). In Figure 4, we have identified and described a number of principles that are common to most approaches to TQM.

Quality Principles		
Principle	What it Means	Questions it Answers
Systems Thinking	Understanding work as a system focused on meeting the needs of those you serve.	What are we trying to do?
Management by Fact	Using data and knowledge of variation to know how you are doing.	How are we doing?
Continuous Improvement	Using an organized and disciplined process to change the way you work.	How are we going to improve?
Trust and Teamwork	Acting like we depend on each other.	Who do we depend on?
Leadership	Having a clear vision of where you are headed.	Where are we going?

Figure 4

Learning, Learning Organizations and TQM   239

While there is a virtual blizzard of names and acronyms describing various quality practices and tools, the quality practices involve three general kinds of activities:

1) **Explicit mapping of systems, processes, and other "mental models" that describe different relationships between us, our work, our organization, and the environment.** These are often referred to as "system pictures," "relationship maps," "flow charts," or simply "mental maps." They usually include the elements of purpose, customers, products and services, processes, resources, and measures. The net result is a map of the key relationships that constitute the organization.

2) **Asking disciplined questions about how the systems are performing.** This involves the use of statistical tools and techniques, and the active understanding of the concept of variation.

3) **Taking action to change systems in a collective and disciplined manner.** This involves the use of trained improvement teams that use a common analytical process and tools.

TQM does not tell educators anything about the <u>content</u> of their decision-making (e.g., what to teach, how to teach, or who to teach). What it does do is give educators a common framework, language, and process to manage the process of organizational change. Because it is a framework of <u>learning,</u> it is applicable across all the academic and managerial disciplines.

As a process of organizational learning, TQM is consistent with the new theories of individual learning because:

• It focuses on understanding the "whole system" and looks at the parts in the context of the whole;

- It emphasizes communities of learners learning together, "getting the whole system in the room";
- It requires that people doing the work create their own understanding of the purpose and quality of that work;
- It emphasizes the role of the manager/leader in clarifying purpose and facilitating learning instead of commanding and controlling individuals and processes; and
- It structures learning around an iterative process of reflection and interaction with the environment (known as the Plan-Do-Check-Act Cycle).

When used as a structured organizational learning process, Total Quality Management has the benefit of creating a common conceptual framework that links management and teaching practices under the overall umbrella of learning. Faculty are challenged to understand their classroom as a system that is connected to—and dependent on—other systems in the institution, and to take responsibility for the management of the whole system. Administrators are challenged to view their work as a learning process, and to open the management process to the same spirit of critical inquiry that pervades excellent classrooms.

Requirements for Success
Using TQM as a vehicle for organizational learning and change in educational institutions requires a number of key developments. These include:
1) **Leaders Become Learners**. All organizational leaders must perceive themselves as learners engaged in the management of their own learning process—the clarification of mental models (particularly their vision of the future); vigorous pursuit of the "truth;" and a constant challenging of the status quo through organized innovation.

2) **Faculty as Learners.** Faculty need time with their peers and others to challenge their assumptions, see new information, and change their behaviors on a continuing basis. This particularly requires structured opportunities to "talk across the disciplines." Faculty need to see themselves less as the "keepers of knowledge" in the classroom and more as facilitators of a learning process.

3) **Learning Becomes the Core Competence of Educational Institutions.** Finally, learning—not social control, economic development, job training, credentialing or research—must be seen as the core competence of educational institutions. The ability to design, create, and facilitate accelerated learning experiences is the foundational capability from which all other activities flow. All of the other "missions" of schools should be subordinated to this primary focus.

Higher education is faced by many external challenges—changing demands, cost pressures, reduced funding, and competing missions. At the same time, many of the assumptions about how we learn and how we can organize for collective action are no longer valid. If approached in the spirit of organizational learning, Total Quality Management can be a powerful tool to help educational institutions make the journey from the learning of the past to the learning of the future, and from the organization of the past to the organization of the future.

References

Barker, J. 1985. *Discovering the Future: The Business of Paradigms.* Lake Elmo, MN: ILL Press.

Bonwell, C. and J. Eison. *Active Learning—Creating Excitement in the Classroom.* ASHE-ERIC Higher Education Report No. 1. Washington, DC: The George Washington University School of Education and Human Development.

Caine, R. and Geoffrey. 1991. *Making Connections—Teaching and the Human Brain.* Association for Supervision and Curriculum Development.

Deming, W. E. 1982. *Out of the Crisis.* Cambridge: MIT Center for Advanced Engineering Study.

Gardner, H. 1983. *Frames of Mind: The Theory of Multiple Intelligences.* Basic Books.

Institute for Research on Learning. 1993. A New Learning Agenda: Putting People First. Unpublished Paper.

Juran, J. 1989. *Juran on Leadership for Quality.* New York: The Free Press.

Kolb, D. 1984. *Experiential Learning: Experience as the Source of Learning and Development.* New Jersey: Prentice Hall.

McCarthy, B. 1987. *The 4-MAT System—Teaching to Learning Styles with Right/Left Mode Techniques.* Barrington, IL: EXCEL, Inc.

JOHN
CLEVELAND

John Cleveland is the director of
continuous quality improvement for
Grand Rapids Community College.
Cleveland also conducts external training and consulting with
community colleges, manufacturers, K-12 school districts,
and other organizations regarding implementing continuous
quality improvement. Cleveland has a degree in city planning
from Yale University.

PETER PLASTRIK

Peter Plastrik is a co-founder
of On Purpose Associates. He is also a
writer and consultant about changing
public systems and organizations. Plastrik holds a master's in
journalism from the University of Michigan and a bachelor's
degree from Columbia University.

Some of Plastrik's leadership positions include: chief
deputy of the Michigan Department of Commerce; president
of the Michigan Strategic Fund; and executive director of the
Governor's Cabinet Council on Economic Development. He
has also served as a state government official, worked as a
journalist, and is now co-authoring a book, *Reinventing Your
Government*, with David Osborne.

CHAPTER ELEVEN:

QUALITY LEARNING TEAMS: IMPROVING STUDENT RETENTION, PERFORMANCE, AND SATISFACTION

Edith Finaly-Neumann
and Yoram Neumann

A brief examination of the Total Quality Management and general business literature reveals an increasing interest in using teams to improve organizational performance and effectiveness. A more thorough review of recent management studies indicates that teams do work. Drucker (1988) predicts that tomorrow's organizations will be organized around teams, which will be where the work gets done. Numerous organizations have adopted the empowered work team approach, since it provides a way to accomplish organizational goals and meet the need of the changing work. Teams offered to American businesses:

    1) improved quality, productivity, and service;

    2) greater flexibility and increased corporate responsiveness to customers and the marketplace;

3) reduced operating cost;
4) faster response to technological change;
5) ability to attract and retain highly qualified individuals;
6) better response to diversified workforce and worker values.

Katzenbach and Smith (1993) have argued that teams are crucial in creating a high performance organization. Their conclusion, based on extensive interviews of hundreds of people working in 50 teams across 30 companies and organizations, is that team performance opportunities exist in all parts of organizations and that teams are the primary unit of performance for an increasing number of organizations. The key for creating the high performance organization lies in the organization's willingness to recognize the unique potential of teams to deliver results and to understand the benefits they provide.

Individuals will benefit from working in teams. According to Mears and Voehl (1994), teams improve an individual's competence in the context of the team. Teams improve an individual's communication ability and increase mutual respect within the team. They improve participation level, "buy in" to changes, and the individual's job satisfaction and organizational commitment. Finally, teams improve each individual's overall effectiveness.

Building High Performing Teams

A self-directed work team is defined as a group of employees who are responsible for a work process that delivers a process or service to an internal or external customer (Wellins et al. 1991). Katzenbach and Smith (1993) defined team as "a small number of people with complimentary skills who are committed to a common purpose, performance goals, and approach for which they hold themselves mutually accountable" (45). A somewhat similar definition is offered by Coffey et al. (1994), who referred to teams as work groups at any level or function in an organization whose members share a common goal, are interdependent, and accountable as a unit to the organization as a whole.

Empowered teams have emerged as a powerful management tool, because they involve and empower employees. Workers are typically more satisfied, committed, and energized, with higher productivity and product quality. Since empowered teams are essential to organizational success, it is management's responsibility to develop and maintain high-performing teams that improve the quality and quantity of outputs and maximize member satisfaction. To help teams become more effective, it is necessary to understand the elements that contribute to team effectiveness and how those elements interact. Katzenbach and Smith (1993) summarized their findings concerning team performance and effectiveness:

1) significant performance challenges energize teams regardless of where they are in an organization;
2) leaders can foster team performance best by building a strong performance ethic;
3) biases toward individualism exist, but need not get in the way of team performance;
4) discipline creates the conditions for team performance;
5) a common and meaningful purpose is essential for team success and sets the tone and aspiration;
6) specific performance goals are an integral part of the purpose;
7) both team purpose and specific performance goals are essential to team success;
8) team success is dependent on a common approach;
9) a successful team needs to specify the way in which it can hold itself accountable as a team;
10) members' strong personal commitment to the team's

and to each other's growth and success is what distinguishes a high-performance team; and

11) Successful teams develop mutual-support, trust-based relationships and opportunities for personal growth.

Quick (1992) suggested nine characteristics of effectiveness teams:

1) information (open and honest, full sharing, flowing freely up, down, and sideways);
2) people relationships (trusting, respectful, collaborative, and supportive);
3) conflict (on issues, not persons; regarded as natural, even helpful);
4) atmosphere (open, non-threatening, non-competitive, participative);
5) decision (by consensus and full commitment);
6) creativity (solution-oriented);
7) power base (shared by all, depending on competence and contribution to the team);
8) motivation (commitment to goals set by the team, belonging needs satisfied, more chance of achievement through group);
9) rewards (based on contribution to group, peer recognition).

The most comprehensive approach for designing high-performing and successful work teams was offered by Hackman (1987), Sundstrom et al. (1990), and Schwartz (1994). Hackman (1987) started by defining what it means for a team to be effective. An effective work team meets three criteria:

1) The services that the team delivers or the product it makes meet or exceed the performance standards of the people who receive it, use it, or review it.
2) The processes and structures used to carry out the work maintain or enhance the capacity of members to work together on subsequent team tasks.

Quality Learning Teams   249

3) The team experience satisfies the personal needs of team members.

To be effective, the team must meet all three criteria.

Hackman (1987) and Sundstrom et al. (1990) defined three major factors that contribute to team effectiveness and success: team process, team structure, and the organizational context. Following Schein (1987), team process refers to how things are done. Team process includes the following (Schwartz 1994):

1) Problem-solving: Two conditions must be met: a) team members use a systematic process for problem-solving, and b) all team members focus on the same step at the same time.

2) Decision-making: Teams are more effective when decisions are made by consensus.

3) Conflict management: Effective teams do not avoid conflict, but deal with it openly and fairly, and resolve it by testing differences of opinion.

4) Communication: Effective teams communicate in a way that uses the full knowledge and skills of members and that maintains their motivation to perform their tasks.

Team structure refers to relatively stable characteristics of the team. Team success is clearly related to the following structural attributes (Schwartz 1994):

1) Clear goals: Goals should be consistent with the mission and vision of the organization, and they should be clear in a way that the team can measure its progress toward realizing them.

2) A motivating task: The team should deal with a meaningful task, and significant outcomes should result once the task is completed. The team should give members autonomy in handling and accomplishing the task.

3) Time: The team should have sufficient time to complete the task (performance and process).
4) Team Culture: Effective team culture includes core values of valid information, free and informed choice, and internal commitment (Argyris 1990).

The organizational context includes aspects of the larger organization that influence the team. The following components of the organizational context affect team success:

1) A clear mission and shared vision that answers the questions "why do we exist?" and "what future do we seek to create?" (Senge 1990).
2) Congruent and supportive organizational culture.
3) Rewards that are consistent with team objectives.
4) Information from the organization, including feedback about performance.

Designing Quality Learning Teams

The basic idea of our paper (i.e., the creation of quality learning teams within each of the classrooms in the college in order to improve the quality of learning, student retention, performance, participation and collaboration), requires substantial role shifts for students as well as for the instructor.

Initial attempts in higher education were aimed at introducing the teamwork into the classroom by means of cooperative learning (Slavin 1991; Johnson et al. 1991; Bechtol and Sorenson 1993; Cooper et al. 1994; Ventimiglia 1994). The basic idea is for instructors to structure learning opportunities so that groups of students work cooperatively. Slavin (1991) summarized most of the research on cooperative learning methods and concluded that the effects of cooperative learning on student performance and achievement are clearly positive. Student performance shows substantial gain when team goals and individual accountability are incorporated in the cooperative model. Furthermore, cooperative learning positively affects other educational outcomes: cooperation, friendship, and interaction among students who differ in race, ethnicity, gender, and achievement, as well as individuals' self-esteem, academic self-confidence, liking for the class, liking and feeling liked by classmates, and psychological health (Slavin 1991; Bechtol and Sorenson 1993). Cooperative learning provides a structure for team work based on the following three elements (Vasquez et al. 1990):

1) Positive interdependence and team success that depends on the efforts of all members.
2) Individual accountability.
3) Interpersonal and communication skills.

Faculty remain deeply committed to the concept of teamwork, but often do not understand that success in cooperative learning is grounded in the structure process, which they design (Ventimiglia 1994).

Beyond Cooperative Learning. Applying teamwork to college teaching requires a systematic approach to designing quality learning teams which transcends the conventional cooperative learning methods (student teams-achievement division; jigsaw; team-assisted individualization). It requires extensive planning, work, and training—before, during, and after actual class time. MacGregor (1990) argued that effective teamwork in the classroom must reframe the student role as well as the teacher role. Students must be trained to deal with shifts in their roles from:

1) listener, observer, and note-taker to active problem-solver, contributor, and discussant;
2) low to moderate expectations of preparations for class to high expectations;
3) private presence in the classroom to a public one;
4) competition with peers to cooperation;
5) responsibilities associated with individual learning to those associated with learning interdependently;

6) seeing teachers and texts to seeing peers and oneself as important sources of authority and knowledge.

Teachers must be trained to deal with shifts in their roles from:

1) responsibility about course coverage to commitment to enabling students to learn on their own;
2) a complete authority over the course and its management to shared responsibility and reshaped authority;
3) organizing, presenting, and directing to facilitating the team, encouraging and energizing team members.

Step One—System Change. The first step in designing quality learning teams is the creation of a system-wide (university) or sub-system (school) culture for change and quality improvement. Quality learning teams will be successful in high performing systems, or sub-systems (Vail 1982). A high performing system has been defined as an excellent human system which performs at an unusually high level of quality (Harvey and Brown 1992). According to Vail (1982), high performing systems or sub-systems in universities will meet the following criteria:

1) excellent performance against a known external standard;
2) excellent performance against what is believed to be the potential level of performance;
3) excellent performance in relation to where the system was at some earlier point in time;
4) judged by objective observers to perform substantially better than other comparable systems;
5) using significantly fewer resources than are believed necessary to do what they do;
6) becoming a source of ideas and inspiration for others.

These criteria lead to the following characteristics of high performing systems (Vail 1982):

1) high level of clarity regarding their broad purposes and regarding the nearer term objectives for fulfilling these purposes;
2) non-perfunctory commitment to the purposes;
3) teamwork focused on task;
4) leadership strong, focused, and clear;
5) existence of clear boundaries which separate them from their environments;
6) functioning as fertile sources of experimentation and innovation, and using new methods within the scope of the purposes and task they have defined;
7) cohesive units.

In order to create a high performing system or sub-systems, leadership has to move from a more traditional, transactional view to transformational leadership (Bass 1990). Transactional leadership has been viewed as a process through which the leader is able to bring about desired actions from followers by using certain behavior, rewards, and incentives. This leadership is based on the premise that a transaction takes place between follower and leader. Transformational leaders, on the other hand, are individuals who envision their organization's future, articulate that vision to organizational members, and inspire and facilitate a higher level of motivation than those members have thought possible. Bass (1990) and Bass et al. (1987) have summarized the characteristics of transformational leader:

1) opposes and strives to change the status quo;
2) idealizes goals quite different from status quo;
3) has long-term perspective;
4) motivates organizational members by inspiring them to aspire to higher-order personal goals;
5) encourages organizational members to innovate and experiment;
6) encourages autonomy and teamwork.

Transformational leaders focus on the process of bringing about significant changes:

1) visioning is the ability of transformational leaders to see the organization's future clearly and completely;

2) valuing is the leaders' adherence to a set of core values around which the organizational transformation takes place;

3) articulating is the ability of the transformational leaders to clearly define and communicate the vision to others;

4) transformational leaders also inspire other members of the organization; and

5) transformational leaders empower their followers by helping them to meet new challenges through shared problem-solving and delegation.

The first step of building quality learning teams consists of a system level intervention by creating high-performing systems (the whole university or a school within an university) and transformational leadership involving at least a college president (for a whole system) or a school dean (for a subsystem). The first step in intervention ought to include training programs for administrators, deans, and department chairs.

Organizing Courses and Class Work. The quality learning team calls for the establishment of heterogeneously formed base teams with an optimal size of five members. When students are assigned to a base team, they know they will be meeting, studying, and working with the same students for the duration of the course (e.g., a semester). The base team should receive formal training from the instructor at the beginning of each course. This team development phase will have the following purposes (Harvey and Brown 1992):

1) to identify objectives and set priorities for the team;

2) to examine the learning and task performance required from the team;

3) to analyze ways the team is functioning;

4) to improve communication and relationships among team members;

5) to improve the ability of the team in solving problems;

6) to decrease competition and increase cooperation among the team members;

7) to increase respect for each other's individual differences.

Team development is an educational process of continually evaluating team functioning and identifying and establishing new and more effective ways of operating (Harvey and Brown 1992). Team building training opens with an explanation of what will be happening and what is expected of participants. The general aim is to help the team understand its own processes and solve it own problems. Team members are given opportunities to share their concerns and clarify their roles. In that process, team members learn how to look at their ways of behaving, diagnosing team's problems, and figure out new and more effective ways of functioning. Realistic goals are discussed and agreed upon. The instructor should follow certain basic steps (Harvey and Brown 1992):

1) initiating team-development meetings;

2) setting objectives;

3) planning the meetings;

4) conducting the meetings; and

5) evaluating the team development process.

The training for teams should start at the beginning of the term and should be designed to enable team members to move along the empowerment process. The following must be included in the training program (Wellins et al. 1991):

1) listening and feedback (summarizing, checking for understanding, and giving and receiving constructive feedback);

2) one-to-one communication;

3) handling conflict (identifying and resolving conflicts and disagreements within a team or with another team);

4) influencing others;

5) team skills (roles and responsibilities of participating in meetings and group process skills).

Quality learning teams need to be trained to follow 15 ground rules (Schwartz 1994):

1) test assumptions and inferences;

2) share all relevant information;

3) focus on interests and not on positions;

4) be specific and use examples;

5) agree on what important words mean;

6) explain the reason behind a member's statements, questions, and actions;

7) disagree openly with any member of the group;

8) make statements, then invite questions and comments;

9) jointly design ways to test disagreements and solutions;

10) discuss undiscussable issues;

11) keep the discussion focussed;

12) do not take cheap shots or otherwise distract the group;

13) participate in all phases of the process (expected of all members);

14) make decisions by consensus;

15) conduct self-critique.

The professor's role in planning quality learning teams includes several critical elements (Johnson et al. 1991):

1) specify objectives;

2) make decisions about placing students in learning teams to ensure heterogeneity and diversity of student membership;

3) explain the academic task and ground rules;

4) provide training in team development;

5) monitor the effectiveness of the quality learning teams;

6) intervene when necessary to teach academic or team skills;

7) evaluate teams' performance and students' academic achievement and contribution to the team.

Angelo and Cross (1993) defined various teaching objectives for professors and grouped them in six different clusters:

1) liberal arts and academic values;
2) discipline-specific knowledge and skills;
3) basic academic success skills;
4) higher-order thinking skills;
5) work and career preparation; and
6) personal development.

These clusters help college professors become more aware of what they want to accomplish in individual courses, assist them in specifying objectives for each course, and enable them to better explain the academic task of quality learning team members. To accomplish the changes in learning modes and to capitalize on the quality of the learning team concept, professors must assume a significantly different role, becoming a facilitator, supporter, role model, challenger, and motivator of student learning. Professors encourage the quality learning teams to engage in self-managing behavior, self-learning, goal setting, creativity, self-evaluation, feedback to one another, new ways of problem-solving, and group problem-solving.

Quality Learning Teams and Student Retention

The problem of student attrition has produced a vast body of literature and has generated interest among policy makers, university administrators, faculty, and students. The attrition phenomenon represents problems for the student leaving and the institution from which he/she departs. College graduates have higher employment rates and, on the average, enjoy higher levels of income than those who did not complete their undergraduate degree. For the institution, attrition represents serious problems. Students play a very important role in determining the college budget. In most private institutions, income is derived largely from tuition and fees; therefore, each student retained maintains the level of income. In public colleges, the majority of income is derived from state appropriations, which are usually allocated in direct proportion to the number of students. In addition, student attrition represents not only a loss of income from tuition, but also a cost associated with recruiting new students to fill the vacated positions.

According to a 1981 study of the College Board, the national dropout norm is between 40 and 55 percent (Raimist 1981). Many reviews of dropout studies have identified variables significantly correlated with student dropout but have failed to describe how they affect withdrawal.

The vast amount of literature emphasized individual-demographic factors which may be associated with attrition, but there have been few attempts to develop theoretical models which explain the process of attrition and guide research.

A. Tinto's Model. Perhaps the most frequently used model is this emerging paradigm proposed by Tinto (1975;1993). Tinto built on Spady's (1970) work to develop an explanatory predictive theory of the withdrawal process. Tinto's core predictors were the concepts of academic and social integration in the institution. Students who enter a particular institution possess different background traits that influence both their academic performance and their level of integration into the institution's social and academic systems. Other things being equal, persistence is positively affected by the level of academic and social integration.

B. Peer Group Influence. One component of social integration in Tinto's framework is peer-group interaction.

The role of a student's peer-group in persistence has received a great deal of attention. Pantages and Creeldon (1978) note that "if the student's social interactions within her or his peer group are positive and satisfying, the chances are that the student will be "successful" in college (i.e., will receive a degree)" (70). Tinto (1993) sees "social integration" and peer-group influences as major determinants of persistence.

Quality learning teams have dominant influence on both academic and social integration into the institution as well as on the peer-group effect. Teamwork in college is expected to significantly increase the level of student retention.

C. Quality of Learning Experience. Once social membership concerns have been addressed, student attrition appears to center increasingly on academic involvements (Neumann and Neumann 1989). Neumann and Neumann (1989) emphasize the "Quality of Learning Experience" approach wherein persistence is conceptually linked to student perceptions of the quality of their learning environments, their learning teams, and their interaction with faculty about learning issues. The significant predictors of student retention proved to be student involvement in learning activities, students' views of the quality of the classroom activities, and their contact with faculty.

Following the Tinto's Model, Peer-Group Influence, and the Neumanns' Quality of Learning Experience, quality learning teams are crucial to improve student involvement in academic activities and thus to increase the level of student retention in college.

Quality Learning Teams and Student College Outcomes
Astin (1993) recently completed a study of over 200 colleges and universities to assess what factors make a difference in undergraduate education. After examining 200 variables, including a large number of curriculum factors, he

concluded that student-student interaction and student-faculty interaction were by far the best predictors of positive student cognitive and attitudinal changes in the undergraduate experience.

Neumann and Neumann (1993) examined the relationships between components of the quality of learning experience and several student college outcomes:

1) Students' perceived performance in their academic program;
2) Students' actual performance in their academic programs;
3) Students' satisfaction with their college experience; and
4) Students' commitment to their college.

The two major and dominant predictors of student college outcomes are students' college involvement and learning flexibility. Both of the predictors are intrinsically related to the concept of quality learning teams.

Let us summarize the major features of the quality learning team (QLT) in college instruction:

1) QLT improves students' effective outcomes, especially their liking of the subject matter, their satisfaction with the academic program, and their commitment to the institution.
2a) QLT improves students' cognitive performance, for all levels of cognitive outcomes.
2b) Although the use of QLT in college teaching will have positive effects for all cognitive outcomes, QLT will have larger positive effects on higher-level cognitive outcomes than on achievement and knowledge. QLT is extremely helpful in facilitating analysis of poorly-structured problems by enabling the members to make specific contributions and help each other in understanding complex problems.

Quality Learning Teams   261

3) QLT improves student retention and initial job opportunities. Members in QLTs are more intrinsically interested in the subject matter and are more satisfied with their college experience than their counterparts and therefore will have a higher retention rate. Members' exposure to QLT will increase their understanding of a variety of situations and their ability to meet future job market needs. Thus QLT will have a positive effect on initial job opportunities.

4a) QLT improves students' cognitive outcomes for <u>all core courses</u>.

4b) Although the use of QLT in college teaching will have positive effect for all courses, QLT will have larger positive effects in courses with higher levels of poorly-structured problems than in courses with well-defined problems.

5a) QLT will improve cognitive outcomes, retention, and initial job opportunities <u>for all student populations</u>.

5b) Although the use of QLT in college teaching will have positive effects on cognitive outcomes, retention, and initial job opportunities for all student populations, QLT will have larger positive effects on the aforementioned outcomes for minority students than for non-minority students. Similarly, larger positive effects are expected for women than men.

QLT will foster socialization into complex situations. Thus, it particularly will help groups with relatively less exposure into complex situations and/or groups having previously less opportunities for high level positions.

References

Angelo, T.T. and P. K. Cross. 1993. *Classroom Assessment Techniques.* San Francisco: Jossey Bass.

Argyris, C. 1990. *Overcoming Organizational Defense: Facilitating Organizational Learning.* Needham Height, MA: Allyn & Bacon.

Astin, A.W. 1993. *What Matters in College: Four Critical Years Revisited.* San Francisco: Jossey Bass.

Bass, B.M. 1991. "From Transactional to Transformational Leadership: Learning to Share the Vision." *California Management Review* 18 (3): 19-31.

Bass, B.M., B. J. Avolio, and L. Goodheim. 1987. "Biography and the Assessment of Transformational Leadership and the World-Class Level." *Journal of Management* 13: 7-19.

Bass, B.M., D. A. Waldman, B. T. Avolio, and M. Bebb. 1987. "Transformational Leadership and the Falling Domino Effect." *Groups and Organizational Studies* 12: 73-87.

Bechtol, W.M. and J. S. Sorenson. 1993. *Restructuring Schooling for Individual Students.* Needham Height, MA: Allyn and Bacon.

Coffey, R.E., C. W. Cook, and P. L. Hamsacker. 1994. *Management and Organizational Behavior.* Burr Ridge, IL: Irwin.

Cooper, J.L., P. Robinson, and M. McKinney. "Cooperative Learning in the Classroom." In Diane F. Halpern and Associates, *Changing College Classroom.* San Francisco: Jossey Bass.

Drucker, P.F. 1988. "The Coming of the New Organization." *Harvard Business Review* (Jan-Feb).

Hackman, J.R. 1987. "The Design of Work Teams." In J. Lorsch, Ed. *Handbook of Organizational Behavior.* Englewood Cliffs, N.J.: Prentice Hall.

Harvey, D.F. and D. R. Brown. 1992. *An Experimental Approach to Organizational Development.* 4th ed. Englewood Cliffs, N.J.: Prentice Hall.

Johnson, D.W., R. T. Johnson, and K. A. Smith. 1991. *Active Learning: Cooperation in the College Classroom.* Edina, MN: Interaction Book, Co.

Katzenbach, J.R. and D. K. Smith. 1993. *The Wisdom of Teams: Creating the High Performance Organization* Boston, MA: Harvard Business School Press.

MacGregor, J. 1990. "Collaborative Learning: Shared Inquiry as a Process of Reform." In M.D. Svinicki, *The Changing Face of College Teaching* San Francisco: Jossey Bass.

Mears, P. and F. Voehl. 1994. *Team Building: A Structural Learning Approach.* Pelray Beach, #1: St. Lucie Press.

Quality Learning Teams   263

Neumann, Y. and E. F. Neumann. 1989. "Predicting Juniors' and Seniors' Persistence and Attrition: A Quality Learning Experience Approach." *The Journal of Experimental Education* 57:129-140.

—. 1993. "Quality of Learning Experience and Students' College Outcomes." *International Journal of Educational Management* 1:4-10.

Pantages, T.J. and C. F. Creeldon. 1975. "Studies at College Attrition: 1950-1975." *Review of Educational Research* 45:49-101.

Quick, T.L. 1992. *Successful Team Building* New York: American Management Association.

Raimist, L. 1981. *College Student Attrition and Retention.* New York: College Entrance Examination Board.

Schein, E.H. 1987. *Process Consultation: Lessons for Managers and Consultants.* Vol. 2. Reading, MA: Addison Wesley.

Schwartz, R.M. 1994. *The Skilled Facilitator.* San Francisco: Jossey-Bass.

Senge, P.M. 1990. *The Fifth Discipline: The Art and Practice of the Learning Organization.* New York: Doubleday.

Shashkim. 1986. "True Vision in Leadership." *Training and Development Journal* 40 (May):8-61.

Slavin, R. 1991. *Cooperative Learning: Theory, Research & Practice.* Englewood Cliffs, N.J.: Prentice Hall.

Spady, W. 1970. "Dropout for Higher Education: An Interdisciplinary Review and Synthesis." *Interchange* 1:621-85.

Sundstrom E., K. P. DeMeuse, and D. Foutrell. 1990. "Work Teams: Application and Effectiveness." *American Psychologist* 45:120-133.

Tichy, N.M. and M. A. Devanna. 1986. "The Transformational Leader." *Training and Development Journal* 40 (July):27-32.

Tinto, V. 1975. "Dropout for Higher Education: A Theoretical Synthesis of Recent Research." *Review of Educational Research* 45: 89-125.

Tinto, V. 1993. *Leaving College: Rethinking the Causes and Cures of Student Attrition.* 2d ed.: The University of Chicago Press.

Vail, P. 1982. "The Purposing of High-Performing Systems." *Organizational Dynamics* (Autumn).

Vasquez, B., R. Slavin, and M. D'Arcangelo. 1990. *Cooperative Learning: Facilitator's Manual* Alexandria, VA: Association for Supervision & Curriculum Development.

Ventimiglia, L.M. 1994. "Cooperative Learning in the College Level." *Thought & Action* 9 (2):5-30.

Wellins, R.S., W. C. Byham, and J. Wilson. 1991. *Empowered Teams: Creating Self-Directed Work Groups that Improve Quality, Productivity, and Participation.* San Francisco: Jossey-Bass Publishers.

Edith Finaly-Neumann

Edith Finaly-Neumann is associate professor of health sciences and the director of the program in healthcare management at California State University–Dominguez Hills. She has a bachelor of arts in behavioral sciences, a master of science in management, and a doctorate in sociology, specializing in health and organizational behavior, from Boston University.

Finaly-Neumann was senior research associate at the Center for Applied Social Science at Boston University, assistant professor of research and policy in Boston University's School of Social Work, director of program evaluation and development at the University Affiliated Programs of the Kennedy-Shriver Center (Waltham, MA), and project director on the assessment of college student's outcomes (Boston University). In addition, Finaly-Neumann received federal grants from the United States Administration on Developmental Disabilities and from the United States Department of Health and Human Services.

YORAM NEUMANN

Yoram Neumann is currently a professor of management and the dean of the School of Management at California State University–Dominguez Hills. He has a bachelor's and a master of business administration in economics and statistics, and a doctorate in organizational behavior and human resources from the New York State School of Industrial and Labor Relations at Cornell University.

Neumann has been involved in many different organizations and leadership positions, some of which include: editorial boards of the *Journal of Business and Management* and the *Quality Management Journal*, chair of the Major Employers Council of Torrance Area Chamber of Commerce, founder and director of the Project on Management of Higher Education at Cornell, associate director of the Center for Applied Social Sciences, and founding director of the H.H. Humphrey Institute.

Neumann has published four books and 80 papers in general management, organizational behavior, survey research, strategic management, and educational management. He has also had significant experience with sponsored projects. During the past 16 years, Neumann has served as the principal investigator in numerous externally funded projects.

CHAPTER TWELVE:

INVOLVING FACULTY IN TQM

K. Patricia Cross

TQM (Total Quality Management) has made its way into the vocabulary of higher education with remarkable speed. College and university administrators, pressed hard by public demands for higher quality at less cost, are taking a serious look at the radical restructuring that is occurring in industry.

Michael Hammer (1990) argues in an article in the *Harvard Business Review* that industry must "radically redesign . . . business processes in order to achieve dramatic improvements in their performance." He observes that "heavy investments in information technology have delivered disappointing results—largely because companies tend to use technology to mechanize old ways of doing business. They leave the existing processes intact and use computers simply to speed them up." The challenge for American industry, says Hammer, is to "stop paving the cow paths."

Education has some cow-paths of its own, and some pioneering colleges are calling for radical re-design, not only to meet what appears to be a continuing budget crisis, but also to meet the dramatically different requirements of the 21st century. Total Quality Management, or something like it, is now at work in more than half of the Fortune 1000 firms, and some college and university presidents are exploring its potential for higher education (Marchese, Seymour, and Mangan).

Total Quality Management (TQM)

Admittedly, TQM has its advocates, agnostics, and detractors, but it appears that education has "hit the wall." State budgetary crises have forced huge reductions in allocations to higher education, resulting in unprecedented rises in tuition, layoffs of tenured faculty members, abolition of entire academic programs, and restriction in admission of students. Even those Draconian measures, however, are not enough. Deeper cuts are required, and higher quality is demanded.

The goal, of course, is to do more with less. Hammer (1990) relates the dramatic success of the Ford Motor Company in reducing costs in its accounts payable department. Management estimated that they could reduce personnel costs by 20 percent through applying new technology and increasing efficiency. That looked good—until they found that they could reduce personnel costs by an astounding 75 percent through revamping the procedures of accounts payable. Not surprisingly, such success stories caught the attention of educators. Daniel Seymour (1991) surveyed 22 pioneering colleges and universities with experience in TQM, finding mixed reactions to early efforts, but concluding that in general the results were promising.

There is considerable irony, however, in the approach of educational institutions to TQM. While the rhetoric of TQM calls boldly for paradigm shifts, restructuring, and dramatic change, with a few notable exceptions (e.g.,Spanbauer), educational practitioners of TQM start in very timid ways. Seymour found, for example, that the five most common applications of TQM in the 22 pioneering institutions were in registration procedures, mail distribution, physical maintenance, construction and remodeling projects, and payroll. While today's practitioners of TQM talk boldly about totally new organizational cultures and about "barrier busting" and the benefits of bringing people together from different departments to work on TQM teams, it appears that the barriers busted so far are usually between employees of different departments in the same management division. Today, the application of TQM in higher education is far from the dramatic reforms that seem called for in the language of TQM and in view of the challenges faced by higher education. TQM, says Marchese (1991), "Is a call to leadership for the reform of American enterprise. Its advocates want more than a change in management practice; they want an entirely new organization, one whose culture is quality-driven, customer-oriented, marked by teamwork, and avid about improvement."

While it is certainly to everyone's advantage for the culture of the mail distribution center to be "quality-driven, customer-oriented, marked by teamwork, and avid about improvement," even total success in the implementation of TQM in the management divisions of colleges and universities would not begin to meet the demands of the 1990s for improved quality in student learning and the increase in faculty productivity that such a goal implies. It is the faculty, after all, who constitute the major portion of any college's budget, and it is the faculty who control quality. If the classroom does not work, the college does not work—no matter how well managed the support services.

Involving Faculty in TQM   269

"But," experienced colleagues in the administrative trenches will say, "everyone knows you can't 'manage' faculty." Right! And the whole point of TQM is to get people to manage themselves—to assume individual responsibility for working toward common ends.

When Miami-Dade Community College started their Teaching/Learning Project five years ago, TQM was not even in the lexicon of higher education. But Miami-Dade's total college push towards improving the quality of education for students is an excellent example of the ideals of TQM. The goal of the Teaching/Learning Project was defined in this way:

> The college would attempt systematically to change the way that it does business in order to raise the status of teaching, improve teaching and learning at the college, relate all of the reward systems to classroom performance, and change the decision-making process such that the first priority is teaching, learning, and the classroom environment (McCabe and Jenrette 1990).

While the major focus of the Miami-Dade Teaching/ Learning Project is on the classroom and improving the productivity of teachers and students, changing the culture of the total institution is clearly the goal. President McCabe (1990) tells a story about changing the decision-making process at the college that captures the essence of what advocates of TQM in higher education are talking about. It seems that since the purchasing department was buying chalk because it came at the best price, but that was too hard to write well, some teachers were buying good chalk and carrying it with them from classroom to classroom. As the Miami-Dade community continued their discussion of quality, other stories about defective light bulbs, dirty classrooms, and the like

Cross

began to surface. The result was the Marriott Plan. Much as "a good hotel does not wait for an irate guest to report a lack of soap or a broken towel rack," so Miami-Dade would not wait for faculty, who were "like hotel guests, constantly passing through an assigned room," to report less than satisfactory classroom conditions; they would send a housekeeper around with a list of standards for classrooms and laboratories (McCabe and Jenrette 1990).

Had TQM been applied to the purchasing department or the physical plant alone, the Marriott Plan would not have been the result. It is only when the attention of everyone who works for the college is directed toward the common mission of improving the quality of education for students that "restructuring" takes place. When someone in the Registrar's Office carries out her bureaucratic duties efficiently, by focusing on the proper procedures and forms to be filed by students, she is doing one job. When she focuses on whether she is contributing to the quality of education at the college, however, she may see her job quite differently—a paradigm shift. TQM requires a paradigm shift throughout the institution, but to date, TQM as applied in higher education has ignored the single most critical element in educational change—the faculty.

TQM and Classroom Assessment

Fortunately, thousands of individual faculty members have been pursuing the quality-oriented activity of Classroom Assessment. (See Cross 1988; Cross and Angelo 1988; Angelo and Cross 1993.) The purpose of Classroom Assessment is to maximize learning through frequent assessments of how well students are meeting the goals of instruction. The procedures of Classroom Assessment involve collecting data from students periodically throughout the term or semester, and then using that information to modify teaching, constantly experimenting to see how teachers can be more effective in maximizing learning.

Quizzes and tests are, of course, one way of assessing learning, but much of the appeal of Classroom Assessment is that it offers a variety of simple techniques that can be used by teachers of any discipline to provide quick and immediate assessments of different kinds of student responses to instruction. The second edition of Classroom Assessment Techniques (Angelo and Cross 1993), describes 50 Classroom Assessment Techniques (CATs) grouped in the following categories:

1) techniques for assessing course-related knowledge and skills,
2) techniques for assessing learner attitudes, values, and self-awareness, and
3) techniques for assessing learner reactions to instruction.

Classroom Assessment is designed to improve the productivity of both teachers and students through continuously focusing the attention of both on the quality of students' learning. Merging the management-oriented TQM with the academically-oriented Classroom Assessment offers an opportunity to address the quality challenge that is the most serious and pervasive challenge to education in the years ahead.

Marchese (1991) has identified 12 major themes of TQM. There is remarkable congruence between the themes of TQM and the principles of Classroom Assessment. Using Marchese's themes as a framework, we can illustrate how faculty would be involved in restructuring education through Classroom Assessment.

1) TQM focuses on quality. "Quality," says Marchese (1991), is "a mind-set, the soul of the company itself, an all-pervasive drive of such intensity that it defines the corporate culture."

Education, like American industry, has come under harsh criticism recently for lack of attention to quality. The often quoted report from the National Commission on Excellence in Education (1983) warned that, "the educational foundations of our society are presently being eroded by a rising tide of mediocrity that threatens our very future as a Nation and a people." Unfortunately, the public's concern about "the rising tide of mediocrity" in the schools arrived at about the same time as the rising tide of red ink in state budgets. Viewed through the old-paradigm lens in which higher quality requires more resources, there is a temptation to concentrate reform in the business office or the office of development. But the quality of a college is determined in its classrooms. If teachers fail to set high standards for learning in their own classrooms, then the pervasive drive for quality in institutional culture that is called for in TQM is impossible.

Classroom Assessment addresses the quality issue by running a continuing quality check on learning, with the intention of finding out how it can be improved. One of the best-known CATs is the Minute Paper, which asks students to write a sentence or two about the most important thing they learned in class that day (Angelo and Cross 1993). This extremely simple technique directs the attention of students to monitoring and articulating their own learning, and it provides immediate information to the teacher about what the class accomplished that day. The total impact of hundreds of students and teachers asking themselves what they had learned or taught that day is potentially enormous; it can result in a cumulative mindset that determines the campus culture.

2) TQM is customer-driven. "The cardinal rule," writes Marchese, "is to identify explicitly who your customers are, know their needs systematically, and commit to serving those needs."

Higher education, of course, has many customers, but first and foremost is the student. The purpose of Classroom Assessment is to systematically determine how well instruction is meeting the needs of students. This requires continuous assessment. Chain Notes is a simple CAT that enables teachers to find out how students are responding to the work of the class at any given moment (Angelo and Cross 1993). The teacher passes around a large envelope on which she has written one question about the class. When the envelope reaches a student, he or she spends less than a minute writing a response to the question, then drops the answer in the envelope and passes it. The question most often used is some variation of, "Immediately before this envelope reached you, what were you paying attention to?" Student responses provide the teacher with a running commentary on the work of the class as it is perceived by students. Other CATs may ask students to evaluate an assignment or an exam. CATs such as Chain Notes keep teachers continually informed about the value of the class to students. Through such information teachers can "commit to serving" the needs of their students.

3) TQM emphasizes continuous improvement.

Classroom Assessment places the emphasis on <u>continuous</u> improvement, on fixing inadequacies in learning as they are discovered. Classroom Assessments are formative evaluations; they provide a continuing flow of information about what students are learning while learning is in process. The question for Classroom Assessors is, "What are my students learning in my classroom as a result of my efforts today?" The point of gathering such information is to enable both teacher and students to monitor learning, and to experiment immediately with changes that will improve learning outcomes.

4) TQM concentrates on making processes work better. "The aim," says Marchese, "is to identify those processes; enable the people who work in them to understand that work in relation to customer needs."
The major "process" of any college or university is learning. And it is the faculty who need to understand that process and take responsibility for improving it. Few college teachers have any formal training in cognition and human learning processes. And yet, teachers have an exceptional opportunity everyday to observe students in the process of learning. Classroom assessment capitalizes on illuminating the "process" of learning for both teachers and students.

David Ausubel (1977), a pioneer in the study of meaningful learning, made the point more than 15 years ago, but the importance of learning as a continuous process is receiving renewed attention today. He said, in essence, find out what a student knows and teach accordingly. Learning is not so much additive, with new learning simply piling on top of existing knowledge, as it is an active dynamic process in which new learning interacts with what already exists in the mind of the learner, reformatting and changing the cognitive structure.

CATs are designed to make teachers more sensitive to the processes of learning. The Background Knowledge Probe, for example, provides information about the level and range of students' preparation for a class, enabling the teacher to know where to start and how to build on what students already know (Angelo and Cross 1993). This use of Classroom Assessment is concerned with the <u>learning</u> process, that is with building connections between new and existing knowledge for individual students.

Involving Faculty in TQM 275

But there is also a use of Classroom Assessment that is concerned with the <u>educational</u> process, that is with assuring that the institution has processes that work for quality in education. TQM, as used in industry, is usually concerned about this kind of process, that is process as a smooth and efficient flow of work. Transitions are important, and therefore teamwork within and between departments is important, as is articulation between the various levels of education. The teamwork and articulation aspects of Classroom Assessment are addressed below under Principles 5 and 8.

5) TQM extends the mind set. "Quality concerns," says Marchese, "reach in all directions ... No longer will it do for automakers to say, 'We know our cars aren't very good, but our lowest bid suppliers send us so-so goods.'"

Today's educators are encouraged to think of education as "all one system" with a "seamless flow" of students from grade school through college. Teachers at all levels need to know the backgrounds, interests, and preparation of students entering their classes, just as they need to know what students take from their class into the next one.

A useful device for helping teachers extend their mindset to the lives of students before and after their class is the CAT, "Interest/Knowledge/Skills Checklists," which asks students to rate their level of interest in various topics and their self-assessment of knowledge or skill in the topics (Angelo and Cross 1993). This CAT was used by a psychology professor, for example, in designing a capstone course where the purpose was to help students integrate and evaluate what they had learned in the previous three-and-a-half years of coursework in psychology. It might also be a useful CAT to assess what students think they need or want to know as they prepare for work after college.

6) TQM involves the discipline of information. "If you're . . . serious about quality," says Marchese, "everybody has to know how they're doing."

The relationship between Classroom Assessment and TQM on this principle is so obvious that little explanation is needed. Classroom Assessment is the continuous collection of information. It becomes a disciplined activity that is used regularly by teachers in the practice of their profession. It may be important, however, to point out that an additional requirement of Classroom Assessment is that the data collected must be shared with students. Feedback on students' learning provides teachers with information about how effectively they have taught the lesson, but equally important, it provides students with information about how well they have learned. Through Classroom Assessment, both teachers and students are continually faced with the discipline of using information to improve their performance.

7) TQM eliminates re-work. "An aim of all this attention to work processes is to ferret out the 'scrap, waste, and complexity' from a system" (Marchese 1991).

Critics of education have been especially sharp in their complaint about the waste in education that exists in remediation. When students fail to learn what they should learn at any point in the educational system, waste piles up and work has to be re-done. Teachers in higher education are all too familiar with the material and human costs that are the result of poor learning the first time around. Because Classroom Assessment involves continuous checking on the quality of learning, it enables teachers and students to identify weaknesses when they first appear.

Every teacher has had the experience of giving what appeared to be a masterful teaching performance, only to be surprised and disappointed at the misperceptions and lack of understanding shown by students' learning. Classroom Assessment, with its emphasis on assessing specific teaching/ learning experiences while they are still fresh in mind, shows both teachers and students what does and does not work. Some Classroom Assessors find that they have been doing things for years that are wasteful and ineffective.

Discovering weaknesses in student learning at the time of the mid-term, or worse yet, the final exam, is wasteful in the extreme. It is too late for students—and too late for the next teacher who receives inadequately prepared students. While teachers may use the results of a final exam to improve next semester's classes, the next class may be different. In any case, when teaching and the assessment of learning are widely separated in time, it may be difficult to pinpoint where and when teaching and learning parted company.

8) TQM emphasizes teamwork. "Teams," observes Marchese, "are not your familiar committees; they are self-directed work groups with their own required competencies and protocols."

While Classroom Assessment was originally proposed as an independent activity that teachers could use in their own classrooms without consulting others, experience shows that independence is not a high value for teachers who become active in Classroom Assessment. Quite the contrary; Classroom Assessment appears to promote interaction and conversations about teaching. It appears that once teachers begin to raise questions about their own teaching and to collect data about its impact on learning, there is a self-generated pressure to discuss findings with colleagues and to form voluntary study groups. Indeed, one of the most common outcomes on campuses where Classroom Assessment is practiced is the voluntary formation of faculty groups who wish to share findings with colleagues and to develop innovative approaches to Classroom Assessment (Cross 1992a; Angelo and Cross 1993, Chapter 7).

Study groups may be multidisciplinary or interdisciplinary, of course, but some of the strongest teamwork in Classroom Assessment is found at the departmental level, in part at least, because members of departments share a set of common values regarding teaching goals and priorities. Our research on the Teaching Goals Inventory (TGI) shows conclusively that teaching priorities are related more to teaching discipline than to any other factor (Angelo and Cross 1993, Chapter 7; Cross 1992a; Cross 1992b).

Departments are also natural sites for teamwork on quality because they are the "key organizational unit within virtually every American college and university" ("Belly" 1993). Indeed, the scholars who participated in the Pew Higher Education Roundtable contend that "departments must be the 'agents of reform' for the quality of undergraduate education." They go on to say that, "We believe that departments, more than individual faculty, ought to be vested with the responsibility for the quality of undergraduate teaching" (4a). If that is the case, then departmental teamwork is required, and Classroom Assessment is one promising route to the development of faculty teamwork.

9) TQM empowers people. "Who, in TQM," asks Marchese, "reviews work processes? . . . not distant managers or external evaluators but the people closest to the processes, those who do the work itself."

Although Classroom Assessment is part of the nationwide institutional assessment movement, it moves assessment into the classroom and under the control of the people who do the work of teaching and learning—students and faculty. The major principle of Classroom Assessment is that it is self-assessment. It shares the assumption with TQM that teachers want to teach as well as they can and students want to do the best job of learning that they can. Classroom assessment empowers both teachers and students to "take charge" of the learning process.

10) TQM invests in training and recognition. "TQM firms invest heavily in human resource development" (Marchese 1991).

Classroom Assessment is a powerful form of faculty development. The major difference between traditional faculty development and Classroom Assessment is that in the former, attention is directed towards the improvement of teacher performance, whereas in the latter, attention is focused on student performance as the ultimate criterion. In traditional forms of faculty development, the teacher is the subject of observation by peers, experts, videos, and the like. Without question, there are many things that experts and peers can point out that will improve teaching performance. Nevertheless, the ultimate criterion of good teaching is effective learning; it makes no difference how perfectly the teacher is teaching if students are not learning. Classroom Assessment places the emphasis on teachers as observers rather than the observed. Through observing the impact of their teaching on students' responses, Classroom Assessors are developing a repertoire of teaching techniques that work for them in their subject matter with their particular students. Classroom Assessment is not, however, a substitute for traditional approaches to faculty development. Rather, the combination of peer collaboration and self-evaluation is a powerful form of human resource development.

11) TQM requires vision. "Unlike the lofty piffle of 'mission' statements," writes Marchese, "TQM urges compelling, down-to-earth language that gets all parties focused on the right things to do."

Most Classroom Assessment starts with teachers making explicit their teaching goals—their vision of what they want students to learn. The revised handbook on *Classroom Assessment Techniques* (Angelo and Cross 1993) provides a self-scorable version of the Teaching Goals Inventory (TGI). The TGI consists of 52 concrete and specific teaching goals. Through taking the TGI, teachers make their teaching goals explicit. The handbook then guides teachers to the CATs that are most useful in assessing their priority teaching goals. The point is that teachers must have some vision about their role in the educational process. Classroom Assessment helps to implement the vision through evaluation of how well concrete goals are being accomplished.

While Classroom Assessment gives credence to the vision of individual teachers, educational quality at the institutional level is more than the sum of the parts. One of the most concrete ways to find out if a college is directing its teaching efforts toward accomplishing the goals of its mission statement is to obtain an institutional profile of the teaching goals of the faculty. If, for example, the "lofty piffle of the mission statement" promises to develop in students "an appreciation of other cultures," but only 15 percent of the faculty members consider such a goal "essential" to their own teaching (our actual finding from administering the TGI to more than 2800 college teachers), then questions must be raised about how well the institution is implementing the collective vision of its mission statement.

I2) **TQM requires leadership.** "TQM partisans want fewer managers, at least of the old type—powerful figures in sole command of vertical authority structures. Instead, they want leaders and of a new type— vision, givers, listeners, team-workers, committed to quality and customer needs, avid but patient for long term ends, orchestrators and enablers of people-driven improvements" (Marchese 1991).

Classroom Assessment is most successful on campuses where it is supported and encouraged by leaders of the type desired by TQM. Robert McCabe, President of Miami-Dade Community College, is the prototype of a TQM leader. His leadership provided the vision and support for the Teaching/ Learning project at Miami-Dade. Faculty were not only heavily "involved" in committees and task forces, they carried out the institution-wide vision of excellence in their own classrooms. It is significant that Miami-Dade requires the development of the human resources of the faculty through the participation of all faculty new to Miami-Dade in a graduate-level course in Classroom Assessment taught by the University of Miami.

Syracuse University is another large complex institution of higher education that is in the process of dramatic institutional change. Under the leadership of Chancellor Kenneth Shaw, Syracuse has newly articulated mission and vision statements that will guide the total institution as they change the institutional culture to that of a student-centered research university. "We shift our focus," claims Vice Chancellor Vincow (1993), "from our current emphasis on our teaching, our courses, our degree programs, our academic department structures, and look at everything we do from the viewpoint of the student, considering its impact on promoting the student's learning experience."

In conclusion, the challenges to higher education for the 21st Century are enormous. Basically, they boil down to offering high-quality education to the widest diversity of learners anywhere in the world, at a cost that will be supported by society. This chapter is not an argument for "squeezing the fat" out of education by cutting budgets and hoping higher education can adjust to under-funding and lack of community support. It is an appeal for careful and systematic analysis of the current processes, procedures, and structures of education to determine how best to meet the changing demands of the 21st Century. Current unprecedented pressures for change require dramatic response. TQM is one possible response that appears bold enough—at least in concept—to meet the challenge. And Classroom Assessment is one way to involve faculty in the substantial restructuring that is required by TQM.

References

Angelo, T. A. and K. P. Cross. 1993. *Classroom Assessment Techniques: A Handbook for Faculty.* 2d ed. San Francisco: Jossey-Bass.

Ausubel, D.P. 1977. "The Facilitation of Meaningful Verbal Learning in the Classroom." *Educational Psychologist* 12: 162-178.

"Belly of the Whale." 1993. *Pew Policy Perspectives* (August).

Cross, K. P. 1988. "In Search of Zippers." *AAHE Bulletin* 10 (4): 3-7.

Cross, K. P. 1992. Classroom Assessment for Academic Departments. Keynote speech at AAHE Assessment Forum, 22 May at Miami Beach.

Cross, K. P. 1993. "On College Teaching." *Journal of Engineering Education* 82 (1).

Cross, K. P., and T. A. Angelo. 1988. *Classroom Assessment Techniques: A Handbook for College Teachers.* Ann Arbor: University of Michigan, National Center for Research on the Improvement of Postsecondary Teaching and Learning (NCRIPTAL).

Hammer, M. 1990. "Reengineering Work: Don't Automate, Obliterate." *Harvard Business Review* July/August: 104-112.

Mangan, K. S. 1992. "TQM: Colleges Embrace the Concept of 'Total Quality Management.'" *Chronicle of Higher Education* (Aug. 12): A 25-26.

Marchese, T. 1991. "TQM Reaches the Academy." *AAHE Bulletin* 44 (November): 3-9.

McCabe, R. H., and M. S. Jenrette. 1990. "Leadership in Action: A Campuswide Effort to Strengthen Teaching." In *How Administrators Can Improve Teaching,* edited by P. Seldin and Associates. San Francisco: Jossey-Bass.

National Commission on Excellence in Education. 1983. *A Nation at Risk.* Washington, D.C.: U.S. Department of Education.

Seymour, D. 1991. "TQM On Campus: What the Pioneers Are Finding." *AAHE Bulletin* 44 (November): 10-13.

Spanbauer, S. J. 1992. *A Quality System for Education.* Milwaukee: ASQC Quality Press.

Vincow, G. 1993. Pursuing the Vision of a Student-Centered Research University: A Progress Report to the Faculty. Unpublished Paper.

The original version of this chapter appeared in *Teaching and Learning in the Community College*, by Terry O'Banion and Associates, Washington, DC: the Community College Press, 1993.

K. PATRICIA CROSS

K. Patricia Cross is the David Pierpont Gardner Professor of Higher Education in the Graduate School of Education at the University of California–Berkeley. Cross received her bachelor of science degree in mathematics from Illinois State University, and her master of arts in psychology and doctorate in social psychology from the University of Illinois.

Cross has had a varied career as a university administrator, researcher, and teacher. Cross is also the author of eight books—including *Beyond the Open Door, Accent on Learning*, and *Classroom Assessment Techniques* (with T. Angelo)—and more than 150 articles and chapters.

Cross has been recognized for her scholarship by election to the National Academy of Education and receipt of the E.F. Lindquist Award for research from the American Educational Research Association, of which she has also been elected president twice. She has been awarded many honors for leadership in higher education, among them the 1990 Leadership Award from the American Association of Community and Junior Colleges, and the Adult Educator of the Year Award from the Coalition of Adult Education Associations.

CHAPTER THIRTEEN:

QUALITY PROCESS MANAGEMENT FOR UNIVERSITIES AND COLLEGES

L. Edwin Coate

The Case for Action

By the year 2000, American colleges and universities will be lean and mean, service-oriented and science-minded, multicultural, and increasingly diverse—if they intend to survive.

In 1992, two-thirds of the nation's public institutions had operating budgets that were less than the previous year. Three years of revenue difficulties and poor public perception has led to increased tuition, higher fees, increased class size, layoffs, and reduced spending on maintenance, library acquisitions and salaries. Over the next ten years, U.S. universities and colleges will continue to face profound revenue shortfalls. We must either increase productivity and effectiveness or the next generation of citizens will face significantly reduced educational opportunities.

What is happening? Why do we need to change now? The first problem, of course, is the current recession or state of the economy. In the public sector, legislators and governors struggle to balance budgets with less revenue. In the private sector, families struggle to pay higher tuition and/or fees.

The second problem is too many students. Demographic forces continue to press for more seats in colleges and universities, and at the same time, more adults are trying to prepare for a new career as jobs of the past disappear.

The third area of concern is the credibility of higher education itself. We are under siege. We are told we cost too much, spend carelessly, plan myopically, teach poorly, and, when questioned, act defensively. According to pollster Louis Harris, only 25 percent of the public have confidence in the "people running higher education."

It is apparent that the current system is simply breaking down—often in ways we do not like—and we must be open to change. But in this department we do not have a good track record—academia has structural difficulties in reacting to change. We are committed to shared governance, to manage by consensus, and we encounter strong resistance to reshaping institutional goals. Yet governors, legislatures, business leaders and tax payers are demanding change. They want and expect us to identify and pursue ways to reduce costs while increasing productivity and effectiveness.

So change we must—the only question is whether we do it by design or by default.

Today, many universities and colleges are looking at the "quality movement" to see if it can provide a template for change. Questions about quality in education get at the "business of the business." In the past, quality in education was linked to the quantity of resources and an institution's reputation. Now the dialogue has changed. How do we assess the outcomes of higher education? How do we measure quality in teaching, research and service? Can we restructure our curricula to be more effective? Can we reduce the time it takes for our students to earn a degree? In what ways can we improve our service internally? Can we process new hires more quickly? Can we pay our bills faster?

Money alone will not provide answers to the these questions. One solution that begins to address these issues is to become a customer-focused institution—using the quality tools introduced by Deming in Japan in 1950 and introduced by Hammer here in the United States in 1990. This change to a customer-focused institution is touching the lives of almost everyone in our world—higher education seems to be one of the last bastions of resistance. But there is evidence that this revolution is touching higher education at last. Over 150 colleges and universities are now experimenting in some way with Total Quality Management (TQM) or Business Process Re-engineering (BPR).

These experiments with TQM and BPR in higher education raise a cadre of questions. Is there really valid evidence that sufficient organizational change is having a lasting impact on the quality of our higher educational institutions? Are there really sincere efforts to change the culture, measurement, infrastructure, motivation, planning, and technology systems in a comprehensive way? Are there serious efforts to be customer driven? Are we sincerely attempting to address the gap between customer expectations and our performance?

The answers are a cautious yes—not a resounding yes—but small steps are being taken by a few brave souls in community colleges and research universities across the nation. At Oregon State University (OSU) we attempted to answer these types of probing questions, and currently at the University of California–Santa Cruz (UCSC) we are attempting to address similar probing questions. This "peaceful revolution" is causing stress and strain in many aspects of our university lives. We are on the cutting edge of change—learning as we go—excited by new opportunities. Even though we are still uncomfortable using terms like "customer," "value added," "touch time," "processes," and "systems," we are trying to change and, in our own way, we are succeeding.

Historically changes occur when there is 1) sufficient dissatisfaction with things as they are, 2) a clear vision of an end goal, 3) a strategy for change to achieve the desired state, and 4) the knowledge and skills to achieve the change. This chapter discusses the need for change in higher education, and provides a vision and a strategy as well as the knowledge and skills to achieve the desired change.

The Vision

In 1776 Adam Smith described the roots of American work styles and organizational structures in his book, *The Wealth of Nations*. His division of labor embodied his observations that more products or services can be provided if specialized employees work in sequence, each performing a single task. This approach to work was improved upon by Frederick Taylor in 1916, but was not significantly changed in America until recently when we realized we were falling behind in world competition.

Today's universities and colleges, as well as private sector companies such as insurance firms and computer chip manufacturers, were all built around Smith and Taylor's central ideas—the division or specialization of labor and the consequent fragmentation of work. The larger the organization, the more specialized and fragmented is the work. For example, in higher education, our registration, admission, purchasing, and facilities management offices typically assign separate staff to

Quality Process Management   289

process standardized forms. They enter data and pass the forms on to supervisors for approval. The supervisor subsequently sends the form to another office for more data to be entered or sometimes for all the data to be re-entered. No one completes the entire job; they just perform piecemeal tasks. As these processes mature and evolve, we build in redundancy and control checks. Many processes now exceed 50 percent in non-value added work in our organizations.

In today's universities the staff may talk about serving customers, but the real job is still perceived as "keeping the boss happy." Many employees feel they are just a cog in the wheel. The best strategy is often seen as "keeping your head down and not making waves." When things go wrong it is the manager's job to solve the problem. After all, that is why he gets paid the big bucks. In turn, the manager is evaluated by the number of direct reports and the size of the budget he has— the one with the biggest empire wins. Sound familiar?

W. Edwards Deming (1992) realized that the way we in America were organizing work was not effective. He found in his research that 85 percent of the problems in organizations were occurring in processes, not people. But his key idea of focusing on process improvement presented a problem for U.S. management because most work is managed by focusing on tasks, jobs, people, and structures—not processes.

Process management was introduced in Japan by Deming in the early 1950s and is the one thing that is most often credited with Japan's business success since World War II. Process Management asks us to realize that customers pay our salaries and that we must provide a product or service that meets or exceeds their expectations. We must recognize that we get paid for value created. All employees must accept ownership of problems and actively participate in resolving them. Employees belong on teams—they fail or succeed together.

This is change in a big way. Getting people to accept the idea that their work lives will undergo radical change is not easy. After providing them with a compelling argument for change, we must give them a clear goal or a vision statement on which to focus. The vision statement for our process management effort at UC Santa Cruz is:

To be the campus known for quality in the best university system in the world. Our administrative goal at UCSC is to provide effective services to our students, faculty, staff, and other constituencies. These services will employ modern technology at the lowest reasonable cost. UCSC's administration will be largely decentralized, placing responsibility and accountability at the appropriate level closest to the transaction or client/customer. Administrative processes will avoid needless redundancy. Technology will enhance communication at all levels of the institution. Staff, faculty, and students alike will save time and money from improved administrative functions.

Customer Driven

Without students to teach, research to conduct, or services to provide, there is no business for colleges and universities. Without value there is no reason for customers to choose our institution over an increasingly large number of similar institutions. The number of colleges and universities in the United States has grown from approximately 1800 to over 3300 in just 40 years! Competition, market niche, empty seats, and empty beds are a new phenomenon to many of us, yet these are problems that have long been familiar to American businesses. What we must concentrate on now is continually increasing the value of our product—our teaching, research and service—to our customers.

The concept of creating value and passing it along to our customers is an approach that can transform rigid institutions into responsive, world-class colleges and universities. We want our customers to feel that they have received exceptional value for their dollar. When tuition was heavily subsidized, almost any level of teaching was of value; but with the cost of tuition skyrocketing, the value is now being scrutinized and questioned.

To be customer driven, we must be able to read our customers' minds, give them caring, personalized service, and provide them with the knowledge and skills they need to be successful. No small task!

So just who are our customers? Students, faculty, taxpayers, parents, legislators, citizens—the list goes on and on. The trick to being customer driven is to first recognize our customers, then identify their needs, wants and desires, and subsequently meet or exceed their expectations.

A New Management Model

Most institutions of higher education have developed around the bureaucratic organizational model. This model is hierarchical, procedural, and dependent on Adam Smith's specialization of labor, narrow delegation of authority, and complex procedures. The problems associated with this model include:

- Substantial organization layering;
- A high reliance on paper and forms to document decisions and transactions;
- Excessive points of control; and
- Excessive redundancy of operations.

Within the bureaucratic model, productivity is significantly reduced by the proliferation of unnecessary tasks while communication is blocked by vertical functional silos.

Quality Process Management

To foster productivity and service, a new management model is evolving on campuses like OSU and UCSC. Built on the concepts of process control (Deming 1992), this new model has evolved from implementing the new management tools of Total Quality Management (TQM) and Business Process Re-engineering (BPR). This new model I call "Quality Process Management."

"Quality Process Management" can be described as a disciplined, structural approach designed to meet or exceed the needs of the customer by improving the efficiency and effectiveness of our processes. This new model reflects the strategies of many industrial leaders, but only a very few campuses. It is meant to eliminate layers of hierarchy by decentralizing the authority for decision-making, by increasing spans of control, and by imbedding minimal internal controls within integrated information systems. The model delegates responsibility and authority to the lowest possible organizational level where the customer first interacts with the institution. It encompasses a set of human resource strategies that specifies expected employee behavior and rewards risk-taking, initiative, personal accountability, outcomes, collaboration, and customer service. Finally, the model uses process improvement teams to improve processes, and rewards teams accordingly.

But what exactly are processes? A process is a sequence of activities that is intended to achieve a result (create added value) for a customer. There are over 150 processes in a typical college or university. There are **academic processes**, which include teaching, research, technology transfer, and tenure giving. There are **auxiliary processes** such as food service, child care, mail service, and book sales. And there are **business** and **administrative processes** such as fund-raising, hiring, assigning space, allocating money, cleaning and maintenance of buildings, and distribution of payments.

The Diagnostic

Quality Process Management begins by identifying those processes that are not adding much value for the customer. A diagnostic is conducted through simple brainstorming by a core team of the best and brightest staff and faculty looking at the work outputs needed to meet the mission of the institution. At OSU and UCSC we began by looking at over 20 critical processes. Each process was looked at in terms of output volume, resource costs, customer satisfaction and customer importance. A diagnostic matrix was then developed as shown in Figure 1.

Figure 1

Process Evaluation Matrix					
Process	**Output Volume**	**Resource Costs**	**Customer Satisfaction**	**Customer Importance**	**Willingness To Change**
Acquire Goods	High	High	Low	High	High
Financial Transaction	Very High	High	Low	High	High
Manage Facilities	Medium	High	Low	High	Medium
Contracts & Grants Management	Medium	Medium	OK	High	Medium
Curriculum Development	Low	Low	OK	High	Low

Coate

Processes which have high output volume, high costs, low customer satisfaction, high customer importance, and recognize the need to change are candidates for radical redesign. At UCSC we found the first three items in Figure 1 to be candidates for Business Process Re-engineering (BPR). Alternatively, those processes which have low output volume, low cost and okay satisfaction (such as the last two items in Figure 1) were identified as candidates for the more gentle approach of Total Quality Management (TQM).

Process Mapping

After processes have been identified and diagnosed, those processes needing attention are then "mapped." Process Mapping traces the path of a service or product request through the organization leading to a final output which is delivered to an external customer. Overall, the objective is to understand the process—the activities, inputs and outputs, resources, costs, and value added work versus non-value added work. This "as is" baseline is established by making a process map.

The process map (or flow chart) is a visual way of recording each activity in a process. Mapping begins by team members going to the department where work is originated and then "walking each activity through the process." Team members observe and record the first activity in the process, then observe and record the physical flow of the paperwork or product. They subsequently identify the use (value) of the output of the activity. They then repeat each step for each activity as the transaction moves on through the process.

Once the process map is completed, the team members go back and add touch time (the amount of time an employee actually works on the transaction), lag time (the amount of time it takes for the paperwork to go to the next step), and error rate. Finally, the team determines if each activity is value added (an activity required by a customer that the customer is willing to pay for) or non-value added (an activity which can be eliminated by technology or is simply not needed).

Each process activity is analyzed by asking questions such as:

- What is being done?
- Is it necessary?
- Can it be eliminated?
- What are the major bottlenecks?
- Where is the work done and/or who does it?
- Is the work done manually?
- How long does it take?
- What are the costs?
- What is the workload?
- What is the quality?
- When/how does the customer interface with the process?

The key issues and questions are then summarized and listed under six headings on a cause and effect (fishbone) diagram:

Figure 2

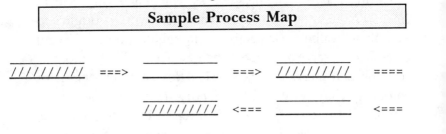

Sample Process Map

//////// ===> _____ ===> //////// ====

_____ //////// <=== _____ <===

//////// Non-value Added   _____ Value Added

Figure 3

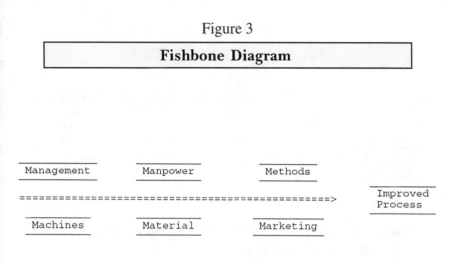

Fishbone Diagram

By adding up touch time and lag time and identifying both non-value added work and the number of people that actually touch each form across campus, a business case for improvement can then be developed. For each process total FTE and costs are determined, and both non-value added work and estimated savings are identified (figure 4).

This data allows us to prioritize our process redesign efforts and determine which process improvement tool to use. The two most popular process improvement tools are Total Quality Management and Business Process Re-engineering.

Continuous Process Improvement/TQM

Total Quality Management (TQM) is a commitment to excellence by everyone in an organization—excellence achieved through teamwork and a process of continuous improvement. TQM requires dedication to being the best in

Quality Process Management   297

Figure 4

| | | | Total | |
| | | Estimated | Non-value | Estimated |
Process	FTE	Costs	Added	Savings
		Building the Business Case		
Acquire goods	97	$4.1M	52-71%	$1.8M
Record trans.	120	$5.2M	30-100%	$1.7M
Manage facilities	72	$7.4M	9-23%	$1.1M
Hire employees	80	$3.4M	11-23%	$0.5M

delivering high quality services which meet or exceed the expectations of the customer.

Total Quality Management is a structural procedure for creating organization-wide participation in planning and implementing a continuous improvement process that meets or exceeds the expectations of the customer. It is built on the Deming assumption that 85 percent of our problems are process problems.

Continuous Process Improvement teams are at the heart of TQM. Better solutions emerge when everyone is given a chance to work on process problems. Just as importantly, solutions are accepted and implemented more quickly and last longer because the people affected have helped develop them. Continuous Process Improvement teams are composed of people who normally work together on the process being reviewed. The team examines a process that can be improved by utilizing resources they already control. Each team includes a team leader—most often the supervisor of the process being reviewed—a facilitator/trainer, and no more than ten team members. The team sponsor is usually the team leader's boss; the team sponsor ensures that the team's work is linked to the university's vision.

TQM teams use a ten-step problem-solving model to guide their work:

- **Step One**: The team identifies and interviews customers of the process to determine which services are not meeting their needs.
- **Step Two**: The team charts customer problems, selects one major problem to work on, prepares an issue statement to direct the study, and uses customer data to set a measure of improved performance.
- **Step Three**: The team constructs detailed flow charts/process maps of the process and sub-processes as they currently exist.
- **Step Four**: The team brainstorms possible causes of the process problem, then uses TQM tools (such as the cause and effect diagram) to select critical causes for further study.
- **Step Five**: The team collects data, graphs it concisely, and uses it to determine root causes of the customer problem. This data becomes a benchmark for measuring future progress.
- **Step Six**: The team develops possible solutions for the root causes that are verified by data, then measures them against criteria that reflect customer needs.
- **Step Seven**: The team identifies benchmarks for the process being studied, i.e., processes used by other organizations or work areas that produce a high quality product or service. Possible solutions are measured against the benchmarks.
- **Step Eight**: The best solutions are implemented, their performance is monitored, and they are adopted if they work.
- **Step Nine**: The team measures the results of the improvement and relines performance measures. If the

problems are solved, the "fixes" are standardized and become standard operating procedure.

• **Step Ten**: The team selects another process to review and improve.

Continuous Process Improvement/TQM is a slow, deliberate way to improve work processes. It is transitional and fits well with the academic culture. Process improvements are often small in nature and build up incrementally over time. Many organizations take over five years to truly achieve significant change.

Within the Quality Process Management model, Continuous Quality Improvement/TQM is used for those processes that are not broken but that can be improved. Most processes contain at least 30 percent non-value added work; Continuous Process Improvement/TQM is very effective in improving these processes over time. Experience to date shows that over 70 percent of work processes in academic institutions can benefit from this form of process improvement.

Business Process Re-engineering

Business Process Re-engineering (BPR) is defined as the fundamental rethinking and radical redesign of processes to achieve dramatic improvements in critical measures of performance such as cost, quality, service and speed. Others say it means simply "starting over" (Hammer 1993). As it relates to higher education, BPR means asking the question, "If we were recreating the university or college, given what we now know and given current technology, what would it look like?" Re-engineering a university means throwing out old systems and processes, going back to the beginning and inventing a better way of doing things. In quality terms, re-engineering is used to achieve major "breakthroughs" in areas identified by strategic or "Hoshin" planning.

How does a university reengineer its processes, both business and academic? Where do the ideas for radical change come from?

Although many corporations are using BPR, to date only four or five universities have experience in this area. At UCSC and OSU we have developed a body of BPR techniques—and our experience has been encouraging. Our results indicate that given intelligence and imagination, these techniques can provide cost savings of from 20 percent to 50 percent in one to three years!

Information Technology (IT) is often the enabler that allows us to re-engineer our processes. This does not mean simply automating existing work. We do not want to repave the cow paths. Rather, IT allows us to enter data only once, send it quickly where it needs to go, and free us from repetitive work.

BPR is the most creative part of the Quality Process Management model. Redesign asks the process team to abandon the familiar and search for the unknown. It demands imagination and vision. Team members are asked to forget about the rules, regulations, policies, and values.

Re-engineering teams use an eight step problem-solving model to guide their redesign work:

- **Step One**: The team identifies and interviews the customers of the process selected to be re-engineered to find out which services are really needed and which services now provided are not meeting the customers' expectations.
- **Step Two**: The team constructs a detailed flow chart of the process and all sub-processes as they currently exist.
- **Step Three**: The team brainstorms new innovative ways to provide needed services to the customer. A new

"process map" is developed which identifies a radical redesign of the process.

- **Step Four**: The team identifies "best in class" processes used by other universities and business organizations. Teams measure performance by "best in class" organizations and benchmark against the new redesign.
- **Step Five**: The team develops needed system architecture to support the redesigned process. An RFP is prepared and a vendor is selected.
- **Step Six**: The team develops an action plan for implementation.
- **Step Seven**: The team develops a training plan for new skills needed by staff and skills needed for any displaced/reassigned staff members.
- **Step Eight**: The team oversees implementation of the redesigned process.

Acquisitions: A Case Study

Acquisition of goods was the first process selected for redesign at both UCSC and OSU. It contains four sub-processes: requisitions, ordering, delivering, and paying. Annually at UCSC we requisition and purchase over 87,000 items. We deliver over 39,000 orders and pay with 88,000 checks. Our major customers include faculty, staff, students, and vendors. Service providers work in all campus units—over 95 FTE are spent annually to support this process.

The redesign team included staff and faculty selected from across campus units such as deans offices, department offices and business offices as well as purchasing and receiving. The team leader was the Director of Purchasing.

When surveying customers, dissatisfaction with process performance was high. It takes seven approvals, five forms, and 50 days to order and receive goods using this process.

During mapping we found data was entered six times. Over 2.6 million dollars was spent in touch time. Non-value activities exceeded fifty percent (52 percent to 71 percent) with a lengthy turnaround time (12 days) to issue purchase orders to vendors. The process was completely manual. No wonder users were experiencing extreme frustration!

The new redesign for acquisition included significant changes in the orientation, values, and work flow of the central purchasing department as well as the overall organization. The new design transformed central purchasing from a reactive paper-driven unit to a contract negotiations unit, arranging for discounted purchase contracts negotiated in advance. By partnering with vendors, the number of vendors were significantly reduced and discounts increased.

As a part of the new process, data is now entered into one data base by the customer; paper forms have been eliminated. Costs/FTE have been reduced by at least 25 percent. Turnaround time has been reduced to five days and customer needs have been exceeded.

Conclusions

Quality Process Management is an exciting new way to improve the quality of work performed for our customers. It puts customers at the top of the organization and asks our leaders to provide direction, empowerment and support for the people who create value for our customers.

Quality Process Management requires significant cultural changes that begin with leadership. It requires leadership to reduce fear of change, encourage open communications, push decision making to the lowest practical level, and build performance around systems that motivate people to grow and develop.

Leadership in a quality university or college is essential to create the vision and provide the direction that will unify and inspire these efforts. A compelling vision has the power to motivate. Clear communication of our campus direction focuses our energies and talents on the shared purpose and common goals of Quality Process Management.

Leadership helps set these shared goals and translate them into action. Quality Process Management provides the structure to planning and implementation that can help leaders focus and direct their energies to improve critical processes.

Significant changes that have been experienced at UCSC and OSU include:

- Elimination of jobs (in some instances, several existing jobs were merged into one);
- Workers' roles changed from controlled to empowered;
- Work is now performed where it makes sense, work steps are performed in a logical order, and redundant tasks have been eliminated;
- Checks and controls were significantly reduced;
- Jobs changed from simple to complex;
- Work units changed from functional departments to process teams;
- Values changed from protective to productive;
- Organizational structures changed from hierarchical to flat;
- Salary structures are changing from salaries based on the size of budget and staff to salaries based on results;
- Systems changed from paving cow paths to enabling radical changes; and
- Work is performed for the customer, not the business.

As described above, this constitutes significant change from the bureaucratic management model currently in use at most colleges and universities today.

One of the enduring characteristics of our national university system has been its stability. But that stability has a tremendous downside: it becomes an excuse to resist change. To believe that we can preserve the American university as it is today is to ignore the reality of our rapidly changing world and its expectations of us. However, change of the magnitude required today can only be made with the use of new methodologies combined with strong leadership and administrative support. Quality Process Management is an exciting new management tool that offers significant improvement over the current bureaucratic model used by most institutions of higher education.

> There is nothing more difficult to carry out, nor more dangerous to handle than to initiate a new order of things. For the reformer has enemies in all those who profit from the old order and only lukewarm defenders in all those who would profit by the new order . . .
>
> (Machiavelli)

References

Deming, W. E. 1992. *Out of the Crisis.* Cambridge: Massachusetts Institute of Technology.

Hammer. 1993. *Business Process Re-engineering.*

Smith, A. 1937. *The Wealth of Nations.* New York: The Modern Library.

Machiavelli, N.1976. *The Prince.* 1st Ed. Indianapolis: Bobbs-Merrill.

L. EDWIN COATE

L. Edwin Coate is vice chancellor for business and administrative services at University of California at Santa Cruz. He has served as deputy regional administrator for the EPA, director of the office of environmental affairs for the county of San Diego, and general manager/chief engineer of a large utility in California. He has also taught at four universities, and was at one time the managing partner of a management consulting firm in San Diego. He continues to work as a consultant for several firms.

Chapter Fourteen:

Continuous Organizational Renewal is Total Quality at the University of Arizona

Vern R. Johnson and Kenneth R. Smith

It would be a mistake to assume that what has served universities well in the past will continue to serve us in the future. An increasing portion of the public does not think universities are doing acceptable jobs with teaching or fiscal responsibilities. University budgets are becoming increasingly constrained and are expected to increase at a constrained rate in the foreseeable future. International competitiveness and the state of the economy have caused the public to need and expect more from universities than in the past.

The University of Arizona recognizes that like many of its peers its past growth has resulted in a certain mismatch between programs, mission, and resources. At his inauguration in May of 1992, President Manuel T. Pacheco addressed a basic need for organizational renewal and how best to adjust present reality to match the requirements of the University of the future. Pacheco's vision of the future for the University of Arizona involves an institution that combines high quality undergraduate education with a steadily advancing reputation for leading-edge research. It involves an institution that has brought its enrollment patterns into balance with its facilities and budgets, that is dedicated to the maintenance of a diverse campus community, and one that is characterized by a strong and constructive sense of community.

Universities are relative newcomers to Total Quality Management. The University of Arizona story mirrors much of what is occurring nationwide, but important differences also exist. With Pacheco providing leadership, and based on a proud history as an innovative and ambitious institution, the UA is working on a complete transformation of its culture and systems. This transformation involves a comprehensive application of total quality principles embracing all seven elements of the Baldrige framework. We refer to the transformation process as Continuous Organizational Renewal (CORe). CORe means total quality at the University of Arizona.

The scope of change being deployed includes: renewed leadership, strategic planning, human resource development, process management, integration of data and analysis for management decisions and planning, and a new desire to achieve results that enhance teaching, research, and public service in support of our customers' needs. This chapter describes the quality transformation that is occurring at the University of Arizona in terms of these seven quality elements.

We started with small steps designed to improve communications and decision-making. The president restructured the administrative organization setting in motion a wholesale examination of all programs, academic and non-academic alike, in light of their centrality, quality, and efficiency. Titled the "Program for the Assessment of Institutional Priorities," (PAIP) this effort provided a current situation analysis of each University unit.

Second, a CORe team was appointed to introduce the campus to the concept of organizational renewal and the principles of total quality. This introduction came with the support and mentoring of Intel Corporation, which provided a full-time loaned executive and access to their extensive experience and well-developed quality training materials.

The value of CORe to the University will be measured by our progress with performance indicators that we are just beginning to define. Our customers, primarily students and research sponsors, but also families, employers, practicing professionals, faculty, staff, legislators, sports fans, and others will tell us how we are doing if we listen. The UA is doing the hard work, doing it the right way, and intends to be among the first universities in the nation to reap the benefits of a transformation in the way we work and deliver value to our customers.

Leadership

During his inaugural address, Pacheco (1992) expressed his concern that, "Business as usual is no longer an acceptable axiom, and along with our sister universities across the country, the University of Arizona is contemplating a certain degree of mismatch between programs, missions, and resources. Our most basic need is the need for organizational renewal. By organizational renewal, I do not mean reporting relationships and organization charts. What I have in mind is the more important matter of collectively addressing the very soul of a university—what it does, why it does it, and how best to adjust present reality to better match the vision."

In July 1992, a partnership to assist in the implementation of an initiative in continuous organizational renewal was created with the Intel Corporation. The University committed itself to implement a quality strategy involving:

- leadership from the top down.
- management via a CORe team that reports directly to the UA leadership.
- leadership by example based on identification of pilot areas for implementation.
- assignment of a senior manager to direct the CORe program, and
- development of a UA CORe quality curriculum and tools for all employees.

The partnership included the provision of an Intel consultant to work full time with a CORe program manager and provide:

- Consulting support to assist in the application of a total quality approach to academic, research, support and administrative services.
- Assistance in building total quality knowledge and skill in leadership, strategic planning, information systems, human resource development, process management, quality results and customer satisfaction.
- Coaching to senior leadership on the role modeling of quality behaviors.
- Facilitation for management and process-improvement teams with training and deployment of the quality materials, systems, methods and tools.
- Consulting on the adaptation of Intel materials to the University culture.
- Training of the CORe program manager to enable the development of an independent UA CORe program.

Once the partnership was initiated, the president and his

Cabinet embarked on a series of training experiences based on the values needed for quality leadership. Since CORe's inception, they have attended a series of leadership workshops averaging more than 10 hours per month. Some of the topics addressed in training include:

- CORe Quality Commitment (an overview of the UA TQM initiative)
- Team Building
- Quality Leadership Series (customer satisfaction, data-based decisions, trust and teamwork, respect and investment in people, and process focus)
- Effective Meetings
- Change Management
- Management by Planning (a strategic planning and operating system)
- Malcolm Baldrige Quality Criteria Assessment
- Managing for Improved Through-put Time
- Process Management
- Quality Tools

This unprecedented commitment has engaged the senior leadership team in a dialog that educates, challenges, and is changing behavior. After a year of training, increased emphasis is now being placed on performance to achieve results.

Starting this fall, the president's Quality Leadership Program begin. This 40-hour course co-taught by the faculty of the business college and the Cabinet members is designed to push down decision-making in the organization by training senior and mid-level managers in the UA quality values and behaviors, to develop knowledge and skills to improve management performance, and to promote a shared culture and vision of management at the University. Additionally, the program will break down organizational barriers and enhance inter-departmental communication by bringing together managers from different areas.

Total Quality at the University of Arizona   311

CORe leadership is provided by the president. Under his direction, the Cabinet CORe Team provides the University community with support services including consultation, training, facilitation, and communication regarding quality activities. These services are designed to support changes in behaviors and attitudes, break down barriers, build communities, and create a culture of trust, teamwork, and respect. Specifically, CORe strategic objectives include:

- Communication: Create a broad understanding of CORe and how it can help improve the University's performance.
- Quality Training: Provide a system of knowledge and skills that empower all employees to contribute effectively through teams to meet the University's quality and operational goals.
- Deployment: Deploy resources and support of quality teams and evaluate CORe's performance in supporting quality improvement.
- Improvement Project Management: Prioritize and support University process improvement projects. Through CORe, the senior leadership has established a set of values for communicating and reinforcing the organization's commitment to quality and customer focus. The following values and the behaviors that support them were used in the development of the President's Quality Leadership Program.
- Excellence: The hallmarks of the products and services we provide are intellectual integrity, fiscal responsibility, and good citizenship. The level of excellence we attain is determined by those we serve.
- Innovation: Academic freedom is fundamental to the ability to embrace change. We must encourage and reward informed risk-taking and develop the insight,

Johnson and Smith

courage, and patience needed to participate at the cutting-edge of innovation.

• Customer Orientation: We will provide quality products and services on a timely basis, and at a minimal cost to those we serve.

• Trust and Teamwork: The University is a place where diversity is applauded and people learn and collaborate across boundaries of discipline and culture. Trust and teamwork will thrive when all employees are empowered and accountable for their actions in meeting the institution's mission.

• Data Based Decisions: Our ability to track and comprehend change is fundamental to our success. Data must be readily available to all employees to support planning, decision-making, and everyday activities.

• Continuous Improvement: We are committed to overcoming barriers and demonstrating the discipline to continuously improve the processes and the organizational structure that support our mission.

• Great Place to Work: Since the treatment received by employees is mirrored in the way they treat those they serve, a long-range outlook, supportive work environment, and adequate infrastructure are key to our success in meeting the needs of our many customers. We strive to create an environment in which respect for each other, positive attitudes, willingness to recognize, and reward behaviors that support our values combine to make us an asset to the community and place where we enjoy working each and every day.

Cabinet members have accepted ownership of individual CORe projects aimed at significant improvements in managing the University and have encouraged the use of TQM principles and methods in their units. In order to implement this program, the Cabinet committed a day a month to project reviews of CORe activities in order to assure that this incredible commitment is translated into performance and results. Pacheco, the provost, the Cabinet, and the Cabinet CORe Team members are regularly involved in public engagements regarding CORe both on and off campus. Working in concert with the Staff Advisory Council, the president and provost have conducted forums open to all employees and have written extensively for the employee newspaper. More than 2,000 of the University's 12,300 employees have received training as a result of CORe initiated efforts. These activities have resulted in general recognition that senior leadership is seriously committed to CORe, that the University has adopted an attractive new way of solving problems and seeking improvements, and that new opportunities exist for all employees to contribute to the well being of the institution.

The serious challenge during the next year is reaching and inviting participation of the remaining staff and convincing the faculty that the culture supported by CORe is an essential ingredient in the University's future success. Total quality principles call for all University employees to become more responsible for planning and decision-making than in the past. The president has acknowledged that faculty members are skeptical as to whether total quality principles are applicable in a university setting after being developed and utilized by industry and business.

Driven by a strategic planning and operation process called Management by Planning (MBP), the University has initiated activities to move our present situation ever closer to our vision. As outlined in Figure 1, the University's mission is the foundation for its quality values which in turn define behaviors which will be rewarded. With the support of CORe quality tools, systems, and environment, employees will man-

Figure 1

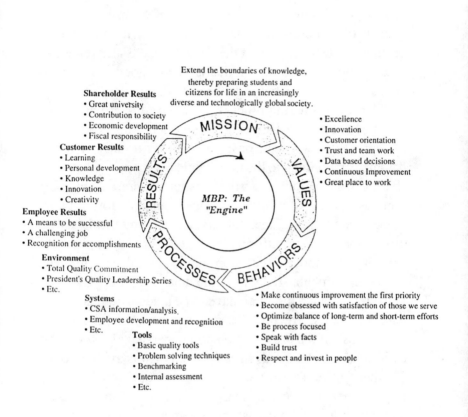

Extend the boundaries of knowledge,
thereby preparing students and
citizens for life in an increasingly
diverse and technologically global society.

Shareholder Results
- Great university
- Contribution to society
- Economic development
- Fiscal responsibility

Customer Results
- Learning
- Personal development
- Knowledge
- Innovation
- Creativity

Employee Results
- A means to be successful
- A challenging job
- Recognition for accomplishments

Environment
- Total Quality Commitment
- President's Quality Leadership Series
- Etc.

Systems
- CSA information/analysis
- Employee development and recognition
- Etc.

Tools
- Basic quality tools
- Problem solving techniques
- Benchmarking
- Internal assessment
- Etc.

MISSION

VALUES

RESULTS

*MBP: The
"Engine"*

PROCESSES

BEHAVIORS

- Excellence
- Innovation
- Customer orientation
- Trust and team work
- Data based decisions
- Continuous Improvement
- Great place to work

- Make continuous improvement the first priority
- Become obsessed with satisfaction of those we serve
- Optimize balance of long-term and short-term efforts
- Be process focused
- Speak with facts
- Build trust
- Respect and invest in people

Total Quality at the University of Arizona   315

age the many processes that produce the products and services needed by our customers, stakeholders, and employees.

Information and Analysis

During the past year, as the University undertook careful analysis of all internal processes in its effort to improve the quality of planning and decision-making, it immediately became evident that one of the most critical issues related to quality improvement was the availability of good, hard, accessible, and reliable data for decision-making.

The data-gathering process has evolved over past years, and now each major University unit collects the data it needs to support its own decisions. The data are usually stored in databases belonging to the unit. Typically there is substantial sharing of data up and down the University hierarchy, but each unit has developed its own rules and standards for defining, gathering, analyzing, maintaining, and sharing the data. Too often these rules are informal and inconsistently applied. As a result, data supported decision-making is both decentralized and compartmentalized within the units. Major decisions by University leadership often have to be made with inadequate data and poorly structured procedures for data analysis.

Because of the proliferation of independent data systems, over 30 major databases have evolved, it was evident to the Cabinet CORe Team that a major objective should be the improvement of data and analysis to support planning, decision-making, and process improvement. Cross-functional teams were formed to address the following questions:

- What decisions need to be made?
- What data are necessary to make these decisions?
- What organizational structure should be used to gather the data from its sources and deliver it to those making decisions?

- What technological infrastructure should be used to gather the data from its sources and deliver it to the decision-makers?

The teams assigned to the first two questions started by gaining a clear understanding of the University's mission and holding discussions with decision-makers and users of data across the University. The teams assigned to the last two questions started by assessing the available technology, human resources, and existing data, giving special attention to the units that make decisions and the units which have the data. In effect, the first two teams focused on what the University needs in the way of data and decision support capability. The last two teams focused on the organizational and technological systems needed to create and deliver in data and decision support. The ultimate decision was to capitalize on the benefit of distributed information gathering and analyses, but develop an organizational mechanism for coordinating analyses and reporting for the institution as a whole.

Creating the necessary technological and organizational environment is a first step toward a system in which all current and historic data of the institution are available in real time to all employees who need them. With an increase in computing power and the advent of client/server software, the University expects to be able to support continuous improvements of its processes based on data. The organizational strategy proposed is one that is amenable to technological advancements, one of the objectives in developing the system. The process adopted takes advantage of the strengths within the various units of the current system and provides coordination among them. It will lead to accurate, accessible, and consistent data for planning and management decision-making throughout the University.

Strategic Quality Planning

The mission of the UA is to challenge and extend the boundaries of knowledge, thereby preparing students and citizens for life in an increasingly diverse and technologically global society. This is operationalized through four University objectives:

- Provide top quality educational programs and services that will attract and graduate an excellent and diverse student body.
- Perform research and creative activity of significant impact in selected areas that are integrated with the educational experience.
- Offer an environment that supports all members of the University community.
- Transfer expertise to address state, national, and international needs.

Strategic planning is the process of moving the University from its current situation toward accomplishment of its mission. In the past, budgeting and strategic planning activities have been isolated from one another, and neither has involved measurement of customer satisfaction, attainment of institution-wide objectives, or active participation of the University community on a continuous basis. The newly implemented planning process seeks to change all of this. Management by Planning is a strategic planning and operating system adapted by the University from the Intel Corporation.

The University's strategic planning approach was created by a cross-functional team of faculty, staff, students, and administrators who determined that:

- strategic planning, budgeting and quality evaluation must be part of the same process.
- all facets of the University community must be continuously involved.

- all activities must be mission driven with direction from the senior leadership of the UA.
- all planning must be cross-functional and avoid being limited to administrative "silos."
- all activities must be data driven.

On the basis of these principles, MBP was adapted to meet University needs and culture. MBP training materials were created and over 200 employees have been trained to develop, implement, and review strategic quality plans. This is the beginning of a plan to deploy MBP throughout the University.

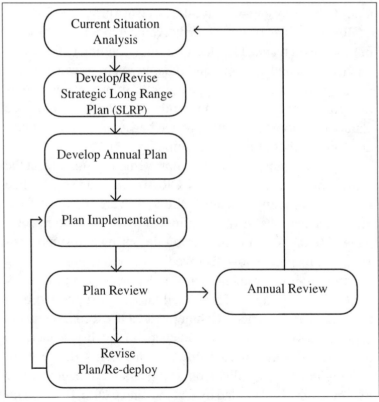

Figure 2

Human Resource Development and Management

The President's Cabinet recognized the importance of employee well-being, and made creating an environment that supports all members of the University community one of the four University objectives to be pursued in coming years.

Prior to CORe, the means available for employees to contribute effectively to meeting University objectives were primarily through service on committees and advisory bodies or through requests from administrators for consultation. The power to take action and correct deficiencies was not usually a part of the process, thus problems were reacted to rather than identified and systematically addressed in a proactive fashion. CORe emphasizes employee involvement in forums, process improvement teams, facilitator training, training in the use of quality tools and systems, and redeployment to value-added work when prior jobs disappear due to improvement activities. Redeployment is supported through the UA Employee Career Development Center, which began operation in January 1993 as part of the CORe initiative.

In order to support process improvement teams and, at the same time, not build up a CORe bureaucracy, part-time process improvement team facilitators were recruited from across the campus. A first contingent of 20 facilitators completed 80 hours of training during the spring and summer of 1993 and many are now deployed to support teams. Training of process-improvement teams is deployed just-in-time by the CORe facilitators. These facilitators are supported by a team of master trainers. Cabinet and CORe Team members also are involved, both as teachers of quality leadership material and as mentors to facilitators and teams. Requests for training in CORe Quality Commitment and Management by Planning are also handled by Cabinet and CORe Team members. All training activities are evaluated to assure continuous improvement.

The CORe strategic objective for training is providing for adaptation of Intel Corporation materials and the training of facilitators. Intel Corporation provides a curriculum with more than 400 hours of training on quality issues which the University can utilize, but adaptation of these materials is critical. Training materials are adapted for the UA culture and then go through alpha and beta testing to assure they meet our needs. As of this writing, CORe Quality Commitment and Management by Planning course materials are completely adapted. Four other programs are in the process of adaptation: Quality Tools, Effective Meetings, Quality Leadership Series, and Internal Assessment. Others will follow as needed.

Management of Process Quality

The quality forums held during the past year, and the PAIP results described above, have resulted in requests for assistance in process improvement and have caused the CORe program to create and pilot a process improvement technique. This is outlined by the following sequence of steps:

1) Develop the management team that is responsible for the process.
2) Identify improvement opportunities. (Identify the opportunity and develop a statement of the problem, its scope, indicators of success, and its customers.)
3) Identify ownership and train. (Form a team of cross-functional employees who have expertise and access to needed resources. Train them in team dynamics, basic quality tools, data gathering, managing for improved through-put time, effective meetings, benchmarking, and problem-solving.)
4) Document the process. (Gather data relative to customer needs, the functions performed by each individual involved in the process, the process flow chart,

through-put time, basic unit of measure and volumes, variations, process times, and documents used.)

5) Evaluate and benchmark processes. (Analyze data and compare to the best.)

6) Develop a plan. (Develop alternatives, select a plan, verify its value based on data, develop a Gantt chart for plan implementation, define new management and process team activities, and get management acceptance.)

7) Execute the plan on a pilot basis.

8) Review performance and make adjustments as required.

9) Standardize changes for cross-campus implementation.

10) Continuously improve. Specific examples of teams using this technique include:

- The Telecom Process Improvement Team implemented improvements in the process of installing analog and digital phone lines on campus to decrease the through-put time for orders from 38 to 3 days. The steps to process all types of service orders are now being handled in a more efficient, effective, and consistent way that enables most of their completion time to be cut by two thirds. This improvement was accompanied by redeployment of three employees.

- The Graduate Student Financial Assistance Process Improvement Team is piloting their new design of a system that will better serve graduate students and the departments that recommend financial assistance for them. The new system decreased the time required to credit awards to the graduate students' accounts from 79 to 2 days. The aca-

Johnson and Smith

demic department will experience reduced paperwork and will know almost immediately which students will receive financial support.

- A pilot project in matrix management was initiated. This management project placed representatives of the Controller's Office and Hillman Resources directly within two University units (the Graduate College and the Animal Care unit) to understand customer needs from first-hand knowledge and provide expert financial and Hillman resource services. Duplicative bookkeeping, databases, and paperwork have been reduced, and seven employees were redeployed to other University jobs. The successes of this project are now being experienced, and business partnerships across functional boundaries are being planned in many operational areas.

Process improvement teams are being initiated with CORe facilitation and support to address many other areas around the University. Several cabinet level initiatives to improve business processes and support services also are currently under way.

Quality and Operational Results

Quality and operational results define the impact of our total quality efforts on the products and services we provide to our customers to fulfill our mission. They also deal with the ability of our customers to better perform their functions because of our products and services.

During the first year of CORe activities we have concentrated on leadership training, implementation of an internal CORe structure capable of supporting continuous organizational renewal, development and empowerment of employ-

Total Quality at the University of Arizona   323

ees, and initiation of a number of pilot process improvement projects that focus on critical University processes. These activities have been aimed at reinventing the University and changing the campus culture to one that focuses on the values and behaviors outlined earlier in this chapter.

In the next few years, this focus will expand to institutional strategic planning, the definition of customer focused performance indicators and goals that assure quality and operational results, implementation of a campus-wide information system capable of supporting continuous organizational renewal, and further progress in developing a CORe culture. The results from CORe activities that have been completed to date have been very impressive indicators of what we can achieve as we concentrate on providing University customers with the products and services outlined in our mission.

Customer Focus and Satisfaction

The customers of the University occur in three primary groupings: students, research sponsors and recipients, and the community, including both state and national communities. Prior to the development of CORe, customer focus was not a matter for institution-wide discussion. It is still difficult for some faculty and administrators to comprehend students as anything other than the products of a system of education. To describe the student as a customer conjures up images of naive students telling faculty what to teach. The idea of students as choice-making individuals whose requirements need to be met for the institution to succeed is mostly held by those organizations that provide direct services, and even there the parental assumption that "father or mother knows best" is still prevalent. Students simply are not asked, nor expected to know, what is best for them. This part of our culture needs to change.

Johnson and Smith

Customer requirements are defined as a result of:
- interaction with employers of graduates.
- career planning and placement activities.
- surveying present and prospective students regarding their expectations.
- participation in national academic organizations.
- focus groups and advisory councils.
- the generation of new knowledge that requires curricular changes.
- faculty task forces studying our present educational offerings.

Historically, the technical expertise of faculty and administrators have determined what would be taught and which services would be provided. Fragmented approaches involving demographic data, placement testing, or surveys determined requirements. The ability to anticipate the lifelong requirements of a university graduate are complicated by the increasingly rapid obsolescence of knowledge. Thus, in recent years the University has put increasing emphasis on learning how to learn and preparing students for lifelong education.

Within the context of CORe training, the Cabinet has begun to address customer needs and satisfaction. The provost has defined customer satisfaction issues to be addressed, and indicators and goals are being established to measure progress toward satisfaction and service. Clearly, this University has only begun to address the issue of customer focus and satisfaction.

It was not until recently that the University began to evaluate interactions that occur across the boundaries of academic units and their consequences to students. CORe is setting up the infrastructure which will make cross-functional customer support more likely in the future through project improvement teams, integrated data-based decision-making, and management of process quality.

While the UA commitment to research and its historic commitment as a land grant university to cooperative extension and other public services has always had a strong customer focus, the University has also begun to recognize the importance of meeting the expectations of students. As a result, the provost recently outlined a series of initiatives with the following targeted outcomes:

- All students will be able to obtain the classes necessary for meeting their general education and major requirements in proper sequence.
- All students will receive adequate advising for their academic programs and career needs.
- Graduates will be trained and educated to compete and excel in their chosen fields.
- The percentage of lower-division courses taught by professorial faculty will be increased.

Of critical importance, indicators and goals are under development for each of these commitments in order to monitor progress.

The University compares itself with the American Association of University (AAU) Institutions both in research activities and in academic programs. However, customer satisfaction benchmarking with other institutions has not yet been done. While CORe is addressing the need to create a system that will support this type of benchmarking, goals and indicators are not yet developed that will tell us how we compare.

Summary

Our disciplined approach has developed a broad based understanding of the importance to the University's future success, of embracing a change strategy built around a total quality philosophy. There is recognition of the need to create a new culture in which the entire university community is brought together in support of those we serve. This culture will emphasize an institutional perspective, an environment of trust, teamwork, and respect for the contributions of all employees, while maintaining the academic values that have produced national class creative achievements.

The leadership of the University accepts this challenge and embraces the values and behaviors that are essential to support this new culture. Due to the work of hundreds of people, the infrastructure for total quality is being put in place at the University of Arizona. We are creating:

- quality leadership throughout the institution.
- data and information to support customers.
- strategic quality planning.
- investments in human resources and training to empower employees.
- process management as means for eliminating non-value added activities.
- recognition and rewards for behaviors that will yield quality results.
- a focus on meeting the needs of our customers.

As our journey toward total quality moves into its second year, our goal is to achieve major breakthroughs in the way we do business, not incremental change. Thus far our activities have been measurable, significant, and surprising! It is our intention to continue on the road of continuous organizational renewal.

The dedication and commitment of many individuals to the total quality initiative at the University of Arizona is the basis for the progress reported in this chapter. The partnership with the Intel Corporation has served as an incredible catalyst for change, and we are indebted to Harry Hollack, Eamon Malone, Jim Grenier, and Susan Strick. The leadership provided by President Manuel Pacheco, Provost Paul Sypherd, and Senior Vice President for Business Affairs Joel Valdez has been a force that is helping the campus to understand and accept the values for doing our business in a new way. The Cabinet and its CORe Team have grown with the program and are making it happen. We especially wish to acknowledge the following for helping to compile the information on which this paper was based: Allan Beigel, Janet Bingham, Jerry Black, Elise Calmus, J.D. Garcia, Martha Gilliland, Andy Heck, Stacy Henegar, Rich Howard, Sue Leverenz, Janice Liebold, Ernie Smerdon, Michael Ray, and Dennis St. Germaine.

References

Pacheco, M. T. Inaugural Address. City of Tucson. University of Arizona, May 1992.

VERN R. JOHNSON

V ern R. Johnson is the associate dean of the College of Engineering and Mines at the University of Arizona. He earned his bachelor of science and doctorate in electrical engineering from the University of Utah.

A few of Johnson's professional experiences include associate dean and assistant dean of the College of Engineering and Mines at the University of Arizona, quality manager (CORe) at the University of Arizona, and visiting fellow in academic administration at Cornell University.

Johnson has also been involved in many professional societies. He has been a senior member of Region 6 Executive Board, a member of the Board of Directors, and a member of the National Consortium for Graduate Degrees for Minorities in Engineering. His recent presentations and course materials deal with quality management, reengineering tools for project teams, lifelong learning for practicing engineers, and introducing new freshmen to engineering.

KENNETH R. SMITH

Kenneth R. Smith is vice provost for academic planning and professional programs at the University of Arizona, where he serves on the president's cabinet and is responsible for the development of an academic plan for the University. He is also chairman of the Continuous Organizational Renewal (CORe) Council. Smith earned his bachelor of arts in economics from the University of Washington and his doctorate in economics at Northwestern University. Following his doctoral studies, he was a visiting research fellow at the Center for Operations Research and Econometrics, Universite Catholique de Louvain, Belgium.

Since 1980 Smith has held the position of dean of the Karl Eller Graduate School of Management and the College of Business and Public Administration, and is a professor of economics. He has served on the faculties of the University of Wisconsin, Northwestern University, and University of California–San Diego, and has held several directorships of academic and research programs. Prior to his tenure at the University of Arizona, Smith was director of the program in hospital and health services management at Northwestern University's Kellogg School.

CHAPTER FIFTEEN:

TQM AT THE UNIVERSITY OF PENNSYLVANIA

Marna C. Whittington and William E. Davies

Total Quality Management at the University of Pennsylvania began in the summer of 1989 as a result of an accident—I rolled the tractor I was driving and ended up flat on my back with a fractured pelvis.

Unable to go to the office, the office came to me. On one such visit, a colleague brought a video tape. It was narrated by Lloyd Dobbins, who had been the narrator of the 1980 NBC white paper telecast "If Japan Can, Why Can't We?" The telecast had described how an American statistician, W. Edwards Deming, had gone to Japan in 1950 and taught the Japanese the concepts of quality management. The Japanese gave Deming and his teachings much of the credit for their overcoming the devastation wrought by World War II. In the subsequent 30 years, they have used these same methods to become a major competitor in a global economy.

TQM at the University of Pennsylvania 331

The video also described how the Ford Motor Company had begun to work with Deming in the early 80s and how his ideas and techniques were transforming Ford. Previously, profitability and competitiveness at Ford had been on a downward trend.

The concepts explained in the video included the importance of customers and the necessity for an organization to focus on satisfying customer needs, the need to measure quality performance and to work at continuously improving product quality and service quality, and the increase in effectiveness achieved by working more as teams than as individuals. The program highlighted the costs of poor quality, the productivity losses attributable to poor process design, and the high frequency of errors or defects accepted as standard practice in many United States industries.

The message resonated with me as I thought about Penn and the problems we were experiencing. The office of the executive vice president was responsible for central administrative services including finance, facilities, human resources, business services, public safety, and government relations. We certainly had our share of dissatisfied customers, long lead times, errors, and bureaucratic procedures.

There were also numerous signs that the future was going to be more difficult financially for Penn as well as for other institutions of higher education. The 80s had been very good to higher education. Each year revenue streams had risen at double digit rates providing significant real growth in the infrastructure and programs of the University.

However, Penn was now experiencing increasing pressures on the revenue streams that had financed the growth in the 80s. Tuition could not continue to be increased at a rate more than double the rate of inflation; the federal government could not afford to continue the same rates of increase in research funding enjoyed during the 80s; the Commonwealth of Pennsylvania was trimming expenditures and the University appropriation was always a target; and the stock and bond markets could not realistically be expected to perform in the 90s as they had in the 80s.

While the rates of growth of our traditional revenue streams were slowing, the costs of remaining competitive were not. The recruiting packages required to entice the very best faculty were becoming more elaborate and expensive. Health-care costs and FAS 106 were making the current fringe benefits package unaffordable. The scientific and information technology required in an increasing number of classrooms, laboratories, and offices was proliferating rapidly and becoming obsolete even more quickly. The need-blind financial aid policy which was at the core of the student recruitment process was becoming prohibitively expensive. Our infrastructure had expanded with the rising revenue streams of the 80s, and now we were faced with the expense of operating and maintaining that infrastructure. Schools were becoming concerned with their ability to balance their budgets, while finding revenue sources for needed investment in academic programs. It was clear that Penn needed to figure out how to do more with its existing resources. It seemed that the philosophy, concepts, and techniques embodied in Total Quality Management could prove useful in dealing with our own changing realities.

In September of 1989, 25 of Penn's key administrators met in a one-day retreat. A director of quality at Eastman Kodak made a presentation about their "Journey to Excellence," the phrase he used to exemplify their approach. This retreat began the process of planning the future of administrative service delivery at Penn.

The planning process involved monthly meetings during which managers agreed on a mission statement for the administrative organization, a vision of the organization as they would like it to be, and a strategic set of goals to be accomplished in the next five years. In December 1990, the first five-year strategic plan was completed.

The mission for the office of the executive vice president as developed by the strategic planning team is:

In support of the education and research missions of the University and the services associated therewith, and in support of our colleagues at all levels participating with us in the fulfillment of those missions, the people of the Office of the Executive Vice President are dedicated to providing leadership, services, and structure to efficiently and effectively:

• Manage the financial, human resource, information, and physical assets of Penn;

• Develop, operate, and maintain a safe, hospitable environment;

• Deliver to the University community and outside entities the policies, standards, and procedures needed to effect their purposes in a consistent, orderly way, and to provide counsel and facilitation in support thereof.

The strategic team's vision of the organization that they wanted to lead was:

We seek to provide leadership in developing an effective administrative support environment, characterized by a unified and well-managed University working together in support of the academic mission. Central to our vision is an open and supportive environment that motivates individuals to act ethically and enthusiastically, that promotes teamwork, and that employs sound

management and analytical processes in the delivery of quality services at least cost. Features of the environment will be:
- A focus on service to customers and satisfying their requirements at lowest cost.
- Respect for individuals, manifested by respect for their diversity and dignity, and by recognition for their performance.
- Maximizing the potential of the individual through fostering personal and professional development and growth.
- A spirit of collaboration, freedom of movement and expression, ethical behavior, and high standards of personal conduct and mutual trust.

Based on the mission and vision statements and the strategic goals, the vice presidents of each of the organizational areas led the development of annual business plans for the organization. The strategic planning group continued to meet monthly to work on particular goals of the plan, increase their expertise with outside speakers, and share specifics on problems or projects in each administrative area. Each quarter, the strategic planning group reviewed progress against the annual business plans. The strategic plan and the business plans taken together described both the longer-term goals as well as the shorter-term courses of action needed to reach these goals.

It is essential before embarking on Total Quality Management that your organization has completed a strategic planning process because it is necessary to have articulated and agreed upon your mission, your core values, and your goals before you can evaluate and improve upon your current processes.

A principal direction set by the planning process was a focus on continually improving the quality of administrative services throughout the University, while containing the costs incurred in their delivery. The primary strategy selected was total quality management (TQM). The TQM literature suggested that approximately 15 to 20 percent of the resources utilized in most work is wasted. By applying the TQ tools, workers can reduce errors, inaccuracies, oversights, sloppy procedures and rework, and this ultimately reduces costs. Penn sought to reduce the administrative costs through quality improvement and thus free up resources for academic investment.

There are many approaches to creating a quality management environment. We chose to employ the concepts and methodologies of Joseph Juran. The Juran Institute for Quality Management was nearby in Wilton, Connecticut, and we invited them in to give our planning group a three-day overview. Though they had not previously worked in higher education administration, their approach seemed reasonable and we decided to test their methodologies at Penn.

We began by setting up a Quality Council, which I chaired and which included my five top managers: the vice presidents of finance, human resources, and facilities and business services, plus the commissioner of public safety and the associate dean of the veterinary school—our "voice of the customer." All of the members of the Quality Council were also members of the strategic planning group.

To begin, we decided on an approach which would include pilot projects and just-in-time training for the individuals involved in the pilot projects. For the pilot projects, we looked for real problems that met four criteria: 1) they were not overly complex, 2) they could be clearly defined, 3) they were potentially easy to address within a fairly short time-frame, and 4) they would have an impact recognized by a broad constituency.

We settled on four pilot projects: 1) reduce postage costs, 2) reduce trash costs, 3) improve accounts receivable in research administration, and 4) improve return rate on employee evaluations. The strategic planning group agreed that after the four pilot projects were completed we would evaluate the applicability of TQM to Penn and determine whether there was merit to further TQM activities. The project leaders and facilitators were selected and team members were recruited. All received training from Juran in applying the TQ concepts. The teams began work, putting in about two hours a week on average. The Quality Council met with each team at least once a month, reviewed status and progress of the project, and provided encouragement and support. The teams were told that they had two tasks: 1) to use the TQ methodology to address the problem areas, and 2) to evaluate the applicability of the tools and process for the Penn environment. No project would be considered a failure as long as we learned from it and documented that knowledge.

The first series of outcomes was very reinforcing for the teams. The postage project quickly resulted in savings of $100,000 annually and generated numerous additional ideas which yielded subsequent savings. The Research Administration project found a $1.7 million billing problem that could be corrected immediately, uncovered 1,100 accounts with negative cash balances, and discovered that we were routinely generating only 70 percent of our potential monthly bills because of errors in the billing process. The trash collection project generated savings of $150,000 annually by evaluating and renegotiating pick-up schedules with outside contractors. The employee evaluation project was disbanded after discovering the problem was larger than anticipated and not appropriate for a trial project.

Even more important than the significant progress made in improving our problem areas was the knowledge we gained from the four pilot projects. Many of our team members were in responsible administrative positions in the University because of their technical competence in specific areas. Few had management training and there was no common set of problem solving tools shared by the group until their TQ training. The TQ training provided them a set of shared tools and approaches to define and solve Penn's problems. It provided an approach that seemed to minimize defensiveness and erode organizational barriers.

The people working on the teams felt good about being able to work together and sharing in solving a University problem. They liked learning the tools and techniques of rigorous problem solving and began using them in their other daily tasks. They also enjoyed engaging higher levels of management on a regular basis and the recognition that went with it. In summary, they enjoyed what every winning team enjoys—the exhilaration of belonging to a worthy cause, sharing the experience, and succeeding.

These early experiences convinced us that TQM had real potential for us, and we were eager to spawn more teams and keep going. However, it was also clear that if we depended on only incremental continuous improvement, it would take too long to realize the productivity increases that we knew were obtainable and that were becoming increasingly necessary for Penn to maintain financial equilibrium and continue to make necessary academic investments. Shortly after completing our first projects, we met Eugene H. Melan, currently an associate professor of business at Marist College, also a long time employee of IBM, where he had been very much involved with their quality initiatives. He introduced us to the concepts of business process quality management or, as some would prefer, business process re-engineering.

Process re-engineering begins with the concept that an enterprise performs a set of work activities that is consistent with the business that it is in. A building contractor will perform a set of construction activities. A Big Six accounting firm will perform a set of auditing and accounting activities. A university will perform a set of teaching and research activities. These sets of activities, or processes, which typically cut across traditional organizational boundaries form the core competencies of the organization. How well organizations perform these processes in satisfying customers at well-managed costs dictates the success of the enterprise. Re-designing or re-engineering these processes in response to customer needs is critical to the organization.

In addition to the core business processes, there are a number of support processes. Traditional support processes are finance, personnel, facilities, equipment, material and supplies, and systems and technology management. In our case, public safety is another. Often, these processes have not been examined for a long time and doing so can lead to breakthrough improvements—dramatic improvements in quality, reduction in error rates, reduction in process time, increase in productivity, reduction in costs—and most important, improved customer satisfaction. The support processes were the processes that the administrative arm of the University had responsibility for and were the subject of our strategic planning process. We thought that our five-year goal of reducing the proportion of the University's budget being spent on administration activities while improving quality could be reached better through a combination of process re-engineering and continuous improvement rather than with TQ alone. Many of our processes had grown substantially over the years in response to new regulations, new administrators, and increasing customer demands without ever being reexamined to make sure all the work done was adding value and that technology was being used where it could add value.

We began searching out opportunities to pilot test process re-engineering. In pilot testing process re-engineering we used the same approach that we had for TQM. We selected problem areas, chose teams comprised of members who each had responsibility for some part of the process, and together had responsibility for the whole process, did just-in-time training and had the Quality Council regularly review progress. On each and every team, we also had a "customer." Often faculty and staff from the academic units were members of teams as representative owners of parts of the process or as customers. Facilities Management used process re-engineering to redesign facilities project planning and construction, and is currently using it to analyze and redefine the facility operating and maintenance process. Finance used the process re-engineering approach to redesign the procurement and accounts payable process.

As more and more individuals became members of process re-engineering or quality improvement teams, individuals across the University began to understand and appreciate the power and applicability of the tools. In fact, there are currently 36 projects underway at Penn addressing either process re-engineering or continuous improvement tasks. Nine of the 36 projects are now in the schools—at Wharton, the School of Engineering and Applied Sciences, and the Graduate School of Fine Arts. Projects range from admissions processing to course pack development and distribution.

The initiatives in the business and engineering schools were spurred by an IBM invitation to submit proposals for IBM-sponsored grants to eight colleges and universities. The grants were to increase interest in teaching TQM principles and techniques to business and engineering students, and to introduce TQM into the research agendas of the schools. Although Penn did not win one of the grants, both Wharton and the School of Engineering and Applied Science adopted the concepts and started initiatives to address school needs. In the Graduate School of Fine Arts, the staff decided that they would like to use the concept in examining the admissions process.

The ongoing initiatives in Finance process re-engineering led us to understanding the need for a third and final component of TQM at Penn—the development and deployment of information systems and technology to support process re-engineering and continuous improvement. Finance had already, through the planning process, identified the need for an improved financial information system. The accounting system was over 20 years old, and while it had served the University well, it did not yield the kind of information needed to manage a large, complex, research university in these times of rapid change.

The traditional approach to acquiring a new university information system is to scan the marketplace of software providers for a package that seems responsive to current needs. A supplier is selected and then, without bothering to examine the policies, procedures and process work flow, the university substantially modifies the software package to meet its "unique" needs (i.e., the way we have always done it). Having done so, the university finds itself maintaining and enhancing the package using expensive in-house systems professionals. In the meantime, the supplier continues to maintain and enhance the software, which is offered to a broad marketplace. The university is unable to take advantage of those enhancements either, because too much retro-fitting must be done to the now drastically modified baseline software or because the supplier has moved to new technology.

TQM at the University of Pennsylvania   341

In 1991, we decided to try a new approach. The computing area had been attempting for some time to define an information architecture to guide future system development, while we were moving forward to re-engineer fundamental financial processes and to develop a new financial management information system (MIS).

If we could develop an information architecture that would support and sustain ongoing process re-engineering and continuous improvement, then quality management practices would become integral to the daily management activities at Penn. We knew what we needed to do, but we did not know how, so we prepared a Request for Proposals seeking the assistance of a firm in designing an information architecture for the University and developing the design for a Financial MIS that would serve as a cornerstone in building the architectural design (NOTE: The project was named "Cornerstone" in recognition of this concept), and assisting in the re-engineering of those financial processes critical to the Financial MIS.

In pursuing this project, at least 30 major research universities were contacted, in addition to colleagues in the commercial and industrial marketplace. We received substantial confirmation that we were on the right track, but we also repeatedly heard an admonition that such a project foretold cultural change; one would be wise to find out up front whether the institution wanted to change, and if so why, and how much—otherwise, a lot of time, energy, and money could be expended with no results.

A Project Manager from our computing area was chosen to lead the effort, and a team of business and technical personnel from the University was selected to work with her. James Martin and Company of Reston, Virginia, was selected as consultant and an initiation phase was launched to

1) develop a preliminary information architecture, consisting of a set of principles, models, and standards in support of four domains—data, applications, organization, and technology—and, 2) to determine, through structured interviews of a broad cross-section of University management, the readiness of the institution to undertake fundamental cultural and organizational change.

As of this writing, the initiation phase of the project has been completed and the University has determined that it is prepared to go forward. Re-engineering efforts in Finance and the development of a Financial MIS are underway in concert with the development of an information architecture for the University. This architecture will be used to sequentially develop replacement information systems for the support processes of the University. The information systems will provide the flexibility and data necessary to support process re-engineering and continuous improvement on an ongoing basis.

What are the relationships between business planning, TQM, and the deployment of information systems and technology? Can one undertake change initiatives in higher education in one arena without consideration of the other two? Before attempting to answer, let us back up and examine the issues facing not only Penn but education in general.

Colleges and universities, together with colleagues in public and private education at primary and secondary school levels, are under siege. Shrinking revenues, rising costs, and public perceptions of bloated, inefficient, ineffective educational institutions face us everyday.

How did it happen? What does it mean? What shall we do? Theories and approaches abound—slash costs, flatten the organization, downsize the work force, reinvent the enterprise, know your customer, empower your people, manage by walking around, break down the barriers, drive out fear, and prioritize functions. The constant barrage of prescriptive solutions is added to the daily trauma of accelerating problems. Too frequently, we reach for a solution that promises to be the silver bullet, and we end up shooting ourselves in the foot. We are reminded of the panaceas of the past—Management by Objectives, Program Planning and Budgeting, Zero Based Budgeting. Now we add TQM to the fix-mix.

There has to be a better way. Not a magic bullet, but a way to think about managing the educational institution in these times and doing so successfully.

First, what is the problem? We think it is the fact that we are doing business as though it were 10, 20, 50, 100 or more years ago. How are we doing business? We start with an organizational structure designed, as Deming instructs us, to assign responsibility and exercise control. This unit takes care of finances, and that—human resources. This school educates budding engineers, and that—lawyers. This one does research in nuclear physics, and that—in economics. It is not designed to satisfy a customer or produce a quality product or service.

Second, we treat our staff people as though they are uneducated and poorly motivated. We give them supervisors to tell them how to do their work and "evaluate" their performance. We provide the supervisors with managers whose job it is to pass instructions from on high down and take problems from below on up. Finally, we give them all "tools"—very sophisticated and expensive tools—PC's and desk top software, networks, and E-Mail. With these tools, the expectation is that we will "improve productivity." We ask our people to work skillfully and productively without the foggiest idea of how their role contributes to the whole. I believe we have learned some f undamental lessons on our own quality journey. Here they are:

Whittington and Davies

- There are two important ingredients in an organization's success—its customers and its people. You cannot satisfy one and not the other.
- If everyone in the organization does not know who the customers are and their level of satisfaction with the services provided them, they will not know what needs improving.
- An organization needs a constancy of purpose and clarity of vision and goals.
- Services are provided to customers through a specific set of work tasks, activities, and processes. Management is responsible for the design of those processes, which tend to flow across organizational boundaries. If they are poorly designed and controlled, no amount of exhortation will make them efficient and effective, most of the average worker's results will not be under their control, and employee evaluations for performance will be counterproductive.
- If the deployment of information systems and technology is simply an overlay on processes that are not well designed nor well integrated, the situation will only get worse.
- If people are not empowered to make the changes they know need to be made to improve customer satisfaction, the bureaucracy is in control.
- If management conceives of itself as directing the work of those below them, and not as supporting those below them so they may perform well and grow on the job, you will not have a productive work force.

How specifically, then, should we go about trying to change our educational institutions? I believe the critical success factors include leadership deciding that the institution needs to be fundamentally rethought. (Leadership must include the Board of Trustees and the chief executive.) A change process or methodology must be adopted; TQM and process re-engineering are part of the methodology, but they do not stand on their own. The methodology should provide a planning process which includes:

- A means by which senior management may be engaged in developing a mission and vision for the institution's future, formed around an underlying set of core values.
- Clear end results to be achieved, with corresponding measures of success.
- A means by which the mission, vision, and values may be communicated to faculty and staff so that they may become truly shared and commonly held.
- Identification of the institutions' customers, their needs that the institution seeks to fulfill, and a means by which satisfaction may be continually measured.
- Definition of the processes through which the direct services of the institution are delivered to external customers and of the support processes required by the direct service providers.
- Assignment of responsibility, authority, and accountability for process ownership and for operational responsibility in performing those processes.
- A means by which each part of the organization may establish its own goals and action plans within the context of the overall plans of the institution.
- Empowerment of people to make changes they know need to be made to improve performance, and a system that rewards and recognizes them for doing so.
- A system of internal control to measure performance against results and enable continual improvement to take place.

• The deployment of information systems and technology aligned with process improvement.

This represents a dramatic re-invention of the enterprise led from the top. If for whatever reason, so comprehensive a change cannot be envisioned and undertaken, what can a given executive or manager do?

I believe it is possible for any executive or manager within a given area of responsibility to take the lead in making improvements within that area. Simply do on a small scale what best is done on an enterprise-wide basis. It is possible to determine who one's customers are and how satisfied, or not, they are with our services. It is possible to define suppliers to the area, and to chart the flow of work. It is possible to empower, reward, and recognize people—regardless of the formal system in place for so doing. In brief, it is possible to lead in the domain over which one has control. This may not be enough for the enterprise as a whole, but it is far better than continuing in a management mode that is no longer functional.

The institutions of higher education are part of a change of monumental proportions taking place in a global society. Those institutions, like their counterparts in a commercial/industrial sector, are being challenged to manage a whole new set of realities. Most are continuing to operate as though this tidal wave of change was not occurring. Highly vertical, rigidly hierarchical, organizational structures, useful in the industrial era, are proving inadequate to cope with the demands of a new age.

Total Quality Management is emerging as a philosophy and concept, complete with a set of methodologies, tools, and techniques that can help an organization re-invent itself. It is not, however, a panacea. It does not guarantee success. In fact, many organizations that have sought to employ it have failed in doing so successfully.

TQM at the University of Pennsylvania   347

Peter Drucker (1993), writing in the *Wall Street Journal,* suggests that every organization must rethink the basic "business theory" under which it is currently operating since every such theory must eventually become inappropriate to the realities of the market and technology. He further suggests that there are two questions that need to be asked: "First: Who are the customers, and who are the non-customers? What is of value to them? What do they pay for? Second: What do the successes—the Wal-Marts, the regional banks, and so on—do that we do not? What do they not do that we know is essential? What do they assume that we know to be wrong?"

Only the leadership can make sure that these kinds of questions are asked and answered. The mission, values, and vision of the people of the organization arise from such questioning. Assumptions about the marketplace and about the people of the enterprise are crucial to designing a desired future and effective means of bringing it about.

TQM is consistent with this mind set, but there is a danger. We cannot cast off everything we have learned in the past about strategic planning, organizational development, human resource development, or the alignment of information systems and technology with business priorities. We need a new synthesis of change management philosophies, concepts, and methodologies that integrates these disciplines.

This new synthesis will focus on meeting the needs of two constituencies—customers and the people of the organization. Emphasis will shift from the sub-optimal approach of meeting the goals of individual organizational components to improving the organizational work processes. The organization will be driven by a shared understanding of organizational purpose, a commonly held vision of the future, and a set of core values that define the norms for organizational and individual behavior.

All of this will require leadership. It will also require re-thinking the system of recognition and reward, i.e., less focus on contributions of the individual and more on contributions of self-directed teams. It will not be easy, but the challenges are exciting, the possibilities endless, and the promises great.

References

Drucker, P. 1993. A Turnaround Primer. *The Wall Street Journal*, 2 February.
If Japan Can, Why Can't We? 1980. Produced by NBC News. 75 min. Videocassette.

MARNA C. WHITTINGTON

Marna C. Whittington joined the investment management firm of Miller, Anderson & Sherrerd in October 1992, and was named partner in January 1994. She currently manages the business core, which includes the areas of client services, marketing, human resources, finance and compliance, and strategic business planning for the firm. She earned a bachelor's degree from the University of Delaware, and received her master of science degree and doctorate from the University of Pittsburgh.

Whittington worked in private industry for seven years prior to becoming deputy secretary of education for Pennsylvania in 1979. In 1981, she was appointed secretary of administrative services for the state of Delaware by Governor DuPont, and in 1983 became the state's secretary of finance. She was named vice president for finance at the University of Pennsylvania in 1984, appointed senior vice president in 1988, and executive vice president in January 1992. In this position, she was responsible for the entire administrative operations of the University, which consisted of finance, human resources, public safety, facilities, government relations, and business services functions.

WILLIAM E. DAVIES

William E. Davies is the head of William E. Davies Consulting Services, where consulting and project facilitation services are provided for clients in higher education, state and local government, and private enterprise. Davies is also assistant to the executive vice president for business and systems planning at the University of Pennsylvania. He received his bachelor of arts degree from Albright College and earned his master's in business administration from Southern Illinois University.

Some of William Davies' experiences and leadership positions include director of office planning systems development, director of operations of the statewide family court system in Delaware, information systems project leader for the statewide criminal justice system, and project leader for marketing and sales information at the International Playtex Corporation. Davies has also had experience in the United States Navy as lieutenant of operations and has served as a special agent for the Federal Bureau of Investigation.

Chapter Sixteen:

The Total Quality Management Movement: Practicing Good Sociology in Educational Settings

Thomas R. Plough

Steady criticism and skepticism about the lack of productivity and effectiveness of United States colleges and universities is widespread, resulting in declining thresholds for annual giving, public funding, and tuition rates. This revenue diet is forcing us to rethink the way in which we deliver our service, and the way we behave in order to reduce costs yet maintain quality and not lose whatever vestiges of community remain intact on the campus.

Today there is a growing sense that the time for diagnosis is past and the time for practical strategies is at hand. What sequence of steps should an institution take to restructure its administrative functions? How can an institution, using both the spirit and procedures of collegiality, return a greater degree of faculty energy and commitment to the classroom? How best can the social contract that binds scholars to the institution be reinforced or perhaps be renegotiated? How much smaller should the staff of an institution be? How should a college or university go about the business of out-sourcing some of its functions, including some of its academic functions? What kind of process should an institution use to design programs for higher education's new majority of non-traditional learners? How can the processes and procedures of restructuring be applied to this seemingly intractable problem of increasing the enrollment and the degree attainment of historically under-representative populations, particularly African-Americans and Hispanics? (Zemsky 1993)

While many educators cling to the notion that American higher education is the envy of the world, they seem to ignore the reality that United States automobile manufacturers and healthcare professionals said the same thing only a few years back. They also seem unshaken by the opinion surveys which indicate that 61 percent of Americans had confidence in people running higher education in the 1960s, but only 25 percent feel that way in the 1990s. The trend is pretty clear. Trust and confidence in higher education is being replaced by cynicism. As Leslie Cochran (1992) suggests in *Publish or Perish: The Wrong Issue*, the belief in the myth that teaching cannot be evaluated makes higher education a public laughing stock.

Still, much affection for individual colleges and universities—as symbolized in America by all the college emblems displayed on the rear windows of family automobiles—and the persistent hope that education can prepare young people for a more successful and satisfying life, is far from extinguished in the heart of the public. It is clear that change is required and that change must make the curriculum in universities more relevant to the problems which exist within the United States, all of which are complicated by the dynamic nature of global realities. Higher education as an industry must find ways to transfer this latent hopefulness held by isolated individuals and their significant others to a more manifest loyalty and support by the public at large. As Daniel Yankelovich says "people are asking questions about affordability and results" (Edgerton 1993). He warns that unless educators respond to these questions, other people will take control of the situation and dictate changes. As he says "the price you pay for not seizing responsibility is to be excluded and to be victimized" (Edgerton 1993).

In our current context, it is abundantly clear that educators must question all the assumptions upon which their current practices are based and be prepared to evaluate and change their behaviors. In the foreword to *Quality—Transforming Postsecondary Education*, Jonathan Fife states:

> The fact is that the role and importance of higher education in society have changed dramatically over the years, but institutional practices have not (Chaffee and Sherr 1992).

Practices that must change include routine evaluation of goal achievement and more specified professional development for all university personnel in best practices found in education. All this must be done, however, without losing sight of the mission of the university, which is to prepare students for earning a living and living a life, not as two processes, but as one.

We need, as Seymour (1993) suggests, the notion of a "university that not only teaches but learns." It is important to note that Total Quality Management as an approach to cultural changes in higher education, is yet to be significantly tested in practice. It does however appear to present a viable methodology to approach change in a service industry. However, as Fisher has observed, the emphasis on process rather than people could result in a failure to properly address issues of accountability and leadership. "At best, TQM in higher education appears to be a process for doing what we do better; but what we really need, is to do something different" (Fisher 1993). Chichering and Potter also warn against a too literal and non-customized application of TQM to higher education. They point out that customer satisfaction cannot come to mean that educators simply provide whatever students want. Rather, educators, as professionals, must make judgments about what students need, both as individuals and also as members of a collective social enterprise. They provide a wonderful contrast that points out the differences between an approach called fast food and an approach called fitness center. In the fast food orientation, efficiency, low cost, satisfaction of the appetite, and no hassles for customers are the organizing principles. In the fitness center orientation, a program is designed based on needs established through examination, followed by instruction from a professional who also assists the customer to reach benchmarks, utilizing frequent feedback which leads to independent continuing fitness training by the individual (Chichering 1993). Marchese (1993) reminds us that "the danger is that we'll be put off by the fervor, the formulas, or the smell of fad and miss the fact that a very important set of ideas about the organizations we work in has made its way through the industrial, service, healthcare, and government sectors of society and is now at our doorstep."

These observations about the potential strength and weakness of TQM from knowledgeable educators are worth our attention, but it seems clear that the delivery of educational service must change. As Seymour has observed, "we are kidding ourselves if we believe that educating people for the year 2000 is essentially the same as educating them for the year 1975. Everything has changed—technology, lifestyles, culture" (Scheuch 1992). John A. White (1990) put the challenge in this manner:

How long would a firm be in business if it rejected parts, materials, and sub-assemblies at an overall rate of 35 percent and rejected a critical component at a rate of 65 percent? How long would a firm be in business if it consistently failed to meet its advertised delivery dates by 25 percent?

How long would a firm be in business if its products failed to satisfy more than half of its customers? How long would a firm be in business if it paid little attention to its cost of production, but instead raised prices at a rate considerably above the cost of living while competitors were entering the market with lower prices?

In a service industry, it is actually more important to be defect-free than it is in manufacturing. For example, 99 percent defect-free means that 12 babies a day are going to the wrong parents and that the Internal Revenue Service loses two million documents per year. Certainly, one problem with TQM is that its language is drawn from manufacturing and tends to generate negative semantic loadings for many in education. A language bridge is needed to effectively utilize TQM in educational settings. On the other hand, TQM draws upon many concepts that are familiar to the behavioral sciences and management which many faculty regularly teach:

The literature on management has taught that three elements are key to the success of a service enterprise: 1) know the customers; 2) commit the organization to specific service goals; 3) establish strong feedback loops that continuously measure the provider's success in achieving their goals. (Zemsky 1991)

The New York State Governor's Excelsior Quality at Work Award was the first state award to recognize quality in three sectors: private, public, and education. The Excelsior Award Executive Committee is composed of union leaders, corporate executives, educators, and public officials. Frequent interaction among these committee members, and staff support from the New York State Departments of Economic Development and Labor, led to both increased understanding of and consensus modifications in the Malcolm Baldrige National Quality Award categories which placed more emphasis on partnering, the management of diversity, and labor-management cooperation. In-depth discussions allowed the committee to reach agreement on some of the special features of each sector (especially language) while holding each sector to common evaluation techniques and standards utilized by examiners and judges. It is interesting to note that the first winners of the 1992 Excelsior Award were the New York State Police, the Kenmore-Town of Tonawanda School District, Albany International, Press-Fabrics Division, and Motorola Automotive and Industrial Electronics Group Plant.

Simone has suggested that we use the term colleagues to replace customers. He identifies core colleagues (students), internal colleagues (faculty, secretaries, trustees, support service administrators), and external colleagues (parents, employers, graduate schools, suppliers of equipment) as one way of expressing TQM in a new collegiality frame of reference (Simone 1992). It should also be noted that TQM is only the latest business practice adopted by the education sector. In the 1960s it was accounting practice, in the 1970s, marketing techniques, and in the 1980s, strategic planning. As Fecher suggests, the "intended effects of adopting business practices and utilizing management strategies in higher education has not been to turn colleges and universities into businesses but

Figure 1

1994 Education Sector Categories and Items

1.0 Leadership   170 subtotal of points
1.1 Senior Executive Leadership (70 points)
1.2 Management for Quality (30 points)
1.3 Partnering (40 points)
1.4 Community Responsibility (30 points)

2.0 Information and Analysis   50 subtotal of points
2.1 Scope and Management of Quality and Performance Data and
Information (10 points)
2.2 Benchmarks and Comparisons (20 points)
2.3 Analysis and Uses of Organizational-Level Data (20 points)

3.0 Strategic Quality Planning   50 subtotal of points
3.1 Strategic Quality and Organizational Performance Planning Process
(30 points)
3.2 Quality and Performance Plans (20 points)

4.0 Human Resource Excellence   240 subtotal of points
4.1 Human Resource Management (30 points)
4.2 Employee Involvement (30 points)
4.3 Education and Training (50 points)
4.4 Employee Performance and Recognition (40 points)
4.5 Employee Well-Being and Morale (30 points)
4.6 Diversity (30 points)
4.7 Employee Partnering (30 points)

5.0 Management of Process Quality   100 subtotal of points
5.1 Design/Development and Introduction of Quality Programs and
Services (25 points)
5.2 Process Management-Instructional and Service Processes (20
points)
5.3 Process Management-Administrative Processes and Support
Service Quality (20 points)
5.4 Supplier Quality (20 points)
5.5 Quality Assessment (15 points)

Plough

6.0 Quality and Operational Results   150 subtotal of points
6.1 Program and Service Quality Results (60 points)
6.2 Operational Results of the Institution (40 points)
6.3 Administrative Process and Support Service Results (25 points)
6.4 Supplier Quality Results (25 points)

7.0 Student and Customer Focus and Satisfaction   240 points
7.1 Student and Customer Expectations: Current and Future (25 points)
7.2 Student and Customer Relationship Management (55 points)
7.3 Commitment to Students and Customers (15 points)
7.4 Determining Student and Customer Satisfaction (25 points)
7.5 Student and Customer Satisfaction Results (60 points)
7.6 Student and Customer Satisfaction Comparisons (60 points)
TOTAL POINTS 1,000

to enable them to maximize their resources and reach their fullest potential (Fecher 1985).

Scheuch's research on quality of life has many implications for dealing with students in education consistent with the TQM principle of listening. "Lifestyle research indicates that both the image of a mass society and of individualistic and fractionalized society are both false. The reality is characterized by something we might call 'ordered diversity.'" (Scheuch 1992) Educators can identify this "ordered diversity" only by careful observation and listening techniques which continuously monitor this campus makeup, share the information widely with faculty and staff, and design learning experiences to take advantage of its characteristics. These characteristics cannot be ascertained by survey data alone, or campus or general media reports about students. "For example, the desire to express oneself, to realize one's individuality, may be central to the intellectuals of our time but it is of secondary importance to the vast majority of the population. The satisfaction derived from the immediate environment is dominant" (Scheuch 1992). For example, good communication skills, as an objective of a university education, may be better facilitated by a program of study which entices the student into the use of written and oral expression rather than assuming students identify with, and are naturally drawn toward, such an educational objective. Chaffee and Sheer argue that resources are not quality. How they are used to produce the intended outcome is the key. "Quality lies in the design, process, and output; inputs are merely appropriate or inappropriate" (Chaffee 1992). They use the example of a library which has an immense collection, but where many students do not use the library or where some academic programs with large enrollments are poorly served by the collections in the library. As Karmarkar argues, educators have to shift some of their time and attention from concerns over process quality (their view of what constitutes a good quality education) to concerns about product quality (the view of students, parents, and employers about what constitutes a quality education) (Karmarkar 1990). Internal specifications are fine and necessary, but satisfaction on the part of the student or colleague is equally important. The two concepts of process and product quality need to merge in any educational approach. Garvin has charted the evolution of TQM in the United States through "eras of quality" from craftsmanship, inspection, statistical quality control, quality assurance, and total quality management (Garvin 1988). Both the eras of craftsmanship and TQM combine the notions of process and product quality, except that craftsmen dealt with small volume, small numbers of parts in any one product, and isolated markets. The tools and methodology of TQM were developed to meet the demands of large lot sizes, with customizing flexibility, many parts in any one product, and global markets. For example, reaching a 99 percent defect-free target for wine barrels made by hand at the rate of several a day is not as difficult as producing a bicycle with 25 parts where if each part is 99 percent defect free, the bicycle produced will be only .7586 defect free (Burr 1979). Elliot has adapted the language of the seven macro categories of the national quality award in the USA, called the Baldridge Award, for the culture of higher education in the USA. The categories are leadership, information and analysis, strategic planning, human resources utilization, quality assurance of curriculum and courses, quality results, and student sponsor and employer satisfaction (Elliott 1991). Lincoln summarized the components of TQM as meeting or exceeding customer expectations, continuous improvement, data-based decision making, leadership committed to quality initiatives,

Cultural Change

From	To
Authority driven	Consensus driven
Short term	Long term
Narrow view	Participative
Internal competition	Cooperation
Unstructured, individualistic problem solving	Discipline, participative group problem solving
Constant work	Right the first time
Ambiguous requirements	Systematic approach
Problem centered	Visionary
Acceptance of the status quo ("Not my job")	Everybody committed to continuous improvement
Power at the top	Power shared by everybody
Intuitive	Analytical/fact-based
Working as individuals	Teams

Figure 2

Practicing Sociology in Higher Education 361

and cross functional teamwork (Lincoln 1992). Nowlin has taken the various conceptions of TQM and developed a cultural change chart for educational institutions in Figure 2 (Blazey 1993).

In this context of applying concepts of TQM in educational settings, there are some promising ideas which seem to allow for increased productivity and quality, while controlling increases in costs and preserving the shared purposes of the academy.The first is that "when placed in the same systems, people, however different, tend to produce similar results" (Seymour 1992). This is sometimes called the 85-15 rule. That is, what goes wrong is 85 percent traceable to the system and 15 percent related to the individual. This leads to the hypothesis that significant change in higher education will only come from rearrangements in the way students, faculty, and staff relate to one another. Teaching and learning is a relationship, not a function. Studies over many years in the sociology of work indicate that most organizational alienation comes from poor worker-supervisor relations and lack of cross-divisional communication and teamwork, rather than from rates of pay or work environment.

Thousands of studies done on college student retention indicate that the lack of connections between faculty/staff and students (alienation) and the compartmentalization of university programs and services allow students to fall between the cracks—and that leads to student attrition. Further, we know that one-third of the entering college students in the United States each year do not return to the same institution the following fall. Three-fourths of those who do not complete degrees leave their institution in good academic standing, and 50 percent of first-year dropouts make that decision in the first six weeks. The system is not working. Clearly, academic institutions need to design new ways to bond students with the academic enterprise.

Many of these students are different from those of past decades in very important ways. Most of the students that arrive on our campuses are smart and full of energy, but they have short attention spans, undisciplined work habits, and unreasonable expectations about the ease with which they will master both the social and intellectual environments they will encounter. Too many of our students have had little experience with difficult materials and complex ideas that must be learned and understood within relatively brief periods of time. Many will be deficient in mathematics, science, and communication skills. From a clinical psychological point of view, they lack readiness for university study and life. Regardless of our students' readiness for collegiate level study and life, once they enter, most of them can stay and succeed if the faculty, staff, and those students who are successfully negotiating the campus already will provide enthusiastic and effective instruction, advice, services, and opportunities for involvement, show personal interest in them, and remain present and accessible enough of the time on campus, to serve as role models or as interested and more knowledgeable sources of information.

This will require a paradigm shift. "Faculty spend more time in activities of their own choosing than they did a generation ago and that time is richly augmented with support services" (Massy 1991). David Riesman (1989) has stated that "the grave problem with regard to the professorate is how invitational the college experience is for undergraduates. Invitational for learning." It would be useful also for faculty to remind themselves that few of these students will ever consider or enter the profession of college teaching. According to the Higher Education Research Institute, fewer than 2.3 percent of all 1991 freshmen indicated a higher education teaching career objective. Students have factors of satisfaction related to their quality of academic life objectives that are

Practicing Sociology in Higher Education   363

different from ours, and we must learn more about these factors in order to draw students along toward broader educational objectives.

Senge (1990) has introduced the second idea relevant to TQM which suggests that, just as individuals have learning disabilities, so too do organizations. One of our learning disabilities is the tendency not to listen to our students. There is a principle that any seller in a buyer's market who does not want to pay attention to the buyer is going to be in for a hard time. In order to listen, you have to pay attention continuously to your customers. In a university, it is easy not to pay attention. More accurately, we tend to pay attention discontinuously. Instead of early warning systems like mid-quarter grades, we wait until the student has failed or done poorly before we try to help. We do not require a professor to schedule and insist on attendance at special study sessions for those students in class who are doing poorly after a week or so. Of course, if we only give an exam at the end of the quarter, we may have no way of listening to the student until it is too late. We tend not to ask students how they are doing.

Recently, several articles by outstanding teachers have suggested that team learning and team assignments are very effective in promoting peer learning, and that the simple practice of taking the last few minutes of each class to ask each student to write on an index card what they did not understand and what they did not hear that they wanted to know more about, enhances student performance. Some have even suggested that faculty should practice their course presentations prior to class to ensure that they are crisp, professional, and right the first time, instead of practicing them on the class. Obviously, input from students on what they want must be balanced by the judgement of the subject matter experts, but the balance cannot be maintained adequately unless there is listening, communication, and relationship. Further, Harari

(1993) suggests that "a true organization-wide listening strategy means that the information gained from everyone's daily dose of reality . . . must be consolidated and available to all hands." Tom Fredericks, biology department head at RIT, spends a fair amount of time each summer reading through the applications of new students which are available in the Admissions Office. He finds the information very helpful in getting to know his students before they arrive on campus. This is an excellent example of a rich data base available on campus which is generally underutilized.

Clark (1987) has written that "professional authority in academia begins with the simple fact that academic subjects serve not only as areas for work and sources of dignity and faith, but also as bases of control." This discipline-based authority can become a disability for higher education if it is not redirected through restructuring. Dean Richard Rosett (1992) of RIT's College of Business has restructured the entire College by abolishing discipline-focused academic departments and replacing them with student-focused program teams. These cross-functional teams of faculty have the responsibility for developing, for each major, a sequence of articulated courses. These teams are responsible for knowing their feeder schools by communicating with faculty from those schools, advising the students—most of whom they know by name through frequent informal contact and continuous feedback—and knowing the employers of their graduates and the faculty of graduate schools where their students continue their education. They are expected to "listen" to their students by facilitating focus group sessions, designing a friendly means to meet with students in their programs at least three times a year as a group to elicit comments about the curriculum, and encouraging students to form their own teams to evaluate learning strategies to share with the faculty team. Rosett writes about one particular learning disability of the academy:

Practicing Sociology in Higher Education   365

Objection to the student as customer is an important reason for academic resistance to TQM, but it is not the only one. Another is the organization of academic disciplines and the corresponding organization of colleges. In a sense, an academic discipline is organized for the purpose of creating a body of literature. Scholars in a discipline read and publish one another's writings, cite one another, dispute one another, hire one another, assess one another's publications for promotion and tenure, and most often are uninformed about what is happening outside their own discipline. But focus on the education of a student, especially an undergraduate student, calls for partnerships that cut across the lines of these disciplines. The more committed a university is to academic scholarship, the more resistant it will be to such partnerships and to TQM. (Rosett 1992)

Harrington (1987) has suggested a third TQM idea which is the proposition that "if you can't measure it, you can't understand it; if you can't understand it, you can't control it; if you can't control it, you can't improve it." The idea of measurement in service industry, especially education, is not one that is readily accepted. And educators, as well as many researchers of the service sector, are right to maintain that service is not the same as manufacturing. One particular reason for this difference is that the characteristics on which the service user bases his/her evaluation may have nothing to do with the delivery of the service. For example, the student may come to the university expecting to get an A average when his/her preparation will not likely allow it. Or the student may expect no waiting when trying to access a service designed for appointments rather than walk-ins. Nevertheless, these expectations can be shaped by the faculty and staff of an institution, and if communication occurs between student and faculty/staff, inappropriate expectations can be clarified. Lincoln (1992) calls this TQM principle, data based decision-making. It is necessary to understand the needs and expectations of the student, to uncover variations between customer expectations and organizational performance, to identify the nature of the variation, and to monitor progress towards reducing variations. Data-based discussions and decision-making develops understanding such as the following: 1) more than 25 percent of an institutions new students enter off-term (not in the fall semester or quarter); 2) not all new students are freshmen (many may be transfer students and adult part-time learners); 3) many students may take as long as seven or eight years to complete a baccalaureate degree; and that 4) many students work more than 20 hours per week. Information such as this should result in new systems for facilitating student orientation, involvement, and academic success through such things as course scheduling changes and support service operating hours and times when faculty must be present in or around their offices.

The assumption, however, is that the outcomes to be measured are valued by the faculty and staff. It is difficult to reach any consensus on outcomes and even more complicated to shape everyone's work toward the successful achievement of those outcomes because in higher education we suffer from what Warren Bennis (1990) calls terminal egocentricity. Special interests and more and more specialization combine to turn people away from common objectives, team process, and embraced vision. Thus, effective and even inspired teaching in isolated courses is a necessary, but not sufficient, condition for generating positive educational outcomes. Team development of a series of coherent educational experiences, or solid design of curriculum in which each course has an interrelationship with the other, is often completely lacking. While the majority of faculty do not really think of themselves as independent contractors, sometimes their approach to educational outcomes takes on that appearance. Therefore, we need to find explicit ways to link incentives to continuous improvement in our student centered approach. Donald Langenberg (1992) has argued that team scholarship and collective responsibility and accountability of each academic department should replace our current values of individual and isolated scholarship and faculty responsibilities for individual courses rather than cohesive curricula. He writes that "when everyone's next salary increase (including that of the department's Nobel laureate) depends on a good evaluation of the entire department, Physics 101 is unlikely to be taught by the new graduate students who can barely speak English."

The cultural value of wide discretionary use of time and energy by faculty is highly prized. The value of almost complete protection from peer review of teaching will also be difficult to surrender. Faculty also have little experience with teamwork, and probably, with the exception of some research, little opportunity for it. The tradition of faculty leaves for professional development tied only to the specialized disciplinary interest of the faculty will also be hard to overcome. TQM principles would suggest that higher education needs to design these leaves to accomplish the objectives of the institution as well as individual faculty. As Boyer (1990) has suggested, scholarship may be redefined to allow a more productive use of faculty talent by expanding beyond the traditional scholarship of discovery to scholarship of integration, application, and teaching. Certainly several faculty could be funded to explore best practices in education every year. It may be that functional literacy across several disciplines will become as useful a competency as in depth scholarship in one. It is easy to identify some of the academic values in our educational settings which need some modification, balancing, or re-emphasis. It is quite another matter to shape a strategy to change any of these values and resulting behaviors.

Chaffee and Sherr (1992) remind us that "most administrations are unaware of the extent to which fear pervades their organizations." Many faculty feel at risk for tenure, promotion, and salary increases by discussing, much less by acting upon some of the new assumptions surfaced by TQM. Unless these matters are addressed in written policy, resistance will continue to be high. Seymour (1992) has suggested that many faculty simply do not perceive any real crisis in higher education that requires this kind of significant shift in their daily behaviors. Leadership must address this factor and present a compelling case while listening carefully to faculty concerns and additional ideas. Whether one talks about students, faculty, staff, or university officers, "it's impossible to feel ignored if someone is paying attention" (Seymour 1992). We need to be able to evaluate the performance of faculty and staff in activities which are coordinated and characterized by attention and follow-up to student needs—personal, social, and intellectual. The idea of utilizing the portfolio method for evaluating both faculty and programs is emerging strongly in the literature. Cheney (1990) writes about the use of "teaching portfolios" to evaluate the professional experience of faculty. These can include everything from peer observations and recommendations, student evaluations, examples of examinations and syllabi, alumni feedback, and self-evaluations which detail the changes faculty have made in approach based on learner performance in class, on exams, and from their remarks during out-of-class conversations.

Brock and Harvey (1993) have applied some aspects of corporate strategies development to the analysis of academic program portfolios. The academic programs of units of the university are plotted on a matrix based on their competitive position in the education market and their attractiveness to students, student sponsors, and potential employers. (Figure 3.)

Practicing Sociology in Higher Education   369

A Hypothetical Portfolio for a University		
Competitive Position of Business/Program		
	STRONG	**WEAK**
I n d u s t r y A t t r a c t i v e n e s s / **S t r o n g**	Engineering Continuing Education STARS	Education Veterinary Science QUESTION MARKS
W e a k	Revenue Sports Undergraduate Program CASH COWS	Non-Revenue Sports School of Design DOGS

Figure 3

James Miller, enrollment management and career services vice president at RIT, uses a similar approach in his collaboration with the deans and the provost to develop an enrollment management strategy for the respective colleges and/or their major academic programs. (Figures 4 and 5.)

As educators begin to seriously evaluate their academic program portfolios, the concepts of quality, competitive position, and centrality will help to make sound decisions about

Figure 4

Fine and Applied Arts				

| Selectivity | Geographic Draw | | | |
	Local	Instate	Regional	National
Low	SUC Buffalo			
Moderate	SUNY Buffalo	Pratt		
			Parsons	
			RISD	Boston Univ
	Temple	Syracuse		
High			O	
			Carnegie-Mellon	

O = RIT

Figure 5

Graphic Arts & Photography				

| Selectivity | Geographic Draw | | | |
	Local	Instate	Regional	National
Low				
Moderate	SUC Buffalo	Bridgeport Univ.		
		Hartford Univ.		
		Cornell	RISD	O
		Ithaca	Pratt	
High	Penn State			
		Syracuse		
		Boston Univ.		

O = RIT

Practicing Sociology in Higher Education 371

which programs to increase in size and quality, reduce or hold in size and increase in quality, and which program to reduce or eliminate regardless of quality.

The fourth idea emerging from some of the literature and practice focuses on the design of our learning experiences for students and our need to define and measure the outcomes of these designed learning experiences. Cochran (1992) has focused on the need to ascertain what faculty do. He maintains that faculty must be able to describe their teaching objectives and strategies, indicate how they maintain their professional competence and identify ways to validate their professional competence. He would ask many questions, for example: What do you try to accomplish with students? What particular emphasis do you bring to the classroom? How do you stay up-to-date in your discipline? How do you improve your teaching ability? In what ways can your technical/content expertise be demonstrated?

The answers to these questions form a portfolio which can be evaluated by peers, department heads, and deans on a continuous basis. Charlene Abshire (1991) illustrates the incongruity of our design of educational experiences with the world our students will confront. She writes:

> Employers have compared the college culture with the work culture, and concluded that many students go through college: studying alone, doing homework alone, being tested alone, producing already-known answers, doing closed-book exams, studying discrete bits of knowledge, moving on before getting feed-back, seeing results as compartmented, and seeing consequences as personal.
>
> Then, graduates get jobs that require: working in groups, conferring with peers, referring to any books or data, tapping consultants, working toward novel answers, seeking management guidance, getting

prompt feedback, working on multi-discipline problems, seeing results as interrelated, and seeing consequences as communal.

Students successfully completing our academic programs should possess a set of applications skills designed for some segment of the employment market, and at the same time a set of transferrable intellectual and communications competencies that minimally include the ability to speak and write clearly, listen effectively, use the computer as a tool, think logically, and be oriented toward team problem solving. Yet technical and professional knowledge alone are not enough. The ability to speak and write clearly, listen, compute, and think are not enough. An appreciation of the liberal arts and sciences is not enough. Even if all these are enhanced by the ability to carry on a lifetime of learning, they are not enough. If we are to make good on our promise to prepare students to earn a living and to live a life, not as two separate processes but as one, we must give them—most certainly the best and the brightest of them—a taste for leadership. This taste for leadership involves both an appreciation for the intended and unintended consequences of technology and a sense of craftsmanship or pride in the quality of one's work in the workplace and in the community.

These outcomes will not characterize graduates of American universities unless we find more professional ways of evaluating our own work and become much more systematic in the design of our curriculum. Each course must be carefully crafted and a majority of courses should fit together. Faculty must be willing to sacrifice some of their prized autonomy and work together to fashion such curriculum. While each student will still receive a unique education based on the special character of relationships with faculty and other students, each student will be able to perform all specified outcomes of the program regardless of the talent level they initially brought

Practicing Sociology in Higher Education   373

to the university. In order to accomplish these kinds of objectives with a diverse student body, education will have to embrace the delivery of instruction in new and novel ways. An example of the kind of innovative thinking required can be diagram/based largely on ideas developed by James Eifert and Gloria Rogers at Rose-Hulman Institute of Technology.

Figure 6

Classroom Relationships			
Classroom Configuration	**Roles**		
	Student	**Teacher**	**Administrator**
Teacher in Front/ Students in Rows	Listener	Lecturer	"Caretaker of the Status Quo"
Teacher and Screen in Front: Students in Rows	Observer	Presentor/ Coordinator	Manager/Agent of Change
Teacher and Screen in Front Students and Computers in Rows	Player	Coach	Resource Procurer
Flexible Learning Spaces	Partners: Same Time/Same Place		Facilitator of Continuous Improvement
Non-site Based Electronic Classroom	Colleagues: Same Time/Any Place		Real Time Interactivity

Classroom Relationships

Obviously, those who initiate change must be held accountable for the results. As Drucker (1993) has written "there is a great deal of talk today about 'empowerment'—a term I have never used and never will. It does not do any good simply to take power from the top and move it to the bottom. Power always corrupts unless it is first earned through responsibility." Bohn and Adams (1993) state that "empowerment isn't doing something to somebody—it's creating an environment where people accept responsibilities and are rewarded for it." Regardless of the terminology one uses, the challenge of accepting accountability for results in educational enterprises must be addressed through some systematic procedure, and TQM offers one such avenue. In higher education, we focus on one of the several factors which lead to success in the world of work. We are good at developing cognitive or conceptual skills. But we are less adept at fostering interpersonal skills and motivational affinity towards group goals. The former can be highly developed in isolation, but the latter two require team learning and collaborative problem-solving experiences. Robert Caruthers (1992) has written that "TQM is spreading so rapidly and being so well received, not because it increases efficiency and productivity in difficult times, but because it also incorporates a philosophy about work, people, and relationships built around human values and shared vision." Fisher (1993) puts it this way: "Any changes of consequence in higher education must include consideration of the following: increased teaching loads; dramatic reduction in emphasis on scholarly publication (it has been estimated that 75 percent of the published research in my field, psychology, is nonsense); required student advisers and posted office hours for every faculty member; dramatically reduced administrative staffs, especially in student services and academic affairs; the elimination of costly advanced graduate programs at hundreds of institutions; wrenching major revisions of general education requirements; the elimination or major modification of state systems; and above all, the adoption of truly accountable college and university governance practices."

These are some selected concepts and ideas emerging out of the TQM literature and practice which may be useful in ensuring that the programs of study in our universities are in touch with life. As Carol Cartwright (1992) has observed, the other trustees of the College of William and Mary were shocked when Thomas Jefferson suggested—in 1779—a complete change in curriculum because what the faculty then offered was out of touch with life.

References

Abshire, C. 1991. Federal Government Panel Summary. In *Quality and Higher Education in the 21st Century*. Los Angeles: USC.

Bennis, W. 1990. "Long Slide from True Leadership." *Executive Excellence* 7 (April).

Bess, J. L. 1988. *Collegiality and Bureaucracy in the Modern University: The Influence of Information and Power on Decision-Making Structures*. New York: Teachers College Press.

Blazey, M. L. 1990. Quality and Retention: The Cause-Effect Relationship. Unpublished Paper. Rochester, N. Y.: Rochester Institute of Technology.

Bohn, E. and B. Adams. 1993. "I'd Rather be Dead Than Empowered." *Executive Excellence* 10 (March).

Boyer, E. L. 1990. *Scholarship Reconsidered: Priorities of the Professorate*. Princeton: Princeton UP.

Brock, D. M. and W. B. Harvey. 1993. "The Applicability of Corporate Strategic Prinipals to Diversified University Campuses." *Journal for Higher Education Management* 8 (Winter/Spring).

Burr, I. W. 1979. *Elementary Statistical Quality Control*. New York: Marcel Dekker, Inc.

Calista, D. J., ed. 1991. "Total Quality Management (TQM) Symposium." *Journal of Management Science and Policy Analysis* 8 (Spring/Summer).

Cannie, L. K. and D. Caplin. 1991. *Keeping Customers for Life.*
Washington: American Management Association.

Carothers, R. L. 1992. "Translating Quality for the Academy." *AAHE Bulletin* 45 (November).

Cartwright, C. A. 1992. "Reclaiming the Public Trust: A Look to the Future." *AAHE Bulletin* 44 (June).

Chaffee, E. E. and L. A. Sherr. 1992. *Quality: Transforming Postsecondary Education.* ASHE-ERIC Higher Education Report, No. 3.

Cheney, L. V. 1990. *Tyrannical Machines.* Washington, D.C.: National Ednowment for the Humanities.

Chichering, A. W. and D. Potter. 1993. "TQM and Quality Education: Fast Food or Fitness Center." *Educational Record* 74 (Spring).

Clark, B. R. 1987. *The Academic Life: Small Worlds, Different Worlds.* Princeton, NJ: The Carnegie Foundation.

Cochran, L. H. 1992. *Publish or Perish: The Wrong Issues.* Cape Girardeau, MO: Step Up, Inc.

Drucker, P. F. 1993. "The Rise of the Knowledge Society." *The Wilson Quarterly* 17 (2).

Edgerton, R. 1993. "The New Public Mood and What it Means for Higher Education: A Conversation with Daniel Yankelovich." *AAHE Bulletin* 45 (10).

Elliott, R. K. 1991. "Employers Demand Improved Quality in Education for Business." In *Quality and Higher Education in the 21st Century*, edited by W. J. Petak. Los Angeles: USC.

Fecher, R., ed. 1985. *New Directions for Higher Education: Applying Corporate Management Strategies.* San Francisco: Jossey-Bass.

Firstenberg, P. B. 1991. "Private Education Competes for Survival." *Management Review* (April).

Fisher, J. L. 1993. "TQM—A Warning for Higher Education." *Educational Record* 74 (Spring).

Garvin, D. A. 1988. *Managing for Quality: The Strategic and Competitive Edge.* New York: Free Press.

Golomski, W. A. 1992. "Social Science Aspect of Quality." Quality at the Crossroads Conference Proceedings. Rochester, N. Y.: Center for Quality and Applied Statistics.

Handy, C. 1992. "Balancing Corporate Power: A New Federalist Paper." Harvard Business Review (November-December).

Handy, C. B. 1990. *The Age of Unreason.* New York: McGraw-Hill.

Harari, O. 1993. "Three Very Difficult Steps to Total Quality." *Management Review* 82 (April).

Practicing Sociology in Higher Education   377

Harrinton, H. J. 1987. *The Improvement Process*. New York: McGraw-Hill.

Harris, J. W. and J. M. Baggett, eds. 1992. *Quality Quest in the Academic Process*. Birmingham: Stamford University.

Heady, S. C. 1991. Cease Dependence on Mass Inspection. In *Applying the Deming Method to Higher Education for More Effective Human Resource Management*, edited by R. I. Miller. Washington: CUPA.

Henderson, R. L. 1991. *An Analysis of the State of TQM in Academia*. Report number ADA 246-966. Monterey, CA: Naval Postgraduate School.

Holt, L. C. and T. E. Wagner. 1983. "An Alternative for Higher Education." *Journal of the College and University Personnel Association* 34 (1).

Jencks, C. and D. Riesman. 1977. *The Academic Revolution*. Chicago: University of Chicago Press.

Karmarker, U. 1990. Quality Management. Unpublished paper. Rochester, NY: William E. Simon Graduate School of Business, University of Rochester.

Keller, G. 1992. "Increasing Quality on Campus." *Change* 24 (May/June).

Langenberg, D. N. 1992. "Point of View." *The Chronicle of Higher Education* 2 September.

Leskin , B. 1991. "Changing Demographics: Issues for Higher Education and the Work Place." In *Quality and Higher Education*, edited by W. J. Petak. Los Angeles: USC.

Lincoln, E. A. 1992. Towards a Better Understanding of the Applicability of Total Quality Management to American Higher Education. Unpublished paper. January. Rochester NY: RIT.

——. 1993. Responding to Faculty Reactions to Total Quality in Higher Education. Unpublished paper. Rochester, NY: RIT.

Luther, D. B. 1993. "How New York Launched a State Quality Award in 15 Months." *Quality Progress* (May).

——. 1991. "TQM Reaches the Academy." *AAHE Bulletin* 44 (November).

Marchese, T. 1993. "TQM: A Time for Ideas." *Change* 3 (May/June).

Massy, W. 1991. "Improving Academic Productivity: The Next Frontier?" *Capital Ideas* 6 (Spring).

Miller, R. I., ed. 1991. *Applying the Deming Method to Higher Education for More Effective Human Resource Management*. Washington: CUPA.

Nowlin, W. A. 1993. Total Quality: Key Concepts. Unpublished paper. January. Rochester, NY: RIT.

Pavela, G., ed. 1991. "Part I: Total Quality on Campus Law and Policy in Higher Education." *Synthesis* 3 (Summer).

Petak, W. J., ed. 1991. *Quality and Higher Education in the 21st Century*. Los Angeles: USC.

Peterson, P. 1992. Total Quality in Engineering Education. Faculty Colloquium. Rochester, NY: RIT.

Riesman, D. 1989. "The Next Academic Revolution." *AAHE Bulletin* 48 (September).

Rosett, R. N. 1992. "TQM in the College of Business." Faculty Colloquium, Rochester Institute of Technology. Rochester, NY.

—. 1992. Realignment Plan. Rochester, NY: RIT.

Rosovsky, H. 1992. "Faculty Citizenship." *Harvard Institutes for Higher Education* 1 (November).

Scheuch, E. K. 1992. The Puzzle of Quality of Life. In *The Annals*, edited by M. Sasaki and Y. Yonebayashi. vol. 3. Kobe, Japan: International Institute of Sociology.

Senge, P. M. 1990. *The Fifth Dimension*. New York: Doubleday.

Seymour, D. T. 1991. "TQM on Campus: What the Pioneers are Finding." *AAHE Bulletin* 44 (November).

—. 1992. *On Q: Causing Quality in Higher Education*. Ace Macmillan.

—. 1993. "TQM: Focus on Performance, Not Resources." *Educational Record* 74 (Spring).

Simone, A. J. 1992. Beyond Buzzwords: Applying TQM in the Public Interest. Plenary Address, Third Annual Eastman Symposium. September. Rochester, NY: RIT.

Thomas, P. R., L. J. Gallace, and K. R. Morten. 1992. *Quality Alone is Not Enough*. New York: American Management Association.

Trow, M. 1988. "American Higher Education: Past, Present and Future." In *ASHE Reader on the History of Higher Education*, edited by L. F. Goodchild and H. S. Wechsler. Needham Heights, MA: Ginn Press.

White, J. A. 1990. "TQM: It's Time Academia." *Education News* 3 (November).

Whittington, M. C. 1992. "TQM at Penn: A Report on First Experiences." *AAHE Bulletin* 45 (November).

Zemsky, R., ed. 1991. "Learning Slope." *Policy Perspectives* 4 (November).

—, ed. 1993. "A Call to Meeting." *Policy Perspectives* 4 (February).

Practicing Sociology in Higher Education

THOMAS R. PLOUGH

T homas R. Plough is provost and executive vice president of Rochester Institute of Technology, having served twice as acting president. Plough holds a doctorate degree from Michigan State University and teaches sociology of work, education, and leadership.

He also serves on the board of the Crestwood Children's Center and the International Museum of Photography at the George Eastman House. He is a member of the Governor's Task Force on Quality of Work Awards and a member of the Consumer Advisory Board of New York Telephone Corporation.

Plough has served in the roles of dean of students, associate dean, vice president, executive dean, vice president of academic affairs, and provost. He has a special research interest in technology transfer and distance learning, and he has lectured internationally on these topics as well as the applications of total quality management concepts in educational settings.

CHAPTER SEVENTEEN:

PRACTICING LEADERSHIP

Thomas W. Davis

Leadership is a topic which many people believe they know a lot about, but in fact, very little is really known. There are no models to follow, and no one can do it right all the time or in every situation. If everyone understood leadership, everyone would be practicing it and we would be doing it all the same way. Principles of leadership can change from organization to organization, from culture to culture, and even from person to person. It is even thought to follow some of the same principles as the theory of chaos and the universe (Wheatley 1992).

Some of the best leaders seem to have an inherent knack or talent to make things happen. They seem to adapt their styles well to a variety of situations, organizations, and cultures, and yet others never succeed in finding the true magic of leadership. One thing is certain: leadership can be learned and even taught. The true leader is someone who practices every day to improve and adapt, sets milestones and feedback mechanisms to measure effectiveness, and then continues to learn new methods, styles, and processes.

There are numerous presentations, articles, and scholarly writings on the concept of leadership. One might then ask why there are not more great leaders. The answer may be in the lack of practice in leadership and developing a daily commitment to improvement of leadership skills. There are almost as many consultants in leadership as there are people trying to implement it. But, the only real way to learn leadership is to do it.

People will develop personal exercise programs to keep their bodies in shape, but do not do the same thing for their minds. Even more difficult is to develop programs to keep and maintain leadership skills. Sure, people go to seminars and read books on leadership, but they return to work the next day and do business the same as usual. They do not change the basic way they do things.

There are many quality buzz words that seem to be a fad. Some of these change constantly. Total Quality Management is now being replaced by re-engineering and Management by Objectives. Management by objectives may never be heard from again. (Deming calls it management by fear!) Quality circles and empowerment will have a place in the past. True leadership will always be needed. As people understand that real contributors do not need supervision, and as middle management is eliminated, more enlightened leaders are needed—more people who can kindle the spark in others and help to invent the future.

Lessons in leadership are all around. There are many to be found in manufacturing and service companies, at the Boy Scout troop, at the church, and maybe once in a while in government. Learning from these experiences is important to the development of a style of leadership that produces results, and it all takes practice.

As with physicians who have a "practice," leaders too must practice. Leadership is a skill which can only be learned through constant and continuous practice and development of a personal dedication and commitment on a daily basis.

While reading this chapter, if you find yourself saying "I already know all of this," then ask the question, "Do I practice this each and every day?"

The Route to Leadership

As in most corporations today, the route to leadership in higher education is not a clearly defined one. Many "leaders" obtained their positions because they were in the right place at the right time, or because they were outstanding educators, or because they were good at fundraising. While there are a few, most have not been promoted because of leadership ability or style. Many people in leadership positions today have not been trained or educated to be leaders.

At a presentation recently, an engineering educator made the following observation: "As a graduate engineer working in industry, my education really paid off. Graduate school further supported my design work and progression in the company. The experience paid off, and I was invited to be a faculty member. Quickly realizing that I knew very little about education, I studied it and became a good teacher. Being a good teacher I was promoted to department chair, and I knew nothing of management; so I studied it. Being a good department chair, I was promoted to dean and knew nothing of leadership; so I studied it. Being a good dean, I was promoted to academic vice president; and I continue to study leadership today, still looking for the right way to do it" (Davis 1993).

Practicing Leadership   383

At the same presentation, the question was asked of nearly 200 college deans, chancellors, department chairs, vice presidents and presidents: "How many people have had leadership training?" The five people who raised their hands did so with great enthusiasm.

Leadership needs constant study, and practice, practice, practice.

Leadership at All Levels

Leadership is not just a skill for the university president. It is a skill needed at all levels in the organization. This also is true in the corporate world as well, but even more so in the university. Faculty, for example, lead more people than 70 percent of all United States company presidents. Not only do faculty have more than 100 employees, but they change every semester. Faculty cannot control or even manage what their students do; they can only lead them in the right direction.

University administrators, therefore, become *leaders of leaders* and need to have even greater skills in this area. Someone once said that "Managing faculty is like herding cats." That same person never attempted to lead faculty and did not have a clue to leading students to achieve their greatest potential.

Leadership is particularly important in the implementation of quality programs. It is truly unfortunate that the acronym TQM was ever developed. It should be Total Quality Leadership (TQL) instead. The essence of management is leadership, not supervision.

Let's Get Rid of Management

(United Technologies Corporation, 1989)

People do not want to be managed.

They want to be led.

Whoever heard of a world manager?

World leader, yes.

Educational leader.

Political leader.

Religious leader.

Scout leader.

Community leader.

Labor leader.

They lead; they do not manage.

The carrot always wins over the stick.

Ask your horse.

You can *lead* your horse to water,

but you can not *manage* him to drink.

If you want to manage somebody, manage yourself.

Do that well,

and you will be ready to stop managing and start

leading.

Some time ago, the opportunity was provided to review the TQM program at another university—a sort of quality audit. This university has all of the right things: quality council, director of quality, and regular "team" meetings. Yet when the meetings were over, everyone took off their "quality hats" and went back to doing things as usual. What they lacked was an *integrated* quality approach, and more importantly, leadership in quality.

Things to Practice in Leadership

Why is it then that some "leaders" can get things done and others have such problems? There are some fundamental philosophies that seem to be consistent in the development of good leadership practices.

Leaders have a vision. In fact, the terms "vision and leadership" often go hand in hand and could be called visionary leadership. Leaders have a vision for the future and what it is to be. It becomes an important characteristic to be able to visualize the future and to help others understand this vision. The mental picture that is created will help to make decisions and to bring focus to an otherwise chaotic environment. Vision also helps to build consensus and to bring focus. When people have a clear vision, decisions become much easier. If it fits the vision, you do it; if it does not, you toss it out.

Leaders maintain perspective. Maintaining perspective is often a difficult task, particularly when there are hundreds of events, questions, complaints, and meetings every day. It is important for leaders to remember, fundamentally, where the organization is headed and what needs to be done to get there.

There is a story, for example, about a university which virtually eliminated their educational assistance program for employees because employees were attending classes over their lunch hours and taking lunch at 10 a.m., 11 a.m., or 1 p.m., to match the class offerings. While most of the education was "related" to their jobs, it was considered to be an inconvenience. These were exactly the same kind of programs that the university sold to local companies.

Yet another university charged department budgets at the full tuition rate for faculty and staff development taken by department employees, regardless of where the course was taken. This, in effect, caused employees to take the same classes at another (less expensive) university across town, where the actual out-of-pocket costs were much greater.

386 **Davis**

Although it is sometimes difficult to maintain perspective, one of the most important things leaders do is to help everyone in the organization to maintain a consistent philosophy, and to discuss the philosophy often and regularly. It even helps to have it written down—to refer to it, and modify it as it develops.

Motorola, for example, developed a small document entitled "For Which We Stand." It described the purpose, vision, and philosophy of the company. It was distributed to all employees and served to guide the operations and dealings of the company (Motorola Personnel Publication, "For Which We Stand—A Statement of Purpose, Principles and Ethics" 1988). Arthur Anderson published a booklet in 1987 entitled *Our Shared Values* that helped both employees and customers to understand their philosophy.

Leaders do the right thing. The saying "Managers do things right, and leaders do the right thing" has been used over and over, but there is still evidence that people are not practicing it. Many people spend their lives trying to do things exactly right, but often entirely in the wrong direction.

There is a simple story which illustrates this principle. A large machine tool manufacturer placed a vast amount of company resources into the development and sales of hydraulic robots. They were a model in new product development. Several years down the road, they found out that the real future was in electric robots, and almost lost the company as they tried to make the shift. They did it right, but it was not the right thing to do.

Leaders are always honest. The cornerstone of effective leadership is honesty. It is one of the more important characteristics of effective leaders. There is nothing which will disenchant someone more in their job than having the boss tell one person one thing and someone else a different story. These two people almost always talk to each other, compare stories, and walk away believing both are wrong and will have to be sold twice as hard in the future.

Honesty helps leaders to build trust and respect. Trust and respect is not something that comes with a particular office, but rather something which is earned.

Leaders motivate and encourage people. People run on motivation and excitement, and it serves as fuel for the entire organization. People need to believe that they are making a difference, and that they are doing something meaningful and important. Also, they want to be included in what is happening.

One of the key elements to motivation is recognition. One officer at a university spends up to 10 percent of the day recognizing the real accomplishments of people in the organization. Some of these people have accomplished seemingly unbelievable things over the years. You cannot change someone's attitude through negative words or actions. It takes positive reinforcement to change someone's attitude permanently.

Leaders communicate. Communication is critical to the role of leadership. Such things as regular meetings to discuss vision and philosophy are as important, if not more important, than meetings called to accomplish a project. Communication on the state and health of the people and the organization are also important. People want to know what is happening and provide their ideas and feedback on how to improve it.

Leaders place decisions at the appropriate level. Giving the responsibility along with the authority to execute a job can go a long way toward developing motivation and the kind of attitude that produces results.

There was the story told by the president of Midwest Express Airlines about one employee checking in passengers before a flight. A woman and her daughter were purchasing tickets, and the woman asked for her senior citizen's discount but had no identification of any kind. The company policy was to require identification, and the employee behind the counter was bound and determined to follow this policy and charged her the full fare. Several weeks later, the daughter wrote to the president of the airline complaining about the situation, and enclosed a picture of her mother who was, and looked to be, 95 years old. From that point on, it was made clear what the new company policy was on these situations. The employee behind the counter had the authority to make the proper decisions and even to set aside company policies that do not make sense for a particular situation (Hoeksema 1993).

Leaders build teams. There are entire books written on the subject of team building and several companies that make a business from teaching others how to build teams. It is not complicated or difficult to learn the concept of team building, but it is difficult for many people to implement. Several references at the end of this chapter can provide more information.

Leaders coach and teach. Many people do not see their role as teachers. Yet teaching must go on at all levels in an organization for it to grow. Growing people is one of the most important roles any leader can play. If we teach everyone everything we know all the time, not only will we help to grow people, but we will grow even more. Intellectual property is one of those things that the more you give it away, the more the giver has.

Things Not to Practice in Leadership

Misplaced recognition. One of those signs that gets photocopied hundreds of times lists the seven stages of project implementation. The last stage is reward for the non-participants. It is true that recognition of the accomplishment must be with those responsible. You cannot reward "A" while hoping for "B.

Too much focus on financial objectives. While it is important for every organization to be financially healthy, it should not be the primary focus. Some manufacturing companies have recognized that customer service is more important than profits as a focus. Good customer service, on time delivery, good quality, and a productive environment for the employees does produce profits.

There is a sad story of a company in Milwaukee that produced consistent profits despite business down turns. At the first down turn, the president cut the company's educational assistance program. During the next period the president cut the research and development staff, and later cut the sales staff. Showing profits quarter after quarter despite declining sales, the board of directors voted a bonus for the president. And, in just three short years the company went bankrupt.

Control. The more you attempt to control people the less control there really is. If anyone believes that people can be controlled, they are very sadly mistaken. You can control processes, control a plant, control a system, but you must lead people.

Short answers and patchwork solutions. In order to achieve long-term progress, problems must be solved at the root cause.

Home runs. Many people try to hit a home run each time at bat. This is also true with many leaders. They look only for the major accomplishments, and fail to realize that the long term health of any organization is in the small and consistent improvements. The difference between a .250 hitter and a .300 hitter, besides $500,000 a year, is one extra base hit every 20 times at bat. Small changes do make a difference in the long run.

"It is not in the plan." This is a common misuse of strategic planning in leadership today. Of course, plans are meant to be followed; however, if there is a better way, change the plan and keep everyone informed.

Someone was once told that "Things are really tight, and we need to follow the budget exactly. Therefore, there will be no new ideas this year."

"That's a great idea, Joe. Let's see what Sue can do with it." People need to champion their own ideas through the system and see the results of their efforts. It is important, too, from the standpoint that someone "assigned" someone else's ideas will not necessarily do the best job to see that they come to fruition.

Problem people. There are some who do not want to learn new things, and others who just want to bring attention to themselves by being part of the problem and not part of the solution. Working with these people can sometimes defocus the real needs of the organization.

A manufacturing company president once told this brief story. As he embarked on new leadership styles, the company's chief financial officer came into his office and said, "I am 55 years old, and I am not about to make any changes in my life." To which the company president responded, "Just one more, I'm afraid . . . A new job! Clean out your desk!"

Change. Change is one of the most effective barriers to leadership. People do not inherently want to make changes in their lives and go through the same emotional stages as with a death in the family. The job of leadership is to help individuals cope with change and risk for the purposes of improvement.

As Bob Galvin (retired chairman of Motorola) once said, "If you do what you have always done, you will get what you have always got" (YPO Manufacturing Conference 1989).

Practice Paradigm Shifts in Thinking

Some basic changes are needed in the leadership of people which are fundamental.

OLD
Involved
Assets are Things
Hold at Arms Length
Economy of Scale
Profit Domination
Hierarchy
Measurement of Judgment
Management
NEW
Committed
Assets are People
Build Trust and Respect
Economy of Time
Customer Satisfaction
Problem Solving Network
Measurement for Improvement
Leadership

There are many great examples of effective leadership in education as well as corporate America. In virtually all cases, there has been a real leap of faith, a leap of faith in people. It has been recognized that people are the real strength and backbone of the organizations, and represent the real opportunity for improvement.

The Tools for Practicing Leadership

There are tools for leadership. Perhaps not as well defined as the tools for a carpenter or the tools of a surgeon, but as critical.

Belief in self. Leaders must first believe in themselves before they can help others. Too, leaders must help themselves first before they can help others. Remember what the flight attendant says before each takeoff: "If the cabin loses air pressure during the flight and the oxygen masks fall and you have an infant in your arms, place the mask on yourself first. If something happens to you, the infant cannot survive." This is true in life too. It is not possible to help others if you are not helped.

Attention to process. Pay attention to process more than to outcomes. If the process if right, the outcome is assured.

There are several manufacturing companies such as New United Motors Manufacturing Incorporated (NUMMI) that have eliminated the inspection process at various stages in manufacturing because the process is so well defined that there is no need to conduct inspections.

There are numerous tools regarding process and process development such as the ones developed by Geary A. Rummler and Alan Brache (Rummler and Brache 1990).

Teaching. Teach everyone everything you know all the time. Building people and helping them to achieve their goals is one of the greatest ways to build trust and respect and to obtain top performance. Help others to achieve what you have, and you will achieve even more.

Remember, too, you really do not learn something until you put it into practice. Practice makes teaching work.

Practice what you preach. Live your life by what you ask others to do. Most people remember a favorite teacher, or someone else in their lives whom they try to mimic or pattern themselves after.

Practicing Leadership 393

Manage risk. It is important to take some calculated risk to achieve what you want. It is also important to help others to risk, and reward that risk even if it resulted in failure. Without the confidence that there will be no punishment in failure, people will not take the risk. The mistakes we make today will be called experience tomorrow.

At 3M, for example, the Research and Development Department rewards failure. Out of every 500 ideas, only two will make money. So every failure brings them closer to the ideas that will make money. And, as Winston Churchill once said, "Success is going from failure to failure without loss of enthusiasm."

Planning. One of the major responsibilities of leaders is to plan the work and let others work the plan. Planning is a tool and, like many other things, needs to be learned and studied.

These are just a few examples of the tools that leaders must develop and improve. Document them in the same way you would document a patent for a new product or an instruction manual for a new piece of software, because without a map of where you are going, any road will get you there.

Practice Life's Little Instruction Book Daily

Here is a takeoff on *Life's Little Instruction Book* for leaders:

Walk around and talk to people • Treat everyone you meet as you want to be treated • Criticize behavior, not people • Practice what you preach • Arrange release time • Strive for excellence, not perfection • Plant a tree on your birthday • Learn three clean jokes • Return borrowed vehicles with the tank full • Compliment three people every day • Never waste an opportunity to tell someone you care about them • Leave everything a little better than you found it • Keep it simple • Think big thoughts but relish small pleasures • Become the most positive and enthusiastic person you know • Play as you practiced • Be forgiving of yourself and others • Overtip breakfast waitresses • Say "thank you" a lot • Say "please" a lot • Help negative people • Buy whatever kids are selling on card tables in their front yards • Wear polished shoes • Remember other people's birthdays • Commit yourself to constant improvement • Measure yourself by what you have helped others to do • Have a firm handshake • Send lots of valentines cards, and sign them "Someone who thinks you're terrific" • Look people in the eye • Be the first to say "hello" • Involve everyone in everything you do • Return all things you borrow • Make new friends, but cherish the old ones • Keep secrets • Sing in a choir • Read a book on leadership • Take a course again • Always accept an outstretched hand • Stop blaming others • Take responsibility for every area of your life • Wave at kids on school buses • Be there when people need you • Feed a stranger's expired parking meter • Don't expect life to be fair • Pay more attention to process than product • Take someone to lunch for no reason • Live your life as an exclamation, not an explanation • Don't be afraid to say, "I made a mistake" • Don't be afraid to say, "I don't know" • Compliment even small improvements • Keep your promises (no matter what) • Rekindle old friendships • Count your blessings • Call your mother (Brown 1991)

Practice, Practice, Practice

The concept of leadership cannot be understood by everyone, but those who do will develop a plan to make it happen. There are many clichés that can reflect this philosophy:

"You will play as you practice." —Vince Lombardi, Head Coach, Green Bay Packers

"People rarely notice the existence of the greatest leaders."—Admiral Hyman George Rickover

"Some use people to build a great company. I use the company to build great people."—Ralph Stayer, Johnsonville Foods

Practicing Leadership 395

The best advice that can be given is to practice, practice, practice.

References

"I will teach thee all my original songs, my self-constructed riddles, my own ingenious paradoxes, nay, more, I will reveal to thee the source whence I get them."—Jack Point

Arthur Anderson & Co. 1987. *Our Shared Values*. Milwaukee, WI: Society Cooperative.

Brown, Jr., H. J. 1991. *Life's Little Instruction Book—511 Suggestions, Observations and Reminders on How to Have a Happy and Rewarding Life*. Rutledge Hill Press.

For Which We Stand—A Statement of Purpose, Principles and Ethics. 1988. Schaumberg, IL: Motorola Personnel Publication.

Hoeksema, T. E. 1993. Presentation at MSOE. 29 October, Milwaukee, WI.

Rummler, G. A. and A. P. Brache. 1990. *Improving Performance: How to Manage the White Space on the Organization Chart*. San Francisco: JosseyBass.

Davis, T. W. 1993. TQM in Colleges and Universities. Presentation, 27-28 September, Chicago.

Wheatley, M. J. 1992. *Leadership and the New Science*. San Francisco: Berrett-Koehler.

YPO Manufacturing Conference. 1989. 5-8 March, Washington, D.C.

Suggested Readings

Belasco, J. A. 1990. *Teaching the Elephant to Dance: Empowering Change in Your Organization*. New York: Crown.

Bennis, W. G. 1989. *Why Leaders Can't Lead*. San Francisco: Jossey-Bass.

Bhote, K. R. 1986. *Supply Management: How to Make U. S. Suppliers Competitive*. New York: AMA.

—. 1988. *World Class Quality*. New York: AMA.

Burt, D. N. 1984. *Proactive Procurement*. Englewood Cliffs, NJ: Prentice Hall.

Byham, W. 1989. *Zapp! —The Human Lightning of Empowerment (and how to make it work for you)*. Pittsburgh: Development Dimensions International Press.

Carlzon, J. 1987. *Moments of Truth*. Cambridge: Ballinger Pub. Co.

Cetron, M. J. 1985. *The Future of American Business*. New York: McGraw-Hill.

Cohen, S. S. 1987. *Manufacturing Matters*. New York: Basic Books.

Cooper, R. G. 1986. *Winning at New Products*. Reading, MA: Addison-Wesley.

Covey, S. R. 1989. *The Seven Habits of Highly Effective People*. New York: Simon and Schuster.

Deming, W. E. 1986. *Out of the Crisis*. Cambridge: MIT Center For Advanced Engineering Study.

Drucker, P. F. 1985. *Innovation and Entreprenuership*. New York: Harper-Row.

Foster, R. N. 1986. *Innovation: The Attacher's Advantage*. New York: Summit Books.

Fukoda, R. 1983. *Managerial Engineering*. Stanford, CT: Productivity Inc.

Goldratt, E. M. and R. E. Fox. 1986. *The Race*. Croton-on-Hudson, NY: North River Press.

Goldratt, E. M. and J. Cox. 1987. *The Goal—A Process of Ongoing Improvement*. Croton-on-Hudson: North River Press, Inc.

Gunn, T. G. 1987. *Manufacturing for Competitive Advantage*. Cambridge: Ballinger Pub. Co.

Halberstam, D. 1986. *The Reckoning*. New York: William Morrow.

Hale, R. L., D. R. Hoelsher, and R. E. Kowal. 1989. *Quest for Quality — Second Edition*. Minneapolis: Tennant Company.

Hall, R. W. 1987. *Attaining Manufacturing Excellence: Just-in-Time, Total Quality, Total People Involvement*. Homewood, IL: Dow-Jones.

—. 1990. *Measuring Up: Charting Pathways to Manufacturing Excellence*. Homewood, IL: Business One Irwin.

Hasegawa, K. 1987. *Japanese Style Management—An Insider's Analysis of Corporate Success*. New York: Kodansha International Ltd.

Hay, E. J. 1988. *The Just-in-Time Breakthrough*. Wiley, NY.

Hayes, R. H. and S. C. Wheelwright. 1984. *Restoring Our Competitive Edge*. Wiley, NY.

Huge, E. C. 1988. *Spirit of Manufacturing Excellence*. Homewood, IL: Dow Jones.

Imai, M. 1986. *Kaizen, The Key to Japan's Competitive Success*. New York: Random House Business Division.

Practicing Leadership   397

Johnson, H. T. and R. S. Kaplan. 1987. *Relevance Lost*. Boston: Harvard Business School Press.

Manske, Jr., F. A. 1990. *Secrets of Effective Leadership—Second Edition*. Memphis: Leadership Education and Development.

Noori, H. 1990. *Managing the Dynamics of New Technology: Issues in Manufacturing Management*. Englewood Cliffs, NJ: Prentice-Hall.

Pascale, R. T. and A. G. Athos. 1981. *The Art of Japanese Management*. New York: Simon and Schuster.

Peters, T. *Thriving on Chaos*. New York: Alfred A. Knopf.

Rogers, E. M. 1983. *Diffusion of Innovations—Third Edition*. New York: Free Press.

Schmenner, R. W. 1984. *Production Operations Management: Concepts and Situations*. Chicago: Science Research Assoc.

Scholtes, P. R. 1988. *The Team Handbook*. Madison, WI: Joiner Associates Inc.

Schonberger, R. J. 1982. *Managing High Technology Techniques*.

—. 1986. *World Class Manufacturing—The Lessons of Simplicity Applied*. New York: The Free Press.

Senge, P. M. 1990. *Fifth Discipline: The Art and Practice of the Learning Organization*. New York: Doubleday.

Shingo, S. 1985. *A Revolution in Manufacturing: The Smed System*. Stamford, CT: Productivity Press.

Shingo, S. 1986. *Zero Quality Control*. Stamford, CT: Productivity Press.

Skinner, W. 1985. *Manufacturing, The Formidable Competitive Weapon*. Wiley, NY.

Steele, L. W. 1989. *Managing Technology*. New York: McGraw-Hill.

Storm, H. 1972. *Seven Arrows*. New York: Ballantine Books.

Suzaki, K. 1987. *The New Manufacturing Challenge: Techniques for Continuous Improvement*. New York: The Free Press.

Thurow, L. 1987. The Management Challenge: Japanese Views. Cambridge: MIT Press.

White, M. 1987. *The Japanese Educational Challenge*. New York: The Free Press.

THOMAS W. DAVIS

T homas W. Davis is presently executive vice president at Super Steel Products Corporation. He received his bachelor of science degree from MSOE and his master of science degree from the University of Wisconsin-Milwaukee. Davis is actively involved in many different committees, organizations, and departments, including the board of directors of 12 manufacturing and service sector companies; the Center for the Advancement of (K-12) Science, Mathematics, and Technology Education; and a corporate member of Curative Rehabilitation Center. He is a registered professional engineer, and has served on numerous advisory committees for local K-12 schools.

Davis has served as a consultant for over 500 companies in the areas of software development, hardware design, the development of test specifications for military equipment, management, leadership, and total quality. He has served the Milwaukee School of Engineering for nearly 28 years.

*C*HAPTER

*E*IGHTEEN:

BEYOND TQM: TOWARD THE AGILE
REVOLUTION IN EDUCATION

Gerald J. Richter and Galen C. Godbey

The United States continues to lead the world in post-secondary education, a vitally important area of intellectual and economic activity. Our nation will not maintain world class competitiveness in what economists coldly call "human capital formation" processes unless we maintain this leading position. In a recent interview, Peter Drucker (1993) recognized this when he stated, "We have a half million foreign students. American higher education has a positive balance of payments of about $5 billion to $8 billion a year . . . Continuous learning is still an American innovation: it is still considered absolutely unimaginable in Japan or in Germany."

The institutions which lead the world in higher education, however, are faced with a significant challenge: economic and fiscal constraints coupled with rising expectations from consumers of their services. They must continue to improve their services—the whole message of this volume—not only to their traditional but shrinking clientele of full-time students, but to K-12 institutions, business, and government as well. This must be done at a time when the increasing cost of higher education is a major concern; indeed, many commentators have expressed pessimism, if not outright skepticism, regarding the viability of the present labor-intensive model prevalent in much of higher education. In short, our institutions must not only improve the quality of their current services, they must simultaneously achieve wider scope of involvements and a broader set of social commitments without achieving greater institutional mass. Greater scale without greater mass? Is this scenario possible? If so, at what cost?

The preceding chapters have considered the important implications of Total Quality Management (TQM) and continuous improvement theory for higher education from a variety of viewpoints. TQM is vital to maintaining the vitality and viability of post-secondary educational institutions. It is, however, but one element of a set of related forces, movements, and strategies which are converging rapidly, and which will have a dramatic impact on the way we organize ourselves to teach and to learn in the future. TQM is a prerequisite for functioning competitively in the emerging environment of "organizational agility," a strategy of competitiveness through cooperation based upon new distance learning and telecommunication technologies. While TQM is necessary for agility, it is by no means sufficient. Educational institutions must not only embrace and adapt TQM strategies to enhance student learning; they also must be prepared to change in other fundamental ways if they are to position themselves as effective competitors in the emerging world order of technology-mediated global partnerships. Tracking developments in the manufacturing sector, the very nature of competition among institutions of higher education must evolve to embrace the concept of simultaneous competition and cooperation between and among partner institutions.

This chapter will describe the forces which are driving this rapid evolution, discuss the strategies required to thrive in the emergent environment, and attempt to provide a picture of what the educational system (K-post-graduate) will look like in the "agile" future. In short, this chapter will place the quality movement in higher education in the context of a fundamentally new organizational paradigm and external environment.

Organizational Agility Defined

Organizational structures, or the way human activity is organized to accomplish goals and tasks, are determined by broad social, cultural, and economic forces, current as well as historic. For the past century, mass production has been the dominant organizational model in the United states, and indeed in most of the industrialized world. The factory model has informed not only manufacturing but education as well: the Carnegie Unit is the perfect artifact of this archaic system. In discussing the impact of the mass production model on society, Steven L. Goldman, Andrew Mellon Distinguished Professor in the Humanities at Lehigh University, notes:

> Back in the 1880s and 90s—when Gustave Swift was creating the Swift Meat Packing Company, and J.P. Morgan and John D. Rockefeller were creating U.S. Steel and Standard Oil of New Jersey—neither the factory system nor mass production nor the steam power-based Industrial Revolution were new, or any longer newsworthy. The factory system was by then 200 years old. Mass production, in textiles for example, was 100 years old, as were improved steam

engines, which had long since been applied to ships and railroads along with factory machinery. Even the telegraph was "old hat." (Goldman 1993)

What Swift, Morgan, and Rockefeller saw, however, was the possibility of integrating existing production, transportation, and information technologies into a new organizational structure: a centrally administered, vertically integrated, hierarchically managed corporation. They envisioned the unprecedented competitive power that such an organization unleashed. And they were right. Companies that adopted this structure—or adapted to it—survived. Few of the companies that had to compete against such companies as US Steel, Standard Oil, General Electric, Dupont, General Foods, Ford, Goodyear, and refused to adapt, survived for long, even if there was nothing absolutely new in what these corporations were doing.

Explicitly, mass production manufacturing defined a system for the creation, production and distribution of goods and services. Implicitly, it defined paradigms for the organization of society to create, distribute, and consume the kinds of goods and services distinctive of this system of production.

The organizational model of mass production, which still informs the structure of education, government, and social services as well as manufacturing, was developed to meet 19th and early 20th century market and technological conditions. These conditions no longer exist. Mass production was an appropriate model for a time when there was a large, stable demand for undifferentiated manufactured goods (stoves, refrigerators, cars, radios, televisions, etc.), when technological change was slow and when the number of competitors was limited by either geography or the market share of dominant producers. The educational equivalent of a stable demand for goods was the concept of a relatively stable body of knowledge, with sharply defined disciplinary boundaries, to be communicated to a largely homogeneous body of students.

The characteristics of the present environment are radically different: rapid technological change; the information and knowledge explosion; new, international competitors; and the elimination of geographic constraints by new communications technologies, among other factors. This new environment threatens the survival of any organization which is structured along mass production lines, particularly if its products or services are information-intensive. The fact that IBM is facing severe pressure from much newer and smaller competitors who are better able to respond quickly to market and technological changes, is a case in point. An educational example is that school districts in many areas pay out-of-state universities to receive courses such as Russian and Japanese by means of new distance learning technology. In many cases, highly qualified faculty in the same fields exist at nearby post-secondary institutions. These local educators, however, are unable to serve such districts either because of logistical difficulties in transporting faculty or students or, more likely, the perceived impermeability of the sectoral boundary between K-12 and post-secondary education, compounded by a limited conception of the college's mission and constituency.

An alternative to the mass production model, "organizational agility," is evolving rapidly. "Agile" enterprise theory and "virtual" organization theory are being developed by such scholars as Roger N. Nagel and Steven L. Goldman of the Iacocca Institute at Lehigh University. The emergence of "agility" as the successor paradigm to mass production has been featured recently in such publications as *Business Week*, *Newsweek*, and *The Educational Record*. It also has been cited in the Clinton administration's industrial policy and forms the basis for many of the recommendations resulting from Vice President Gore's National Performance Review. Again quoting Goldman (1993):

Today, a new system for the production of goods and services is emerging, one that coordinates new production technologies with a new structure for the industrial corporation. This new system threatens to displace mass production corporations from the century-long dominance they have enjoyed. By implication, the new system, too, will define paradigms for the organization of society to create, distribute, and consume the goods and services distinctive of the agile manufacturing system. In the process, it will evoke from society new institutions, new values, new sensibilities reflecting the spreading influence of this new system of production.

Goldman further characterizes "agility" as a metaphor for a new means of organizing technical, human, social, and natural resources into what is likely to become the dominant world industrial order of the 21st century.

In the mass production model, single producers design, market, and provide standardized products and services in mass quantities based on their **conception** of the long-term needs or, at least, acquiescence of a large, homogeneous customer population. In the agile model, resources from many (usually small or small elements of large) producing organizations (a community of competitors) combine to form a "virtual organization" to develop a new technology or to provide a discrete number of **customized** products or services designed to respond to the rapidly changing, **articulated** needs of a particular customer or group. The resulting virtual organization may exist as a partnership only as long as needed to address a specific market need and may reconstitute itself as needed to accommodate other customer or client groups.

Beyond TQM   405

In the manufacturing area, a virtual corporation composed of agile organizations might include the research departments of a computer company, a television manufacturer, and a cellular phone manufacturer who join forces to develop a color flat screen display for a portable communication/computing device. The technology developed through this partnership may then be incorporated into products marketed by each partner in competition with each other. In this case, no single partner by itself commanded the resources (knowledge and experience) to bring this technology to the product stage.

One also can envision such partnerships developing in the world of higher education. A hypothetical example: due to budget constraints, four independent colleges in Eastern and Central Pennsylvania, located up to 120 miles apart, have reduced their East Asian studies faculties to 1, 1, 2, and 3 respectively. While each institution has highly qualified faculty, none has a sufficient number of faculty in this area to offer an undergraduate concentration in East Asian Studies, due to low student demand at each institution. These four institutions, through personal contacts between chief academic officers, presidents and department chairs, create a shared East Asian Studies undergraduate major by pooling the talents of the available faculty from each. Some of the courses are team-taught by faculty from different institutions. The four institutions have reached agreement regarding transfer of credit and grades in this area, and the degree is awarded by the home institution of each student. Each of the four also participates in other partnerships for other programmatic purposes.

Just as the mass production model was replicated in non-manufacturing fields, so too the agility paradigm will come to influence all elements of society, particularly those which are heavily dependent on the exchange of information. Agility will force the restructuring of large, traditionally organized school districts and universities as well as manufacturing companies. It will favor those institutions that concentrate on strengthening their core competencies and form productive partnerships with other institutions to create new, or expand small, programs.

Technology

Agility essentially means the pooling of experience and expertise (human and information resources) by geographically separated institutions. Consequently, it is dependent upon the ability to communicate interactively and casually in all digital modes (voice, video, data, text, and graphics) and to move large volumes of information quickly and easily. Since an agile institution may cooperate within different, or multiple, virtual organization partnerships, either sequentially or simultaneously, it is also dependent upon the ability to configure high speed, high capacity, multi-media networks on an ad-hoc basis without requiring long-term investment in dedicated institution-to-institution links. A ubiquitous, state-of-the-art telecommunications infrastructure is the sine qua non of organizational agility.

The use of technology to extend the reach of teachers (both geographically and in the number of students reached) is no longer new. Closed-circuit television has been used for at least 20 years by large, land grant universities to link a faculty member to several hundred undergraduate students in one or several large lecture auditoriums. Mind Extension University delivers college courses to the homes of literally millions of cable television subscribers. More recently, the delivery of low demand courses (such as Russian and Japanese) to high school students through satellite services like the Satellite Educational Resource Consortium (SERC) is becoming commonplace. In fact, within the next few years, one can expect entering college freshmen with this high school background to become less accepting of limited curricular choices, especially at small liberal arts colleges. They will be conditioned to expect courses to be provided from sources other than their home institution if that institution cannot provide it directly.

On the surface, SERC and other distance-learning examples given above seem to be innovative, and indeed they do serve a purpose. However, at a deeper level they are still firmly rooted within the paradigm of mass production. Such providers engage in market research or simply make assumptions about the characteristics and needs of what is clearly a mass market. Offerings presuppose student registrations in the thousands. Interaction between the subscribing and producing institutions remains limited to the level of course registration and payment, perhaps with the opportunity to submit evaluation forms. The continuing interaction between provider and customer which characterizes the TQM aspect of organizational agility is, for the most part, missing.

Clearly, the most effective teaching tool remains the direct, face-to-face interactive relationship between a talented teacher and a motivated student. The recent attempts, such as those discussed above, to extend the reach of such teachers through distance learning technologies (one-way video satellite, computer and graphics networks, etc.) have sacrificed this special element of the educational relationship. Some of these technologies allow for limited feedback from students through telephones. However, this is frequently under so much artificial constraint as to be reactive rather than interactive; each client school may be permitted to phone in only one question every several weeks on a rotating basis. Such situations eliminate the "teachable moment," those instances in a classroom when a teacher's presentation is guided and directed by interpretation of the non-verbal signals of the students. This lack of interaction reinforces the reliance on the one-way lecture format in spite of pedagogical research that suggests that this is the least effective teaching methodology. Donald J. Stedman (School of Education, University of North Carolina) and Louis A. Bransford (ESATEL Communications) (1992) state that:

> Vicarious interaction may satisfy many distance learning authorities, but it doesn't necessarily stimulate spontaneous, critical and creative thinking . . . success of distance learning . . . is built on interaction that depends heavily on the professional skills and competence of the instructor.

Recent technological advances have now made it possible to extend not only the teacher, but the classroom environment itself to combine students at remote locations with those in the teacher's originating classroom. Through compressed digital interactive video conferencing technology, it is possible to transmit live, high quality, color interactive video and audio simultaneously between several sites. Teacher and students maintain the face-to-face contact inherent in the traditional classroom while the digital transmission medium allows the incorporation of computers, graphics, video tape, etc.

The use of digital circuits provided by local phone companies and long-distance carriers allows these two-way signals to be switched in a manner similar to the voice telephone network. The implications of this are important. Since dedicated, fixed links between sites are not required, the network architecture is highly flexible, allowing connections between sites in various configurations at various times. In other words, the creation of "virtual institutions" on an ad hoc basis.

Specific benefits of such a network include:
• expand the menu for learners of all ages;

- provision of a basis for avoiding future, or reducing current, needless duplication of courses and other services;
- reduction in the professional isolation of faculty and facilitation of professional development programs;
- reduction in travel expenditures for staff and students and facilitation of in-plant training of business employees.

In recent years, the use of this technology in the higher education community has been rapidly expanding. The Universities of Oklahoma, Kentucky, California, Northern Virginia Community College, Penn State, and the University of Pittsburgh are only a few now using this medium. In fact, Minnesota now requires that interactive video be used in order to grant credit for distance education courses ("Two-Way" 1990).

In the previously described hypothetical East Asian Studies example, the colleges are connected by a high-speed data network capable of transmitting interactive compressed video, and each of them has an electronic classroom equipped and configured for two-way video conferencing. Students use the classroom on their own campus to take the desired course, regardless of the physical location of the professor. The professor teaches his/her own students and, simultaneously, through a video monitor at the rear of the classroom, sees and hears the distant students in the same way that they would be seen and heard if they were in the classroom. The distant students have the same ability as those present with the faculty member to interrupt, question, engage in dialogue, etc. The integrated fax and computer capabilities permit the transmission and return of tests, quizzes, and homework assignments. Following the class, the connecting link is maintained to permit the distant students to converse informally with the professor or with students at the professor's location. Outside of class hours, the interactive technology is used for office hours with students, consultation among faculty, student conferences on team projects, etc.

The importance of these emerging networks and new ways of communicating was emphasized by Arnold Brown, Chairman of Weiner, Edrich, Brown, Inc. (1993):

> The world is being re-ordered along lines defined, not by geography or governmental authority, but by telecommunications. When information is the most important resource in the world—and the least subject to control—geography and sovereignty [governmental and institutional] become increasingly less relevant. Networks are everything.

The ability of distance learning to reach students anywhere at any time presages a serious challenge to any institution's concept and definition of its market and of its competitors. If geography is irrelevant, only quality education and satisfied learners matter. It is no longer possible to be the "only game in town." Distance learning presents moral questions as well as market questions: Is it fair to students to continue to offer mediocre programs or courses, if high quality, real-time interactive alternatives are available?

Relationships: Foundation of Agility

The ability of institutions which are electronically linked to pool their resources to offer programs which none could support alone (i.e., attain organizational agility within a virtual organization); to provide on-campus students with additional curricular choices from distant sites (as institutions are pushed toward narrower on-campus curricula due to cost); and to combine expertise to meet customized professional development needs of business, government, and the K- 12 sector, are obvious. Just as obvious, however, is the fact that technology alone will not bring about the increased sharing and organizational agility envisioned here. Stedman and Bransford (1992) make the vital point that:

In the real world, technology isn't just a medium of information but a medium for relationships. Information matters, but it's the relationships—the formal and informal networks of people—that really govern how the organization runs and how value is created.

The importance of formalized relationships as the basis for developing networks for educational sharing is also emphasized by Richard M. Millard in his important work, *Today's Myths and Tomorrow's Realities: Overcoming Obstacles to Academic Leadership in the 21st Century*. In discussing what he terms the "myth of the technology threat," Millard states:

The new technologies make the extended classroom, even extended colleges and universities, realities, and with appropriate planning provide an infrastructure for cooperation, coordination, and liaison among institutions for sharing resources and meeting the educational and research needs of the broader society.

Given the range of technologies, their costs, their inter-institutional implications (including their relevance to institutional cooperation and reinforcement), and their potential for network development, it may well be that the most effective use of them cannot be achieved by any institution in isolation.... If this is the case, then the potential role of the state, or of consortia of institutions in making their institutional use possible, is critical.

Some of the defining characteristics of an agile educational institution, as described by Professor Goldman are:

- routine inter-institutional information and education exchanges;
- a recognition that cooperation both within and between institutions can be a powerful tool for competitive advantage;
- a pervasive ethic of mutual trust on the parts of administrators, faculty, and staffing the conduct of institutional and inter-institutional operations;
- the routine formation of "virtual" educational institutions (in effect, creating new educational resources through electronic inter-institutional alliances).

These characteristics are not new to higher education, nor is the concept that competition and cooperation can co-exist within the framework of an institutional strategy. One can easily point to numerous examples of inter-institutional cooperation which enhance the competitiveness of participating colleges and universities. The primitive but still widespread notion that competitors cannot collaborate effectively is disproved by the under-publicized work of the nation's approximately 130 general purpose post-secondary consortia. In fact, one could make the argument that any time there are a number of post-secondary institutions in proximity, cooperative relationships are likely to evolve, sometimes at extremely high levels of activity and significance. The Five Colleges, Inc., in Amherst, Massachusetts (Amherst, Smith, Mount Holyoke, Hampshire and University of Massachusetts at Amherst), and the Lehigh Valley Association of Independent Colleges (LVAIC) in the Allentown/Bethlehem/Easton area of Pennsylvania (Allentown College of St. Francis de Sales, Cedar Crest College, Lafayette College, Lehigh University, Moravian College and Muhlenberg College), are cases in point. In the case of LVAIC, cooperative programs include cross-registration, transfer of credits and grades, faculty exchange, joint purchasing, joint study-abroad programs, and library cooperation among others. Both of these organizations are exploring the use of telecommunications technology to strengthen consortial relationships.

Lacking an adequate information infrastructure, such high levels of cooperation would remain limited to groups of institutions located close enough to each other to permit casual travel between them. The new technologies discussed above will remove this geographic restriction and increase the opportunities for cooperation to regional, state, and national scales. However, the consortia described above have succeeded to a great extent because their proximity made it possible for the leadership of the institutions involved to build relationships of trust over time. These human networks of acquaintance and trust are fundamental to the growth of cooperation and will not result merely from having access to new technologies. The technologies are facilitators of relationships; they cannot function effectively in the absence of such relationships or in the absence of a culture of sharing. The key to attaining agility, which is enabled by the technology, is to foster a culture of trust and sharing among the partners: cooperation is the choice of agile organizations. The hypothetical example of the East Asian Studies Program works because the presidents, academic deans, and other administrative and academic leaders of the institutions relate to each other within the human framework of a broad-based consortium of institutions interested in the potential of cooperation facilitated by distance learning. Without the human network of relationships upon which cooperation is based, having the most sophisticated teleconferencing equipment available is like having the only telephone in town. There is simply no use for it.

Some would question whether such close working relationships with competitors would dilute an institution's identity and threaten its autonomy. Institutional autonomy will not disappear in the emerging context; rather, it will be transformed. Institutions that employ cooperative strategies wisely will be more encumbered, yet stronger. Cooperative relationships create obligations, but they also create options that institutions almost by definition could not have by any other means. Go-it-alone strategies for important aspects of both instruction and institutional advancement are fading and will not survive the year 2000 for the majority of institutions. For example, alumni will not be loyal to an institution which does not provide an education which prepares them for a vocation and a full life. If high quality education will require institutional agility, then institutions must commit to the agile strategy to maintain alumni loyalty.

Implications for Exportability

This chapter began with a quote from Peter Drucker (1993) which suggests that American higher education offers a highly exportable service. In fact, at a time when government officials and economic theorists decry the nation's trade deficit, higher education represents a positive trade balance.

There are essentially three ways in which colleges and universities currently "export" to other countries:

- Foreign students attend United States colleges and universities;
- United States college and university faculty visit foreign institutions to teach for a period of time; and
- United States colleges and universities maintain divisions in foreign countries.

Current capabilities of distance learning technology, including interactive two-way video, combined with the creation of virtual institutions can significantly broaden the scale and scope of these activities. Through an interactive network, foreign students could receive video taped campus tours and meet with faculty advisors, financial aid counselors, and host families, prior to traveling to the United States. Regularly scheduled interactive video conferences between consortia of United States institutions and foreign locations would increase the flow of international academic exchanges and make it easier for foreign students to benefit from the United States higher education system.

Another hypothetical example: a consortium of agile institutions could create a specialized academic program combining economics, engineering, business, and entrepreneurship specifically designed to meet the needs of the developing economies of Eastern Europe. Given the ability to combine the resources of several United States colleges and universities and present them face-to-face to international students, the possibilities are endless.

Looking at it from the opposite side, the capability of connecting institutions worldwide by a variety of sophisticated telecommunications media would have dramatic implications for the internationalization of the curricula of our own institutions.

Inter-Sectoral Relationships

The sharp and distinct boundaries which previously separated business, K-12, and higher education are rapidly breaking down as more leaders and policymakers come to realize the interdependence of these sectors. The language of TQM and continuous improvement theory has become the Lingua Franca for the interactions among leaders of these sectors and is helping to prepare the ground for the agile revolution. Organizational agility abetted by interactive telecommunications will institutionalize this interdependence and will create dramatic changes in the structure and nature of the educational process. The following hypothetical examples illustrate important parts of our future educational environment.

K-12 Enrichment. Once or twice a week, students at a center city high school decide to use their study hall periods for real time interactive video conferences with faculty from colleges and universities. Prepared collaboratively by college and K-12 faculty, each of these 45 minute "intellectual appetizers" focuses upon one specific historical event, cultural artifact, famous person, or scientific idea through which students are introduced to the purposes and modes of thinking of different academic disciplines. These "micro courses" fulfill an important public service need by stimulating the intellectual curiosity of inner city students. The recruitment benefits to the participating colleges are obvious.

Inter-Sectoral Articulation. The new academic dean at a community college starts tracking by discipline the academic experience of students who transfer to colleges to complete their undergraduate education. She discovers that students who have majored in computer science have been significantly less successful than students who have transferred to other fields at four-year institutions. This surprises her, since her institution's faculty are well-credentialed and, seem to her, highly motivated classroom performers. Moreover, "comp sci" grads have done very well at certain institutions but have consistently struggled at others. She suspects that the problem is one of programmatic articulation, not professional capacity. Consequently, she organizes a video conference involving all of her institution's computer science faculty and the deans and chairs of computer science departments at those five colleges and universities where her graduates have experienced difficulty fairly consistently. The point of the video-conference is to make sure that her faculty know what these four-year institutions are looking for and for her to communicate the college's ability, or inability, to meet those expectations with current resources. During a subsequent video conference, the five four-year institutions agree to create a pool of faculty who will work with their community college colleagues to provide a special "bridge" course for students who will transfer to their institutions.

Choice/Equity. In a small, rural school district in Central Pennsylvania, three 11th grade students want to take Advanced Placement (AP) Calculus in their senior year. Although small, the professional staff of this district is dedicated, talented, and provides high quality instruction within the bounds of a narrow curriculum restricted by a small student body and declining local tax base. The district is not able to provide an AP calculus course for just a few students every few years. Some of the parents consider exercising choice under a new state choice plan to send their children to an affluent suburban district 25 miles away which provides a broader curriculum. This plan was implemented in order to meet the state's constitutional requirement for a "thorough and efficient system of public education." However, they are constrained by transportation problems and a reluctance to abandon many of the positive educational and social aspects of the present school. The Curriculum Director of the district, which is a member of an inter-sectoral consortium, contacts his counterpart in the suburban district, also a consortium school, and arranges for the three students to electronically join the larger district's regular AP calculus course in the 1995-96 academic year. The students literally become part of the class through two-way audio and video, use integrated fax capability to submit homework and to receive and return quizzes and examinations, and never leave their home school and community, solving the parents' choice dilemma.

Other potential applications include: college courses for advanced high school seniors; a high school physics (or interdisciplinary) course taught by a team, including a certified teacher and a scientist from a distant manufacturing corporation; regular video conference meetings of purchasing directors from several colleges to plan joint purchases and grant preparation; delivery of college courses to corporate employees who remain at their workplace for the interactive class session; and evening noncredit programs of general interest to adults in local centers.

The concept of agility, which presupposes advanced telecommunication technology as well as TQM, has the potential to change radically the way education happens by bringing learners into direct contact with high quality resources which would otherwise be out of reach. The impact of this new organizational model will cut across traditional sectoral boundaries and create the environment envisioned by Peter Drucker (1993) in his recent book, *Post Capitalist Society*, in which he describes schools that look more like businesses, and businesses that look more like schools.

Summary

Total Quality Management and its allied concept of continuous improvement present academic administrators, faculty, and others with important tools for understanding and, presumably, strengthening the processes through which institutions provide services to learners. Clearly, every institution must and will adapt these theories in light of its mission, culture, and character, although there are limits beyond which this process of adaptation cannot go, lest the quality process be denatured into a public relations exercise.

If the process of adapting TQM to institutions, and institutions to TQM, poses great risks for those with responsibilities in this area, an even greater risk is to view the implementation of TQM—as important and complex and threatening as this process inevitably is—as a "stand alone" reform. The chief argument of this chapter has been that post-secondary institutions must view quality processes as one ingredient—albeit an indisputably essential ingredient—in the revolutionary convergence of quality processes with:

- the blindingly rapid integration of telephone, television, and computer into powerful real-time interactive communication centers;
- the emergence of the global student markets (perhaps in graduate or continuing education markets first) dwarfing current assumptions about "foreign students" and "internationalization";
- the growing acceptance of collaborative or self-directed learning on an equal footing with traditional pedagogical assumptions in organizing and supporting the learning process; and
- the growing, unavoidable acceptance of inter-institutional collaboration as **first** choice strategy for fulfilling mission and maintaining competitiveness.

Institutions will be reconceptualizing the very nature of their production processes and the markets they serve through those production processes, not simply how they assure quality in their current production processes for their current clienteles. In short, institutions are about to become agile partners and competitors in a virtual educational system that will be bounded only by the capacity to move voice, video, data, and document, and limited only by the ability of organizations to partner wisely and responsibly.

References

Brown, A. 1993. "If You're On the Bandwagon, Jump Off Now." *On the Horizon* (February).

Drucker, P. 1993. "Post Capitalist: A Conversation with Peter Schwartz." *Wired* (July/August).

Drucker, P. 1993. *Post Capitalist Society*. New York: Harper Collins.

Goldman, S. L. 1993. Agile Manufacturing: A New Production Paradigm for Society. Unpublished paper.

Millard, R. M. 1991. *Today's Myths and Tomorrow's Realities: Overcoming Obstacles to Academic Leadership in the 21st Century*. San Francisco: Jossey-Bass.

Stedman, D. J. and L. A. Bransford. 1992. "Educational Telecommunications Infrastructure: Ferment, Flux and Fragmentation." In *A National Information Network: Changing Our Lives in the 21st Century*. Institute for Information Studies.

"Two-Way Video is the Trend for Distance Learning in the 90's." 1990. *TeleConference* 9 (1).

GERALD J. RICHTER

Gerald J. Richter serves as associate director of the Lehigh Valley Association of Independent Colleges (LVAIC) and of the Pennsylvania Educational Telecommunications Exchange Network (PETE net). Richter has a bachelor's degree in business administration from Fordham University, a master's degree in folklore and mythology from the University of California–Los Angeles, and studied in the folklore and anthropology doctoral program at the University of Pennsylvania.

Richter has worked in the area of community and educational applications of interactive video technology since 1975, serving as executive director of Berks Community Television in Reading, Pennsylvania, the non-profit successor to a major National Science Foundation experiment in the social uses of two-way cable television. He has served as a policy and implementation consultant to municipal governments, educational institutions, businesses, and trade associations. Prior to joining LVAIC, he served as executive director of an intersectoral cooperative of K-12 and post-secondary institutions and business on issues of educational restructuring and reform.

GALEN C. GODBEY

Galen Godbey has served as executive director of the Lehigh Valley Association of Independent Colleges, Inc. Godbey has bachelor's degrees in history and philosophy, and a master's degree in speech communication from the Pennsylvania State University. He earned his doctorate in the study of higher education from the University of Pennsylvania with a dissertation on faculty incentive systems and intercollegiate cooperation.

Prior to assuming his duties with the Lehigh Valley Association, Godbey served in staff positions in education with both legislative and executive branches of state government in Pennsylvania, and as a research fellow with what is now the Institute for Research in Higher Education at the University of Pennsylvania. Godbey is past president of the Association for Consortial Leadership, the national professional organization of post-secondary consortium directors. He is a member of the boards of the Lehigh Valley Distance Learning Cooperative, and the Pennsylvania Legislative Task Force on Distance Education. Most recently he became executive director of the Pennsylvania Educational Telecommunications Exchange Network.

CHAPTER NINETEEN:

CONTINUOUS QUALITY IMPROVEMENT: IMPLEMENTATION IN THE ACADEMIC HEALTH CENTER

Thomas C. Robinson and Ann Dalzell

W. Edwards Deming (1900-1993) was the expert in quality who helped Japan rebuild its shattered industries after World War II and urged United States corporations to treat their workers as associates rather than adversaries. Deming's philosophy was delivered in his "fourteen points for management." His theories were based on the premise that most product defects resulted from management shortcomings rather than careless workers, and that inspection after the fact was inferior to designing processes that would produce better quality. After his success in Japan, United States companies actively sought his help to catch up to Asian competitors. Because of his constant devotion and dedication to the principles of quality, he is considered one of the "fathers of quality" and the Continuous Quality Improvement (CQI) effort.

Robinson and Dalzell

CQI at the University of Kentucky A. B. Chandler Medical Center

Four years ago the concepts of Continuous Quality Improvement were introduced to our Medical Center with mixed reviews. We are a teaching healthcare environment composed of a College of Allied Health Professions, College of Pharmacy, College of Nursing, College of Dentistry, College of Medicine, a 473-bed tertiary referral hospital, and ambulatory care facility Kentucky Clinic, which serves over 300,000 outpatient visits each year.

Health care is a rapidly changing environment. Continuous Quality Improvement is a philosophy and approach that provides the skills and awareness to manage change. It promotes a process of organizational improvement through employee participation and team-building. Health care is also entering a time of heightened competition and increased scrutiny. In order to maintain and increase our share of patients, we must meet, even exceed, our customers expectations. It was clear that CQI was the best way to help us identify our customers, define their needs and expectations, and ensure we meet or exceed them. CQI represented an organized strategy for improving health care services. The hospital and clinics embraced this philosophy more readily—they understood who their "customers" were. Our colleges were less enthusiastic partners. Why?

Colleges certainly face difficulties; however, this does not necessarily mean we must change. The academic side of our Medical Center viewed the CQI philosophy as just another management guru's "flash in the pan" that will not work in an academic setting. Additionally, nothing causes more heated discussion with faculty than the dreaded "C" word— customer—and there is good reason for this. In the academic setting this term signals a commercialized view of knowledge and the service it provides. Additionally, when applied to instruction it implies that the student "customer" may lack the knowledge to determine what he or she actually needs and or how to get it. Even our Medical Center's mission became a "triple threat" to our CQI vision of working together in teams to change processes. Which was more important, teaching, research, or patient care?

Our Quality Steering Council made an important decision to address each one of these diverse functions by forming a Quick Start Quality Action Team in each area. Following is a brief description of our journey with CQI and our Quick Start Teams as case studies in the process.

Initial Experience

The commitment of the chief executive officer of the institution for any endeavor is vital to its success. The introduction of a CQI initiative into an organization represents a shift in corporate culture. In the case of an academic health center, CQI will not get off the ground without the chancellor or vice president's commitment and active participation. In the case of the University of Kentucky Chandler Medical Center, it was the chancellor who was the catalyst for this cultural change in the Summer of 1989.

An important development activity that was undertaken in the Medical Center was that the leadership of the Colleges, the Hospital, and the various service units were involved very early in the process. The chancellor employed his Cabinet meetings to introduce the concept of CQI and educate the deans and hospital director about the importance and the value of the CQI approach. Moreover, the chancellor and his staff facilitated the training of the leadership of the Medical Center. One example of this was the training of this group by attending the workshop, "The Disney Approach to Quality Service," at Disney World in Orlando.

The chancellor also committed funds to establish an Office of CQI in March of 1990. This office has become institutionalized and has been responsible for training employees at all levels in the concepts of CQI.

A consulting firm, Organizational Dynamics, Inc., was hired in January of 1992 to work with the leadership of the Medical Center to ensure the development of consistent corporate values and strategies for CQI. The consultants conducted many workshops and consultations with the leadership and the middle management of the Medical Center. It was through this contract that the model and infrastructure was established for the CQI system within the Medical Center.

Continuous Quality Improvement at the University of Kentucky Chandler Medical Center: The Fade Process and Quick Start Teams

The chancellor established a Quality Council to demonstrate commitment and to monitor CQI activities. This council was then merged into the chancellor's Cabinet, thus guaranteeing attention to the work of the staff and the employees on CQI. The Quality Council decided to take on a limited number of projects to not only improve what was done on a daily basis at the Medical Center, but to allow people to get their "feet wet" with the concept and break down existing paradigms. It was important to choose issues which had a good potential for success. The FADE Process and the establishment of Quick Start teams to identify the issues and work on solutions to the problems were the methodology recommended by the consultants.

Quick Start teams generally consist of about 10 to 12 people including a team leader (a person who goes through a two-day training), a facilitator (a certified trained facilitator who is well versed in the CQI methodology), and a process owner (someone who has responsibility administratively for the area under examination). The terminology "Quickstart" was employed initially in order to jump-start the organization. Although the term, "Quickstart," was used and is employed in this narrative, the Medical Center has returned to the more general term Quality Action Teams (QAT).

Deming promoted the use of data to understand a process and to use that data to uncover the problems and determine alternate methods to improve the processes. The FADE process accomplishes that. The Quick Start team employs the FADE process (Chart A). (The "FADE" process was developed by Organizational Dynamics, Inc.) In simple terms, it is the application of the scientific method.

FADE Process
  • Focus
  • Analyze
  • Develop
  • Execute

The **FADE** process consists of four steps. The first step in the FADE process is the **FOCUS** phase. This represents the traditional first step in any problem-solving exercise, i.e., identify the problem. The team determines the "current state" and identifies the impact on the institution. They go beyond the traditional problem-solving step of identifying the problem because they then identify the "desired state." It is during this part of the process that the Quick Start Team focuses much as one does with a telescope or microscope and delimits the area of study. It is here that ancillary issues are culled out and a clarifying process takes over. It allows everyone on the team to ensure that they all agree on the same vocabulary, definitions, and issues. It is critical to complete this part of the process cleanly and crisply because if there is any ambiguity

Copyright by Organizational Dynamics, Inc.

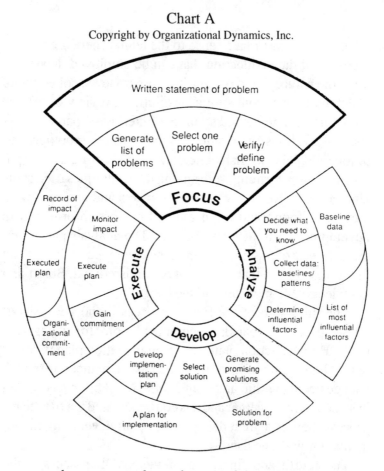

amongst the team members, the rest of the process will be in vain.

The second step in the FADE process is the **ANALYSIS** phase. This is the data gathering part of the process. It is here that the team flows out the current process in order that the team members thoroughly understand the current system and its problems. It is at this point that the data is gathered to determine the productivity of the current process and the capacity of the system. The team members can delegate responsibilities to their members to collect this information in

CQI in an Academic Health Center

whatever formats make sense to the team. There are various methods of data collection that can be employed depending upon the nature of the issue. Literature reviews, collection of benchmark data from similar institutions, review of official guidelines, usage statistics, surveys, interviews, pareto analysis, observations, evaluations, focus groups, photographs, tours, field surveys, fish bone diagrams, charting and graphing, and brainstorming were among the techniques used at the University of Kentucky. The team meets and analyzes what they have found and often return for more information to develop new and different formats. The analysis part represents the best of the brainpower of the employees. It is here and in the next phase that the membership is crucial. Smart and knowledgeable members do the best job.

The third step of the FADE process is the **DEVELOP** phase. It is here that the recommendations for change are made. Both an action plan and communication plan is developed. This again differs from the usual manner in which change occurs within an organization. Most often a new plan or system is put together and it is communicated via fiat. In this process there is a great deal of time spent developing implementation with the users.

The fourth and final step of the FADE process is the **EXECUTE** phase. It is here that the traditional feedback loop is employed. There is a measuring and monitoring plan laid out in the documents prepared by the Quick Start team. It is data-focused and systems-oriented.

It should be noted in this phase the concept that is underscored in this process is the "Parking Lot." As in most problem solving-processes, there surfaces all kinds of permutations and side issues that are important but do not relate to the core of the project. So often these are allowed to blur the discussions and proposals for change. In the FADE process, they are labeled "Parking Lot Issues" and are placed figuratively in the parking lot to be resurrected later. They are given this status because they are important and should not be swept under the rug and indeed may need Quick Start teams of their own.

Four Case Studies: Manageable Solutions To Definable Problems

The Quality Council of the University of Kentucky Chandler Medical Center identified several issues for Quick Start teams. Each team reported back to the Quality Council after the completion of each phase of the FADE process in order to eliminate the surprise effect that traditionally occurs. This monograph will choose four examples. These were chosen as case studies because they relate to the tripartite mission of the University, viz, instruction, service and research. The four Quick Start Teams were established in March of 1992 at the University of Kentucky Chandler Medical Center.
- Classroom Scheduling—Instruction
- Wayfinding for Patients and Their Families—Service
- Wait Time in Radiology—Service
- Core Research Facilities—Research

Classroom Scheduling

The Classroom Scheduling Quick Start Team dealt with a very thorny issue for the Medical Center, i.e., the assignment of classrooms to departments for their instructional programs. The vice chancellor for academic affairs for the Medical Center provided leadership as the process owner for this Quick Start team and secured the appointment of faculty and staff from all of the Colleges in the Medical Center to participate on the team. A faculty member and associate dean from the College of Pharmacy became the team leader. During the

FOCUS phase, the team identified the current state and the problems and impact on the institution. They found that the current system was in fact a non-system. Many faculty and staff believed that the room scheduling process lacked uniform and equitable policies and procedures. Some of the classrooms were "owned" by various Colleges. These were assigned within the Colleges and the conventional wisdom was that they were "released" too late in the process to help other colleges. Hence, some classrooms were indeed thought to remain vacant. The frustration and resentment that some faculty felt was debilitating to the collegial nature of the Medical Center. In summary, the impact was confusion, low morale, inefficiency, conflict, frustration, no predictability, resentment, wasted time, negative influences on quality, inability to plan for the future, and poor understanding of reality. The desired state was identified as the establishment of a scheduling system that meets the demand for scheduled courses and improves room utilization with the most efficient expenditure of time and effort.

The **ANALYZE** Phase represents the Data Collection and Analysis of the problem. The Quick Start team employed many different kinds of methods to conduct this phase of the operation. They reviewed the current literature in facilities planning and operation. They collected information and data from the University's benchmark institutions in regard to how they schedule available classroom space to academic programs. The team inquired as to any institutional or statewide guidelines that might exist in regard to classroom usage. The team did a thorough analysis of the past experience, i.e., room use statistics. This involved a compilation of room use statistics from six schedulers for a sample week in Fall 1991 and Spring 1992. The members of the team also called the faculty of record for courses taught in the Medical Center to verify

432   **Robinson and Dalzell**

meeting patterns. Several members investigated Central Scheduling systems in use at other institutions. In order to get a sense of the mood and potential of the users, the team conducted surveys of the Colleges for constraints. The team also thoroughly reviewed five computer applications to classroom scheduling.

In the **DEVELOP** Phase, the team established the Action Plan and the Communication Plan. This included the recommendation of the Wang Office Meeting Scheduler and the PACE Program Designed for Wang System. Both these software programs accommodate one to six schedulers, control access to view only, and training is provided at no cost. The team recommended certain policies for implementation in order to employ the system:

1) Establish consistent deadlines between the five Colleges.
2) Initiate a priority system for room distribution.
3) Establish a schedule coordinating team.
4) Develop a centralized—computerized scheduling system.
5) Hire one scheduler to handle scheduling after STEP I.

The team recommended a two-phase implementation plan. The first phase was established for Fall 1992 and set as its objective the institution of the New Coordinate Scheduling Process, utilizing numbers 1, 2, 4, and 5 above. Phase II was implemented in the Spring of 1993 and employed number 3 above— computerized/central program for room scheduling for Fall 1993.

The Phase I of the Communication Plan was instituted in the Fall of 1992. Upon official approval of the action plan by the Quality Council, the Quick Start Team sent letters to the Academic Deans, the Schedule Coordinating Team (SCT) and the Department Coordinators advising them of changes in procedures for the 1993 Spring room scheduling process. General notices were sent via E-mail to the Medical Center constituencies informing them of the change in procedures. The SCT assumed responsibility for reminding the constituencies of deadlines through E-mail and written notice.

Phase II of the Communication Plan was implemented in the Spring of 1993. The SCT sent letters to the academic deans, department coordinators, and department chairs advising them of the new policies for room scheduling and outlining the Phase II procedures. When invited, the College representatives on the SCT attended College and departmental meetings to explain the changes in procedures for room scheduling. Flyers were provided to organizers of various events. These flyers also outlined the deadlines and procedures. Students were advised through the Student Affairs Offices of the various Colleges. All of the pertinent information was published in the Medical Center's in-house newsletter. Posters were displayed in each classroom detailing how the room will be scheduled and monitored. A phone number was publicized for central scheduling—233-ROOM. Printouts of the schedules were posted on a weekly basis outside each classroom in the Medical Center to ensure that everyone there knew who was scheduled at any given time.

In the **EXECUTE** Phase, the team promulgated the Measuring and Monitoring Plan, i.e., the PROPOSED SYSTEM:

Five Colleges: Allied Health Professions, Dentistry, Medicine, Nursing, Pharmacy
    All use room priorities to handle needs
    (Two weeks prior to SIS Deadline)

Schedule Coordinating Team
    (One week prior to SIS deadline)

All Schedules Available
Handles All Negotiation
Prioritizes Requests
Uniform Procedures

Central Scheduler
Computerized Process
Search/Print/Provide Data

All individual Department, Faculty/Staff
All Cancellations, Changes/ Outside Requests

The requirements of the system were one half FTE schedulers, the hardware and software programming, and the 233-ROOM phone number. The chancellor allocated these resources, resulting in a visibly improved system, bringing order from chaos.

Patient Wait Time in Radiology
There were 14 members on this Quick Start Team, representing Diagnostic Radiology, Hospital Administration, Orthopedic Surgery, Pediatrics, Neurosurgery, Medicine, and Dentistry. The Team leader was from Hospital Administration and the Owner was the College of Medicine Associate Dean for Clinical Affairs. The first or **FOCUS** Phase concentrated, as did the other teams, on the current and desired states. The team identified the "Current State"/ Problem and Impact on the Institution as follows: When a clinician requested radiology services in the Kentucky Clinic (The UKMC's outpatient facility), there was an inadequate coordination and communication between the clinics, the patients, and the Radiology Department. The impact of this problem was that there was an increase in patient wait time and dissatisfaction

by patients. Employees were frustrated and physicians were unhappy. They found that waiting rooms were crowded and even unnecessary examinations were done. In the final analysis there was decreased productivity and increased staff turnover.

For an institution that espoused quality and a service orientation, this was unacceptable. In order to improve patient care it was imperative that the Hospital continue to work on systems improvement. The team developed a statement representing their desired state in Radiology—i.e., when a patient arrives for radiology services, there should be coordination and communication between clinics, patients, and the Radiology Department, resulting in the reduction of unnecessary patient waiting time.

In the **ANALYZE** Phase, the Team implemented flow charts, brainstorming, surveys, charts and graphs, and the Fish Bone Diagram technique. (Charts B, C & D). The basic data gathering consisted of the flow charts for procedure related to requisitions and registration, and the establishment and filing of film jackets. Requisitioning and registration take place in Orthopedic Surgery, the Medicine Clinic, and General Surgery. Film jacket activities take place in Radiology, the Medicine Clinic, Orthopedics, and the Film Library.

After the flow charts were reviewed, the team brainstormed for types of data that were needed to verify identified problems and to pinpoint influential factors. This resulted in a 28-item list of influential factors leading to problems. The three most illustrative were that not all patients were properly registered, that some requisitions were improperly filled out, and that jacket utilization was not congruent with requests or deliveries.

During the **DEVELOP** Phase, again using the brainstorming technique, the Team identified more clearly their prob-

Robinson and Dalzell

Chart B

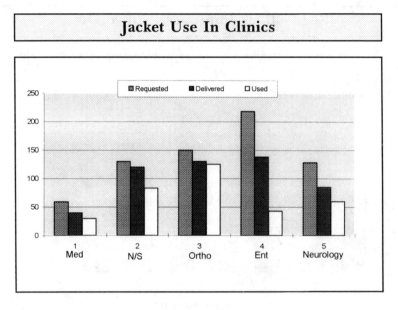

Jacket Use In Clinics

Legend: ▣ Requested ■ Delivered ☐ Used

| | 1 Med | 2 N/S | 3 Ortho | 4 Ent | 5 Neurology |

Chart C

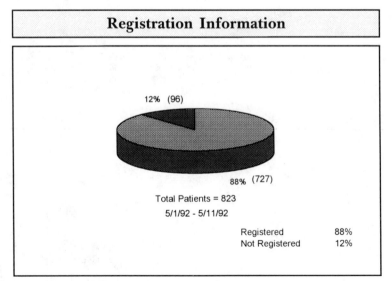

Registration Information

12% (96)

88% (727)

Total Patients = 823
5/1/92 - 5/11/92

Registered	88%
Not Registered	12%

Chart D

Requisitions Improperly Filled Out

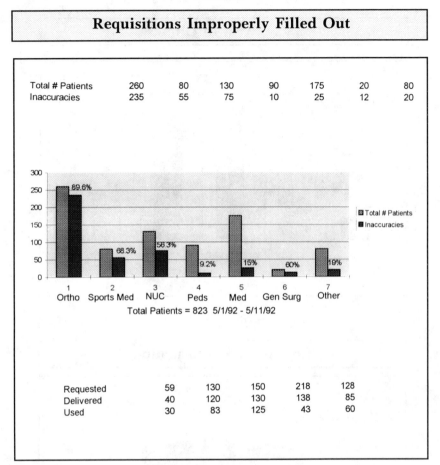

Total # Patients	260	80	130	90	175	20	80
Inaccuracies	235	55	75	10	25	12	20

Total Patients = 823 5/1/92 - 5/11/92

Requested	59	130	150	218	128
Delivered	40	120	130	138	85
Used	30	83	125	43	60

438   **Robinson and Dalzell**

lems and clustered them into five main categories—patient registration/requisition problems, resource issues (staff, phone, etc), patient related issues, film jackets activities, and scheduling issues. After review by the Team, solutions were identified and those that were appropriate were placed on the Implementation Action Plan. The team selected and proposed solution strategies for 13 major problems:
- unstamped requisitions
- no phone number on requisitions
- missing necessary patient information on requisitions
- 12 percent of patients reporting to Radiology are not registered
- patients required to report to clinic for registration prior to going to Radiology
- unnecessary clinic requests for film jackets
- too much time spent searching for film jacket
- inefficient use of Radiology personnel in transportation of paperwork from reception area to film assembly area
- insufficient computer hardware in the film library to manage the volume of film loans
- inefficient use of personnel in Radiology during peak times
- long wait time when making telephone calls between Radiology and the film library due to busy phone line
- inappropriate use of library and Radiology personnel to transport jackets
- inordinate amount of waiting by patients resulting in dissatisfaction

Each included a recommended solution, methods for communication, and monitoring of the specific problem.

During the **EXECUTE** Phase, a measuring and monitoring plan was initiated. Each change in procedure in the areas cited above was to be evaluated. Monitoring began in January of 1993 and was scheduled to go through July of 1994. In all, 16 activities were to be monitored against baseline data to measure improvement.

Core Research Facilities

An integral part of an academic health science center is its capability to conduct cutting edge research. Moreover, research programs need to be eligible and successful in federal and private funding. Ultimately it must transport new knowledge into the mainstream of the clinical practice in order to make a difference in the health and well being of people. Academic health science centers then must make the best use of its space and equipment. It is axiomatic that there never is enough space and equipment to satisfy faculty and researchers at academic health centers, so that the people who manage the research agenda must make decisions on maximum use and payoff for future grants and contracts. The establishment of Core Research Facilities is one method used by research management to maximize these expensive facilities.

The Quick Start team put together a rather improbable group of researchers and administrators to deal with the CRF issue. The team leader was Chair of the Department of Microbiology and Immunology. The Owner was the Vice Chancellor for Research and Graduate Studies. Members represented Nursing, Pharmacy, Biochemistry, Surgery, the Cancer Center, Dentistry, and Nutrition and Dietetics. The **FOCUS** Phase identified the current state and the desired state of affairs. The "Current State"/ Problem and Impact on the Institution was identified as there is an inadequate process for assuring budgeting stability, guidelines for use, evaluation and awareness of core facilities. The impact of the current situation is reduced research productivity and a negative environment, impacting recruitment of research faculty. There is the reality and potential of duplication and poor utilization of equipment. The University's ability to maintain cutting edge technology is reduced. Conflict is created within the institution and the morale of support staff is affected. There is a decrease in publication output and an increase in maintenance costs.

The Desired State was defined as a situation where there will be an improved process to assure consistent and stable core resource management, evaluation, and funding.

During the **ANALYZE** phase, the Team employed feedback from the CRF Directors Survey, the initiation of Focus Groups of researchers in the Medical Center, a User Questionnaire, and utilization of a Benchmark Questionnaire. The core research facilities used in the Team's investigation were:

- Macromolecular Structure Analysis Facility
- Flow Cytometry
- Trangenic Mouse Facility
- Electron Microscopy
- Nuclear Magnetic Resonance
- Mass Spectrometry

The questionnaire developed was used to validate the problem statement that the Team had developed above. After receiving the completed questionnaires, two team members conducted a focus group with the facility directors. The group discussed the answers to specific focus group questions. As a result, the group identified four main areas of immediate interest. These were:

- Criteria for evaluation of the facilities. The Team realized a need to include productivity, number of grants generated as a consequence of the facility, grant dollars, publication, and the percent of the total budget provided by user fees as measure for subsequent evaluation.

- Potential areas for support. The Team determined that adequate resources needed to be identified to maintain stable technical support, backup for technical support, support for maintenance, and the necessity of a plan for equipment upgrades and the replacement of equipment.
- Recharge mechanism and purpose. The Team recognized that a mechanism to compensate unfunded investigators would be necessary. It also included the need to develop a more global effort to secure support by servicing commercial accounts. Consensus was that money should be placed in grant proposals to support these facilities and that there would be a different expectation of percent recovery for different facilities.
- Advisory committee/user groups. There were mixed feelings about the utility of advisory committees/user groups. It was suggested that there should be an oversight committee for all core facilities to deal with management issues.

After reviewing the data from the interview, questionnaires, and focus groups, the Team, in the **DEVELOP** phase, published a document entitled "Guidelines for Core Research Facilities in the Medical Center." This document laid out the policies and procedures required for the CRF. The table of contents follows as an illustration of the issues that were addressed in the document.

1. Purpose of the Guidelines
2. Definition of Core Research Facility (CRF)
3. Organization—Administration—Management
4. Description of Facility: Equipment, Services, and Operation
5. Awareness/Promotion/Assurance of Open access

6. Budget
7. Educational Opportunities
8. Annual Report and Evaluation

The communication plan was laid out for August and September of 1992. The Team Leader sent letters to the core facility directors thanking them for their support. In August, the vice chancellor provided the guidelines to the core facility directors and met with them to discuss the plans. The facilities were scheduled to be reviewed in the fiscal year 1992-93. The vice chancellor informed the dean's council and the department chairs of the guidelines by memo. In September, the vice chancellor consulted with the chancellor regarding the budgetary ramifications of the guidelines.

As a mechanism to measure and monitor the plan—the **EXECUTE** Phase—the vice chancellor was scheduled to review the status of the facilities by January 31, 1993. At that time at least two facilities should have submitted their proposed budgets and documentation. The CQI staff was scheduled to reconvene the team during the week of January 26-30, 1993 to evaluate the first submissions. A final committee meeting was to be held during the week of May 25-29, 1993 at which time all reviews should be completed and the committee planned to assess the status of the process and recommend any changes which appear necessary. The process owner was ready to convene the team in the future if necessary to address problems associated with the guidelines.

Advancements in science are highly dependent upon cutting edge equipment and technical expertise, often beyond the scope of resources available to the independent investigator. In recognition of these factors and to fulfill its unique role within the flagship research institution of the Commonwealth, the Medical Center at the University of Kentucky has developed the following guidelines for establishing and continuously involving CRF's designed to address these needs. The University recognizes that CRF's not only enhance the research enterprise of individual faculty, but also provides a cost effective approach to equipment utilization while reducing duplication.

Wayfinding for Patients and their Families

At the outset we should define "wayfinding." Wayfinding is the process an individual goes through to help him or her make navigational decisions in moving from one place to another. Academic Health Centers are very complex organizations and, in most cases, very complicated places in which to find anyone or any thing. There are plenty of places that are "off limits"; the medical centers are usually concentrated in many, multi-story buildings that are connected together by tunnels, hallways, and bridges; many of the visitors are under stress because they or their families are ill or injured; and there are thousands of people in and around university medical centers at any given time. They are, indeed, confusing places in which to find someone or some office. The Team Leader was the Hospital director of planning and the Owner was the dean of medicine.

During the **FOCUS** Phase, the Wayfinding Team discovered that many patients and visitors have difficulty "finding their way" to and from their destination throughout the Medical Center. The desired state is that patients and visitors will be provided appropriate information in a friendly environment enabling them to take the most direct route to and from their destination. The Team felt that their goal was to provide the foundation for the continuing improvement of wayfinding at the Medical Center, not solve the entire problem.

The Wayfinding Team is considered the most successful of four successful and initial Quick Start teams. In the early stage of the development of a corporate culture which has CQI as an integral value, this team did an outstanding job.

In the **ANALYZE** Phase, the Team employed interviews, surveys, and exit interviews. Pareto Analysis was used as well as observation by team members. Various evaluation protocols were established. As with the previous case, the team contacted the University's benchmark institutions and surveyed them as to their problems, solutions, and systems in wayfinding. This team also successfully used Focus Groups to determine consumer satisfaction. The literature in the area was also reviewed. The team very effectively used photographs to demonstrate the unfriendly environment for visitors showing unattractive entrances without adequate lighting as well confusing and nonfunctional signage. They implemented the use of tours to give members first hand knowledge of the complexity that a visitor faces upon entering Medical Center facilities. They also used Field Surveys and maps to examine the situation.

The Team in the **DEVELOP** Phase had eight foci of intervention and over 50 interventions. (Charts E).

In summation, they involved a change in emphasis at the hospital's main Information Desk to include better signage, better training for volunteers, and more graphics. There was a general improvement in the resources for the info desk to include better maps and the introduction of phone headsets. Better signage was introduced to improve parking in correct facilities. Exterior routes were improved with kiosks and "You are here" maps. Entrances were enhanced and more consistent signage improved interior routes. Training was introduced to ensue continued acceptance of CQI principles and priority information was placed in appropriate places.

The final recommendations for this Quick Start Team were:

- Maintain the role of the Central Information Desks as a key component of the integrated wayfinding system.
- Expand the application of established Wayfinding principles to the visual element of our facilities and expand the role these elements play in the integrated wayfinding system.
- Incorporate specific wayfinding information into patient pre-appointment and staff orientation processes.
- Reallocate funds budgeted for additional overhead walkway signage at Hospital's North end for "You are Here" map production and mounting at six exterior sites. Computerized Map Library: complete base map development and print ready copies.
- Dissolve the CQI Wayfinding Team effective February 1, 1994.

As a part of the **EXECUTE** Phase, the effectiveness of the more than 50 interventions were monitored and measured with 12 distinct evaluation activities including surveys, interviews, structured observations, log of frequencies and events, and the use of focus groups. The results are most enlightening.

There were three evaluation activities aimed specifically at measuring the overall impact and effectiveness of the Team's work. The Team employed the use of an Exit Survey at the two major parking structures as patients and visitors were leaving the Medical Center. They also used a "Hot Spot" survey inside the facilities at the major intersections and known trouble spots. Finally, they surveyed the Medical Center staff on their familiarity with the new wayfinding aids.

The Exit Survey determined that the greatest improvement was in the Hospital parts of the Medical Center. In 1992, 46 percent of the visitors indicated that they had trouble finding their way; after the improvements the figure was reduced to 20 percent. The survey of "hot spots" showed a drop from 42

Robinson and Dalzell

Chart E

Summary of Wayfinding Team's Action Plan/Implementation	
Focus of Intervention	Description of Intervention
Main information desk emphasis	"On Center" article on Wayfinding. Three posters on Main information desk locations/services periodically posted. 24 informational meetings on WF with MC staff. Hospital signs direct to "? Information." "? Information" sign over each main info desk. Graphic emphasis with "?" at KY Clinic phones
Information desk resources	MC Information Desk Advisory Group established/operational. Standard Routes for all high volume outpatient services. Hospital Main corridor & sidewalk map. Med Center Campus map. Kentucky Clinic Campus map. Kentucky Clinic main corridor Map. Laminated reference sheets of landmarks, logos, etc. for desks and unit clerks. Phone headset introduced at Hosp information desk.
Information desk organization and management	Job/Position Standards tailored to information desk needs. Inservice training in phone skills, listening, computer use, stress management, medical terminology and emergency policy.

CQI in an Academic Health Center 447

Information on correct garage in which to park	Reduction of phone calls at Hospital information desk. Meeting with UK Operators.
More clear exterior routes	Supervisor on transferred calls to Hospital. Hospital Garage labeled "Hospital Parking." Memo sent to all admin/directors regarding "Hospital Parking" and "KY Clinic Parking" name/ labeling. Three Posters about "correct garage" and name periodically posted. "On Center" article on Wayfinding interventions. Assistance to Dentistry in pre-appointment info. development. Kiosk near Hospital garage revised to read "Hospital (not visitor) Parking." Hospital garage walkway over-head signage added. Hospital Entrance and "? Informa-tion" emphasized. Three Pedestrian kiosks in Dental/ Markey area. Outdoor "Bridge" entrance identified at base. "You Are Here" maps as variation of campus map (in progress).
Interior navigational decision aids	MRISC blue wall line and signage. Clinic Annex Kite and Sun graphics. Bridge logo developed and added to all approach signage.

Robinson and Dalzell

	Addition of "?" to "Information." signs. Main patients elevators in Hospital labeled: A, B, C. Enhancement of entrances to Surgery Center, KHI, Markey CC, Neurosensory, Neurology and Psychiatry with light, color and contrast.
Continuing use of wayfinding principles at Med Center	3 Educational sessions on Wayfinding held with D & C architects and project managers, PPD Engineers, dept managers. Endorsement of Wayfinding principles by MC sought. Standard section developed for architectural programs requiring consideration of Wayfinding on all projects.
Priority information emphasis on all signage/directories	All Hospital corridor/directory signage revised for priority legend emphasis. Ky Clinic 3rd fl lintel and ceiling signage added. Some Ky Clinic (new) corridor signage revised. "Reassurance" directional signs added inside the Bridge. Emergency Room entrance signs made more clear.

percent having problems to only 24 percent. Where patients indicated in the Hot Spot survey that they had received directional information from some source, there was an overall reduction in those still lost from 30 percent in 1992 to 18 percent in 1993. A high percentage of patients and visitors continued to report that they did not know which parking structure was the correct one for them . A high percentage of patients and visitors reported that they used an information desk on that day (more than 60 percent). Structured observations of Informational Desk Staff and Volunteer performance at all locations showed that they improved their reception, interaction, and information giving skills.

Patients and visitors now have an easier time finding their way, and there is a significant improvement in wayfinding aids, including a more systematic approach to wayfinding at the Medical Center. There is also increased awareness among staff at the Medical Center and University levels of the principles of wayfinding and the benefits of systematic application. There is also general agreement that continued improvement is needed.

Conclusions: Reflections on the CQI Process

Although CQI is a fairly simple philosophy, putting it to work in a teaching health care institution was, and is, a challenge. Nevertheless, CQI is considered a success at the University of Kentucky Medical Center, in large part due to our Quick Start Teams. The following are recommendations and observations on our process for those who are beginning their journey in CQI:

Focus closely on the problem. Given our environment, spend considerable time in the first phase of the process (the FOCUS phase), in order to narrow the scope of the problem or process to a manageable size that fits the team's resources. If

450   **Robinson and Dalzell**

the scope is too broad, team members will lose commitment because of the length of the project.

Recognize the time commitment for the team and the organization. Leadership/supervisory support to this effort is crucial for success and commitment of team members. Team membership and contribution should be recognized in the individual's distribution of effort and performance review.

Team Training before the team begins is essential to success. The Office of CQI in our Medical Center provides one and a half days of training for each team.

Continually train new facilitators to support Quality Improvement teams. Our CQI Office provides a week-long facilitator workshop every quarter.

Is it all worth it? From our perspective . . . yes. As with any major cultural change, CQI is dependent upon strong leadership at all levels. This philosophy will not happen overnight, especially in a teaching health care facility, but it will happen gradually. Our advice is to begin in an area that needs help and wants to be helped, then let the successes build . . . in other words, "just do it!"

THOMAS C. ROBINSON

Thomas C. Robinson has been the dean of the College of Allied Health Professions at the University of Kentucky since 1984. He received his bachelor of arts in history and his doctorate in the department of higher education administration.

Robinson has held many administrative leadership positions, some of which include dean of the College of Allied Health Professions, associate dean for academic affairs, associate dean for the School of Health Related Professions, assistant director for administration, and admissions officer for the Office of Admissions and Records.

Robinson has been a member of numerous professional activity organizations, as well. He has been involved with the Association of Schools of Allied Health Professions (ASAHP) since 1975, where he has served as president (1991-94) and on the board of directors (1991-95). Robinson is also a member of the Kentucky Hospital Association, Kentucky Allied Health Consortium, Kentucky Primary Care Association, Southern Association of Allied Health Deans at Academic Health Centers, American Association for Higher Education, Association of American Colleges, and associate member of the Kentucky Association of Health Care Facilities.

ANN DALZELL

Ann Dalzell is director of Continuous Quality Improvement at the Albert B. Chandler University of Kentucky Medical Center in Lexington, Kentucky. Dalzell has a B.A. in speech and theater from Georgetown College and has done master's work in communications at the University of Kentucky. Since beginning the Medical Center's quality initiative in 1990, Dalzell has studied with Dr. Joseph Juran and is a certified facilitator with Organizational Dynamics Incorporated in Boston, Massachusetts. Dalzell travels extensively, speaking to various professional groups and health care organizations throughout the United States on Continuous Quality Improvement.

PRESCOTT PUBLISHING CO.
Order Form

_____ *TQM: Implications for Higher Education* $29.95

_____ *CQI: Making the Transition To Education* $22.95

_____ *The Culture for Quality: Effective Faculty Teams* $24.95

_____ *Applying Quality to Education* $24.95

Missouri residents add 6.725 % sales tax.

Name_____

Address_____

City _____ State _____ Zip _____

Personal Check Enclosed_____

Invoice Me_____

        Please charge my   ___ MasterCard

                      ___ Visa

                      ___ American Express

                      —— Discover

Card #_____

Exp. Date_____

For RUSH delivery: Call toll-free 1-800-528-5197 Monday through Friday between 9 a.m. and 5 p.m. central/standard time or FAX your order—816/582-4532.

Prescott Publishing Co.
106 S. Main Street
Maryville, MO 64468